Quantitative Trading Systems

Second Edition

Quantitative Trading Systems

Second Edition

**Practical Methods
For Design,
Testing, and
Validation**

Howard B. Bandy

Blue Owl Press

AmiBroker is a trademark of AmiBroker and Tomasz Janeczko.

ISBN-13: 978-097918383-6
LCCN: 2011928444

Published by
Blue Owl Press
3700 S. Westport Avenue, #1876
Sioux Falls, SD 57106

Published 2011
Printed in the United States
16 15 14 13 12 11   1 2 3 4 5 6 7 8 9 10

Disclaimer

This book is an educational document. Nothing in this book is intended as, nor should it be construed to be, investment advice.

The views expressed herein are the personal views of Dr. Howard B. Bandy. Neither the author nor the publisher, Blue Owl Press, have any commercial interest in any of the products mentioned. All of the products described were purchased by the author at regular retail prices.

Investing and trading is risky and can result in loss of principal. Neither this book in its entirety, nor any portion thereof, nor any follow-on discussion or correspondence related to this book, is intended to be a recommendation to invest or trade mutual funds, stocks, commodities, options, or any other financial instrument. Neither the author nor the publisher will accept any responsibility for losses which might result from applications of the ideas expressed in the book or from techniques or trading systems described in the book.

The programs used as examples have been tested and are believed to be correct. Results will depend on the specific data series used. Please verify the accuracy and correctness of all programs before using them to trade.

Contents

Preface and Introduction

QUANTITATIVE TRADING SYSTEMS focuses on three topics:
- Quantitative analysis techniques as applied to stocks, mutual funds, exchange traded funds, futures contracts, and currencies.
- An introduction to the AmiBroker program.
- Design, testing, validation, and implementation of trading systems.

EMPHASIS is given to:
- Techniques that have mathematical grounding – for example, equations rather than chart patterns.
- Techniques that are mechanical and testable rather than discretionary.
- Selection of issues to be traded, optimal holding periods, and expected drawdowns.
- Analysis of entry methods, exit methods, stop placement, money management, and position sizing.
- Analysis of intermarket variables.
- Methods for broad market timing.
- Methods for validation of trading systems, including whether a trading system is sufficiently reliable to trade.

THE AUTHOR, Dr. Howard Bandy:

- Has university degrees in mathematics, physics, engineering, and computer science.
- Has specialized in artificial intelligence, applied mathematics, modeling and simulation.
- Was professor of computer science and mathematics, and a university dean.
- Designed and programmed a well-known program for stock selection and timing.
- Was a senior research analyst for a CTA trading firm.
- Is also the author of:
  - *Modeling Trading System Performance*, a sequel to this book.
  - *Introduction to AmiBroker.*

THE PROGRESSION of trading system development that most people use is:

1. Invent, guess, read about, or buy a trading idea. Usually that means little more than an entry technique.

Then either:

2A. Begin trading using the idea or system tomorrow.
    The market lets them know whether it works or not.

2B. Program that idea into AmiBroker or some other language, test the idea using historical data, and evaluate whether it would have worked.
    Try to improve the idea.
    Probably repeatedly.
    Either reject the idea or eventually begin trading.
    The market lets them know whether it works or not.

The purpose of this book is to guide you through path 2B so that when you begin trading there is a higher likelihood that it is profitable.

WHAT YOU WILL FIND IN THIS BOOK

- An introduction to many aspects of technical analysis and quantitative analysis. Emphasis is on removing the mystery from things that work that you should know about, and debunking things that do not work so you do not need to spend time finding them out for yourself.

- A thorough explanation of methods used to measure the goodness of a trading system, and useful metrics to incorporate into the objective function.
- Identification of the key aspects of trading system development, and techniques to incorporate them into your own trading systems.
- Detailed explanation of data splitting into in-sample and out-of-sample periods, and the proper use of each.
- Enough mathematical rigor to (hopefully) be convincing without being overwhelming.

WHAT YOU WILL NOT FIND IN THIS BOOK

- No Gann, no divergences, no chart patterns, no flags, no pennants, no trendlines, no Fibonacci retracements, no Elliott waves – nothing that relies on subjective judgment. All indicators and signals will be expressed in terms of unambiguous mathematical statements.
- No indicators or trading signals that change when additional data is received. All indicators and signals that are created will depend only on data already available.
- No guarantees of great wealth in a short time with little effort.
- No investment advice. This book is intended to be an educational text. Trading systems described are meant to be examples which readers can experiment with, expand, and develop for their own use. Neither the author nor the publisher will be held responsible for losses that result from application of the techniques described herein.
- No pricing for exotic derivatives. This is elementary quantitative analysis. The title was chosen to distinguish it from fundamental analysis and that part of technical analysis that focuses on subjective analysis.
- No vague statements. I am regularly frustrated by advertising or jacket copy that tells me a book explains 18 profitable trading systems in complete detail, only to find a few hand drawn charts, an incomplete set of vague entry rules, and no performance summary. It is my sincere hope that none of you feels this book falls into that category.

COMMENTS ABOUT THE EXAMPLES

The examples of AmiBroker statements, systems, and programs are intended to be educational. Whenever there was a decision to be made whether to write code that was clear and illustrative of the point being made, or efficient in terms of minimizing the number of lines of code or the execution time, the choice was always made in favor of the educational clarity rather than the computational efficiency. Experienced users of AmiBroker may wish to recode for execution efficiency. But, in my experience, if the program is clear and correct, recode it for efficiency only if the execution time is unacceptable.

Every example has been carefully checked and rechecked. Nevertheless, some errors are likely to slip through. With regard to AmiBroker code, refer to the AmiBroker documentation and help files. When in doubt, the AmiBroker compiler itself is the ultimate arbiter of correctness.

Readers should be able to reasonably replicate the results of the programs listed. Exact replication would require using exactly the same data.

CONCEPTS AND TECHNIQUES

Many of the concepts and techniques described can be applied in many different applications. Usually, the concept or technique is described in detail, often including an example, when it is first mentioned. This book would be many pages longer than it is if every possible reference to every possible alternative was explained in detail. To save space, and to allow the focus to continue to be on new material as the book progresses, later references to concepts explained earlier may be mentioned briefly, or may be omitted completely, with the expectation that the reader will remember them and apply them as desired.

ORGANIZATION OF TOPICS

It is difficult to describe all of the features of AmiBroker and all of the concepts of quantitative trading system design in a linear manner. Capabilities of the programs, techniques for using the programs, and concepts of trading system design are introduced in an interwoven manner, in what is hoped to be a more natural flow than a traditional user's manual.

This book is not intended to be a user's manual for any program. There are many features of AmiBroker that are not covered.

1

Quantitative Analysis

By QUANTITATIVE ANALYSIS, I mean the application of mathematically based trading system models to financial data.

Quantitative techniques can be very sophisticated, require advanced mathematics, and be applied to exotic financial instruments. But many of the concepts can be applied to trading stocks, mutual funds, and futures using readily accessible data, computers, and programs.

This book presents some techniques that should help traders expand from fundamental analysis and the chartist aspects of technical analysis to more mathematical techniques that lend themselves to statistical validation.

I may be preaching to the choir in this first section, but I think it is important to clarify some distinctions about trading, investing, and the sources of information.

FUNDAMENTAL ANALYSIS

Fundamental analysis is based on the premise that a stock, bond, fund, commodity, or a market as a whole has an underlying intrinsic value. By analysis of the fundamental characteristics, such as the assets, liabilities, income, supply, or demand, that value can be determined.

Fundamental data for a company includes earnings, sales, inventory turnovers, price to earnings ratios, price to sales ratios, dividend payout ratios, and any other information that might be reported on a balance sheet or income statement. Fundamental data extends to government and private research bureau reports, including gross domestic product, inflation, balance of payments, and any other data reported periodically. In general, fundamental data is only gathered, summarized, and reported — it does not represent trades.

Economists and security analysts who focus on fundamental information have developed mathematical models of the fair price for one share of the stock — it is the current book value of the stock plus the present value of all future dividends that will be paid to that one share. Any difference between the actual price of the stock and this fundamental value of the stock represents an opinion on the part of shareholders.

The fundamental analyst uses data that is reported by a company or agency to create subjective models. She may use charts to gauge overall price activity, but with few mathematically defined indicators.

While fundamental analysis may have value in its own right, there are several problems associated with incorporating it into trading models.

1. There is a great disparity in the granularity of the data. Mutual funds trade every day. That means there are 252 data points, each representing a mutual fund trade, or trading opportunity, in a year. Stocks and futures trade every minute — even every second. There are thousands or millions of data points per year for each stock or future. But there are many fewer data points for each fundamental data stream. Four in the case of quarterly GDP, twelve in the case of Michigan Consumer Sentiment, and so forth. If we want to use some fundamental data along with our daily stock prices, we have the problem of deciding which day is the fundamental data value assigned to and what to do with the days in between. One solution is to work with monthly data rather than daily data. Any data reported any time during the month would be assigned to the last day of the month. Using monthly data would mean we have only 12 possible trading opportunities each year, and this would make validation more difficult.

2. There is a lag between the time period being described and the release of the report. First quarter company earnings are released some time after the end of the first quarter. Similarly for GDP.

3. There is often revision of previously released data. For government reports, these revisions are well publicized and expected. As an example, the unemployment rate is released the first Friday of each month, reporting on the previous month. The data representing August is reported around September 5. There are usually two revisions to the employment report. The first revision is in October, and the final revision is released the first

Friday in November. If I am building a trading system that uses the unemployment rate in some way, I have three very serious problems. First, the reporting granularity is monthly. Second, the reporting date is inconsistent and does not readily align with other monthly data, such as end-of-month closing prices. Third, the data point for August is very preliminary on September 5. The final number is released on about November 5. When I download the historical data for monthly unemployment, the figures reported are the final revision figures. To use this series properly, I must provide for a three month lag — August activity to November reporting. If I want to trade at the release of the August data, I must use a preliminary figure; if I want to backtest the trading system, the data is all final figures. These are two distinct data series, but only one of them is easily obtained. Granted, the revisions to the monthly unemployment rate are usually minor, but other series are often revised so extremely that the sign of the reported number changes.

For corporate reports, before about 1980 revisions and restatements were unusual — about 3 of the S&P 500 companies each year. Since 1995, and particularly since 2000, revisions have become much more common — about 200 of the S&P 500 each year. Assume we are following the XYZ stock. And assume we are basing our investment and trading on their earnings per share. We open Value Line, Moody's, or an Internet site and see quarter by quarter earnings from the most recent quarter back for twenty years – eighty data points. Tomorrow, the CFO of XYZ announces that the earnings for the past three years will be revised and gives the restated figures. Next month when we open Value Line, we will see only the new, revised earnings. That causes us to wonder which of the figures we see are original data and which are revisions. The revision of the previous three years data might cause buy and sell signals that were based on the original data to change when the revised data replaces the original data.

In company reports, there is the regular use of one-time entries that seriously distort data. A company may have failed to successfully incorporate a new subsidiary into its parent. Its earnings statement reports $1.25 per share profit from ongoing operations. In a footnote it reports a one-time charge of $0.80 per share due to the problems with the subsidiary. The first question we ask is "which figure fits into the definition of our data series — $1.25

or $.45?" The second question is "will the historical earnings data as seen a year later show the $1.25, or the $.45?" And how will we know without reading the footnotes? Some companies report a one-time exclusion almost every year.

Corporate reorganization also causes data to be revised. When a company sells or spins off a subsidiary or makes an acquisition, the operations of the company from that point forward can be considerably different. Is the historical data (sales, inventory turn-overs, etc) revised to reflect the new organization? If revised, is the revised data made public? If it is made public, is it reported by the data service you are using? Whether the data is revised or not, does your data service inform you?

4. There is an unknown, and for outsiders unknowable, agenda behind the release of fundamental data. Leaving aside any conspiracy theory, every government and company official (or accounting clerk) hopes the numbers released will project a particular image. Who wants us to be bullish and who wants us to be bearish? What are net revenues? What are operating earnings? What are costs? What has been set aside in some accrual account? How have options been treated? Which figures are real and which are fictional? A company might want a report to appear robust (say, to win confidence of investors) or weak (say, to appear to be uninteresting to a hostile takeover). A government might want a report to appear strong (say, going into a presidential election) or weak (say, because there is already bad news, worse news will do little more damage now and will set up for good news for the next report). Except for those with the most inside knowledge, no one knows the true agenda and the resulting bias.

Public statements by company officials and Wall Street analysts can be very misleading. Those of us outside the Enron (Tyco, WorldCom, Quest, Health South, Fannie Mae, Cendant and others yet to come) finance department will never know what the real earnings were.

There is wide spread distortion and lack of standardization of earnings due to accounting rules. For example, the extent to which a company uses options as employee compensation and the methods they use to report that information. Are different metrics required to evaluate different accounting practices? Can we even identify which companies fall into which category?

5. Be aware of survivor bias. Survivor bias occurs when something that would eventually be undesirable is removed from an index or a report and replaced by something else.

   The Conference Board provides an example of subtle survivor bias where the report did not stop, but changed. In 1995, the Conference Board revised their *Index of Leading Indicators, LEI*. (The fact that the index was being revised indicated that the old one did not work.) Among all the government and independent agencies there are literally thousands of data series that could be combined into such an index. There is no way for us to know how the components of the new version were selected and what validation techniques were used, but imagine the difficulty of reserving several years of monthly data for out-of-sample testing and not contaminating it during development of the new index. Could the Conference Board possibly risk releasing a curve-fit index? Could they avoid creating an index that was not curve-fit? We were planning to wait several years after the revision to completely evaluate the new index, but that proved unnecessary. The new index did not lead well enough to be useful, and the LEI was revised again in 2005 — this time to avoid showing a bearish forecast. Perhaps this index should be called the Index of Misleading Indicators, but the point is that the series is meaningless, even though it is regularly reported and widely followed.

As a consequence of these five points, I feel that fundamental data is unusable, particularly in developing trading systems that will be subject to tests of statistical significance. For a more extensive analysis, refer to: *http://www.blueowlpress.com/Use of Fundamental Data in Active Investing.pdf*

TECHNICAL ANALYSIS

Technical analysis and quantitative analysis are based on the belief that several conditions are true.
1. The price and volume reflect all available and necessary information about the company, fund, or market.
2. There are patterns in the records of price and volume that regularly precede profitable opportunities.
3. We can discover those patterns.
4. Those patterns will continue to exist long enough for us to trade them profitably.

5. The markets we model are sufficiently inefficient for us to make a profit trading them.

TECHNICAL ANALYSIS BEGAN AS CHART ANALYSIS, and has developed a large body of subjective interpretation of chart artifacts such as flags, retracements, head-and-shoulders, and trend lines, to name just a few. We traders are all very good at selective vision – we see what we want to see. We can look at a chart and see examples of a big gain following, say, the breakout of a triangle pattern. Thinking we have found a good trade entry technique, we can define those conditions in very precise terms and have the unbiased computer search all the data for instances of that pattern. The results do indeed show a profit for the pattern we saw so clearly. It also shows loses from many similar patterns that we either did not see or chose not to acknowledge, and it shows signals that appear, and then disappear as additional data points are added to the chart.

QUANTITATIVE ANALYSIS

Quantitative analysis refines technical analysis by:
*   Removing the judgment associated with ambiguous chart patterns
*   Defining unambiguous, mathematically precise indicators
*   Requiring that no indicator or signal may change in response to data that is received after it has been initially computed
*   Making extensive use of mathematical models, numerical methods, and computer simulations
*   Applying statistical validation techniques to the resulting trading models

REGRESSION ANALYSIS

Many relationships encountered in science and social sciences can be analyzed using regression analysis. While some regression models are used for prediction, most are descriptive. Political scientists build models that describe voting patterns, for example. Sociologists study the relationship between diet, height, and weight and develop models to explain the relationships. One of the distinctions of these studies is that there is no time order among the individual data items being studied.

TIME SERIES ANALYSIS

A time series is a sequence of data points that occur in time order. A chemical process follows laws of chemistry and physics. During the process, temperature, pressure, and concentration of chemical components vary over time. Models, such as these process models, are said to be stationary, meaning that the expected values, standard deviations, and correlations are constant throughout the series. Stationary time series lend themselves to being models by several well known techniques, including regression and auto-regressive integrated moving average (ARIMA).

FINANCIAL TIME SERIES ANALYSIS

Financial models differ from models of other time series processes. For one, financial time series are not stationary. In some cases, stationarity can be improved by taking first differences (bar-to-bar changes) of the data points, but that is usually not sufficient. For another, the very act of understanding financial time series, and in particular of trading them, changes the characteristics of the series.

Generalized auto-regressive conditional heteroskedasticity (GARCH) models are used to estimate volatility in financial time series so that it can be used in risk analysis and derivative pricing. But theoretical models potentially useful in predicting future prices are hampered by the lack of stationarity and by the low signal to noise ratio.

Unfortunately, modeling of financial data is not a science – it is impossible to build theoretical models or to carry out controlled experiments. But it is possible to apply computer simulation and statistical techniques, and to estimate the robustness of the empirical relationships our trading systems detect. These topics are the main focus of this book.

EFFICIENT MARKET HYPOTHESIS

There is a large body of discussion devoted to whether the financial markets are efficient or inefficient. Efficiency, in this context, refers to the question of whether variations in prices are just random noise, or whether they represent potentially profitable trading opportunities, and what categories of information are valuable to a trader.

Those favoring the point of view that markets are *strongly* efficient say that even insider information is already reflected in the price of the stock and is not valuable enough to create profitable trades. The capital asset pricing model and mean-variance portfolio construction follow from strongly efficient views.

Those favoring the point of view that markets are *semi-strongly* efficient say that public information, including both fundamental information and historical price information, is already priced into the market and cannot be used to make profitable trades.

Those favoring the point of view that markets are *weakly* efficient say that historical price and volume information is not valuable enough to create profitable trades.

Clearly, insiders do very well trading on information that only they have, so the markets are not strongly efficient. And there is enough controversy about the validity of all three forms of the efficient market hypothesis that all three forms may be disproved. In order for quantitative trading systems to be profitable, the market must have some inefficiency. If there are not persistent patterns and trends that we can identify and trade profitably, then we are all wasting our time.

Warren Buffett is reported to have said, "I'd be a bum in the street with a tin cup if the markets were efficient."

INVESTING

The characteristics of an investment and an investor are:
- The objective of the investment is income.
- There is an expectation of a predictable rate of return.
- The securities held are primarily bonds and dividend paying stocks.
- The decision to buy or sell is based on macro information related to the business model of the company, or fundamental relation between supply and demand for a commodity reported some time after the information was collected.
- The status of the investments is reviewed daily or less frequently.
- Management of the investment is passive rather than active.
- If capital gain is anticipated, it is because the investor believes that the market has mispriced the investment.
- Holding periods are longer for investments than for trades.
- Drawdowns are larger for investments than for trades.
- An investor is more likely to use subjective judgment to make buy and sell decisions.
- Statistical validation of investing models is not possible.
- There is no concern about when the position will be closed.
- No criteria have been established to decide what will cause the position to be closed.

TRADING

The characteristics of a trade and a trader are:
- The objective of the trade is capital appreciation.
- The decision to buy or sell is based on price and volume information from transactions that take place as frequently as or more often than the trading activity, are recorded at the time of a trade, reported very shortly thereafter, and seldom revised later.
- The status of the trade is reviewed daily or more frequently.
- Management of the trade is active rather than passive.
- Majority of the information used is technical.
- Traders are more likely to hold short positions than investors.
- The trader believes that the market is always right.
- Holding periods are shorter for trades than for investments.
- Drawdowns for trades are smaller than for investments.
- The trader will more likely, but not necessarily exclusively, use mechanical trading rules.
- Statistical validation of trading systems is possible.
- The trader is aware that each position will be closed out in a relatively short period of time.
- The trader is anticipating the conditions that will cause the position to be closed.

Trading includes day trading where several trades may be made per day, swing trading where a trade may last a few days to a few weeks, and position trading where a trade may last months.

A speculator or trader is a person who takes positions expecting to make a profit from price changes. His investments are primarily non-dividend paying common stocks, index funds, commodities, real estate, and other growth items. A person who buys a stock with the expectation of selling it at a profit is a trader, regardless of what he thinks at the time. I believe that almost everyone who owns stocks, bonds, mutual funds — even real estate — is a trader; just one who has not yet planned the exit from his position.

With the exception of an investment made with the explicit intention of passing it on to heirs, all positions will eventually be closed out. Even investments made during prime working years which are intended to fund expenses in the far future, such as retirement, will eventually be sold.

TRADING SYSTEMS

A trading system is a combination of a trading model and a market or a group of markets. When it causes no confusion, trading system and model are used interchangeably.

Models, in general, are sets of rules, written as formulas (or at least well defined descriptions) that either describe or infer a relationship, or help predict future behavior. Trading models, models that describe market behavior, can be written as computer programs and used to give buy and sell signals.

A trading model is a static representation of a dynamic underlying market. As long as the model and the underlying market remain in synchronization, then the model will continue to issue profitable buy and sell signals. As the market changes, the model will be less well correlated to the market and profitability will drop and perhaps fail completely. It could be that the market is undergoing some transient or cyclic behavior and it will eventually return to the state where the model was accurate. It could also be that the market will never return to that state, and the model will never be profitable again. Whenever the market characteristics change in a way that the model does not recognize, for whatever reason, then that model has failed. There are so many dimensions to the market that we will not be able to understand why it changed characteristics, or to identify when it has changed back, except through the actions of our trading system.

One of the reasons that financial time series are so difficult to model is that profitable trading systems identify inefficiencies in a market and, in trading it, change that market and make it more efficient.

Let me give an example of a system that might trade the corn market. It buys, using a stop order, a one average true range breakout of the 20 day high, and sells a one average true range breakout of the 20 day low. If I am the first trader to get the signal from this system and get my buy order in, I will raise the price. The next trader will get a worse fill than I did, and less profit. The third trader gets a still worse price and still less profit. Eventually, the inefficiency that this system identified will be completely removed by the profitable trades taking advantage of it.

Clearly, the historical price and volume of a tradable item are lagging indicators — they tell us where the price and volume were. Can price and volume be leading indicators, or be manipulated in such a way that they provide leading indicators? If we hope to develop profitable trading models, then the answer must in some quantifiable way be yes. Indeed, the basis for technical analysis is that there are patterns in price and volume, that patterns occur repeatedly, that we can detect them, and that we can make profitable trades based upon them.

The patterns we identify must:
- Precede changes in price large enough to be profitable even after deducting commissions and slippage
- Lead by enough time so that we can act
- Repeat with enough regularity to be statistically significant
- Occur often enough to allow tests of statistical significance
- Correctly identify the future price change a high percentage of the time
- Continue to act in the future as they have in the past
- Be completely objective
- Never be subject to revision as additional data points are received
- Never be subject to revision if the price splits
- Never depend upon a unique method of displaying the data

TRADING SYSTEM DEVELOPMENT PLATFORMS

In order to have a model give buy and sell signals, it must be coded as part of a trading system development platform – a computer program specifically designed for analysis of financial markets. The platform must be able to read historical price and volume data, use the model to generate buy and sell signals, compute and report statistics related to the trades, and perform searches for profitable trading systems. Throughout this book we will use AmiBroker as our trading system platform. It is described in more detail in Chapter 5.

CONCLUSION

Why study trading systems? Only one answer is rational — to make a profit trading. Someone who treats this just as an intellectual exercise would do better taking up chess, bridge, or crossword puzzles. Playing at backtesting is little different than computer solitaire. The only true measurement of mastery of trading systems is to trade with real money.

Whether *you* are trading for fun or for profit, expect your competitors to be trading for profit. Many of them have very high levels of education, training, and experience. They are equipped with fast computers, advanced software, and high quality data. They are paid a salary plus performance bonus, are well capitalized with other people's money, and take their monthly profitability reports very seriously. There have been occurrences of manipulation of various aspects of trading, always to the detriment of outsiders and small players.

Trading is a hard problem to solve. Barriers to entry are low. Competition is tough. But the rewards to the successful — whether skilled or lucky — can be immense and are worth pursuing.

Trading the market changes the characteristics of the market. The change is permanent; and once the markets have changed, the trading system that caused the change will never be profitable again.

Against a problem that difficult, against an ever-changing marketplace, and against competition that unforgiving, it is extremely important that your trading systems are well designed, robust, and have a high probability of profitability. These topics are the focus of this book.

My opinion is that there is enough inefficiency in the markets for all of us to live well from our trading systems.

If it is not possible for anyone to design and trade quantitative models, then we had all better keep our day jobs and find a new hobby.

2

Data

EACH TRADE is the result of a buyer and a seller making a transaction at a price. The exchange where the trade took place records the transaction, reports it, and broadcasts it to everyone who subscribes to the data service of that exchange. A single trade is called a tick. The series of ticks that take place over a specified period of time is treated as one bar of data. The bar may be of any length – five seconds, one minute, 30 minutes, one day, one week, or any other length.

For stocks (also options and exchange traded funds), the data point describing a trade consists of a symbol, date and time of execution, price of execution, and volume for that trade. The details of each trade are reported very shortly after the execution and are represented by a single tick.

For commodities, the data point describing a trade consists of a symbol, the contract month, date and time of execution, and price of execution. The details of each trade are reported very shortly after the execution and are represented by a single tick. No trade-by-trade volume is reported or available.

For mutual funds, the data point represents the trading price for that fund as determined by the fund's sponsor. While most funds are priced only once per trading day – at the close – some are priced at two or more times during the day. Regardless of the number of times a mutual fund allows buying and selling of its shares, most data vendors report only the closing price for mutual funds.

If your trading system is based entirely on a single price for a day – most commonly the closing price – then end-of-day data is adequate.

End-of-day data is published by the data vendor after the markets have been closed; typically a few hours after. The data vendor has collected the ticks throughout the trading session and summarized them into a single bar which you receive.

If your trading system computes its signals during the day, then you must bring intra-day data (bars whose duration is anywhere from a few seconds to several hours – anything less than the full open to close day) into your program — AmiBroker, if you are following the examples in this book. Most commonly, the program receives every tick that is reported and builds intra-day bars according to a time scale that you define. Intra-day data can be real-time, collected as soon as it is reported, or delayed real-time, after a delay of about 20 minutes.

End-of-day data is least expensive, delayed real-time more expensive, and real time most expensive.

TICK DATA AND DATA REVISION

While it is possible to work with individual ticks, be aware of several difficulties:

- Since every tick represents a single transaction, there will be a lot of data.
- For a given tradable and a given exchange, the ticks usually arrive (real time data) or will be reported (historical data) in the order in which the trades took place. But out-of-sequence trades and trades that are reported late do occur. Either degrades the series and reduces the value of whatever models use them.
- If the exchange wishes to, or needs to, reduce the amount of data being transmitted – such as when the tape falls behind or when the communications channel fills up – the data provider will omit some ticks.
- When there are multiple trading agents – such as multiple market makers, or the simultaneous trading through open outcry and electronic systems – then the time order of the ticks is less reliable.
- A tick often represents only the price and does not report the volume. Two successive ticks for corn futures could represent a trade of one contract followed by a trade of one thousand contracts.
- In real-time data, there will be erroneous ticks. Sometimes these will be corrected after a few seconds or a few minutes; sometimes never. Even historical tick data includes erroneous ticks.

Using bars removes some, but not all, of the difficulties with ticks. There is still uncertainty about the sequence, but only four points are specifically identified – open, high, low, and close.

If intra-day bars are used, there are more bars for a given number of trading days. This means the model can be more sensitive, detecting changes hidden within daily bars. The greater number of data points gives potentially more trades per calendar period, which allows more robust statistical validation.

But intra-day data is more difficult and more expensive to acquire. Note that building models using intra-day data does not necessarily imply day trading (where entry and exit are made during the same trading day). But if a model is designed and tested using intra-day bars, it will be necessary to trade it using intra-day bars, which means being willing and able to pay attention to the market while it is open.

Sometimes one of the agencies reporting data will make a mistake. A trade is reported at an incorrect price (a bad tick), and a corrected price is reported later. If you are collecting intra-day data and building intra-day bars, the bad tick could cause your trading system to give an erroneous buy or sell signal. When the corrected data comes in and the previously bad intra-day bar is corrected, that signal would disappear. Of course, this can also happen with end-of-day data, but you will have hours to detect and correct the problem, not seconds or minutes.

SNAPSHOT DATA

Many financial websites and brokerage firms offer market data during the trading day or after closing. End-of-day, delayed real-time, and real-time data are provided as single quotation snapshots, or with a short history. Access to some requires a brokerage account, some a free membership, some a paid membership, and some are completely free of cost. These data sources are valuable, particularly in checking the intra-day price of a position, but do not provide the historical data needed for model development.

Here is a partial list, along with their web addresses:
- Google. *www.google.com/finance*. Free real-time quotations and fundamental data.
- Yahoo. *finance.yahoo.com*. Free real-time quotations and fundamental data.

- msn money. *money.msn.com*. Free delayed real-time quotations and fundamental information.
- Market Watch. *www.marketwatch.com*. Free real-time quotations and fundamental data.
- CNN Money. *money.cnn.com*. Free real-time quotations and fundamental data.
- Reuters. *today.reuters.com*. Free real-time quotations and fundamental data.

HISTORICAL DATA

If you are using the AmiBroker program, it includes a data acquisition program named AmiQuote. AmiQuote can communicate with almost any data source in the world to bring daily or intra-day data into a database where it is available to AmiBroker.

In order to get historical data into AmiBroker, a subscription from a vendor of historical data is required. A detailed list of vendors will eventually become out of date, but some vendors who are well established in business and whose data files are easily accessed by AmiBroker include these:

- Yahoo. *finance.yahoo.com*. Free end-of-day data for indices, stocks, and mutual funds. Automatic downloading through AmiQuote.
- msn money. *money.msn.com*. Free end-of-day data for indices, stocks, and mutual funds. Automatic downloading through AmiQuote.
- Premium Data. *www.premiumdata.net*. Subscription end-of-day data for stocks, funds, and futures. Covers major world markets.
- Commodity Systems, Incorporated (CSI). *www.csidata.com*. Subscription end-of-day data for stocks, indices, futures, and mutual funds. Covers all world markets.
- Quotes Plus. *www.qp2.com*. Subscription end-of-day data for stocks, indices, futures, and mutual funds.
- TC2000. *www.tc2000.com*. Subscription end-of-day data for stocks, indices, and mutual funds.
- FastTrack. *www.fasttrack.net*. Subscription end-of-day data for stocks, indices, and mutual funds.
- Reuters Datalink. *www.equis.com*. Subscription real-time and end-of-day data for equities, indices, mutual funds, and futures. Covers all world markets.

DATA QUALITY

HIGH QUALITY MODELS DEPEND on high quality data.

AmiBroker has a utility that will test and purify the database. Let it identify missing data, extra data, inconsistent data (such as open less than low), and price changes that might be unadjusted splits. Examine the data for each and every report that could be a possible data error. Use AmiBroker's Edit tool from the Symbol menu to change one or more prices or delete an entire bar. Be particularly aware of exchange traded funds and trusts that pay (or have paid, at some point in their history) large dividends – junk bond funds, for example. Many of these are not adjusted for those distributions in historical data.

If there is an unadjusted split, use AmiBroker's Split tool from the Symbol menu to adjust all earlier data.

Some of the choices you have when you find data errors are:
- Have AmiBroker / AmiQuote reload the data. Reload it from a different vendor if the problem persists.
- Look up the data and manually enter the correct values.
- Make an arbitrary decision. For example, if the open is less than the low, but the two differ by an insignificant amount, give the open the value of the low or the low the value of the open.
- Make a reasonable adjustment. If the high for bars before and after the problem bar are about 40, and the high on the bar in question is 4003, assume the decimal point is off and adjust the high to be 40.03.
- Delete the data for the entire bar. Let AmiBroker duplicate the preceding bar when it needs data for that bar. (The program will simply skip that date when processing a single issue, but will fill in the data when synchronizing multiple issues.)

How do you know what values are correct? You probably do not. Using a data provider with a good reputation is the best you can do. Once you pick a vendor for historical data, use that vendor's data exclusively. This may be one of those cases where consistency is more valuable than accuracy.

COMMODITY CONTRACTS

Unlike stock shares which have an indefinite life, commodity contracts are very short lived. New contracts are formed on a regular schedule, such as once a month or once a quarter, depending on the commodity. Each new contract specifies the month and year that it will expire. For each commodity, there will be several contracts that are actively traded. Immediately after the newest contract is created, it is the farthest in time from its expiration – nine months, perhaps longer – and there is relatively little trading volume in it. As time passes, this contract comes closer to its expiration, until it becomes the front month contract – the contract that is closest to expiration and accounts for most of the trading volume. Usually the volume for the front month contract drops off after first notice (notice that delivery of the physical commodity is imminent) in the final week or two before its expiration. The process of one contract losing volume, expiring, and being replaced as the front month by another contract is called rollover.

When two or more contracts are being traded for the same commodity, their prices are different due to expectations of supply and demand, and to the costs of carrying the physical commodity or borrowing the money necessary to purchase it in advance.

When designing a trading system to trade a commodity, what data should be used? Each individual contract has only about three months during which it would have been the one you traded – not enough time to develop and test a system.

If the individual contracts are spliced together, there are discontinuities every three months as a new contract becomes the front month. These discontinuities would result in what looked like profitable price changes and the trading system would regularly be long or short and record a profit or loss when, in fact, that result was never possible.

If the individual contracts are joined in a manner to smooth the transition from one contract to the next, the result of the joining is called a continuous contract, and the system designer must be aware of the technique used to join them.

One method forms the continuous contract by adding or subtracting the difference between the outgoing front month and the incoming front month. Using this method, the prices reported in the historical data will differ from the actual transaction prices by the cumulative amount of the adjustments. This can cause the historical data for some commodities to be much higher or lower than they actually were, or even to appear to have been negative. In any event, any indicator used in the trading system that relies on a percentage change or ratio will be inaccurate, and worse, will change when the next contract is added to the series.

Another method forms the continuous contract by taking the ratio between the outgoing and incoming front months and adjusting all previous data by that ratio. Using this method, indicators that are based on prices and ranges of prices (such as the average true range indicator) will be inaccurate and will change when the next contract is added to the series.

A third alternative for those commodities where both a cash market and a futures market exist (such as the S&P 500 index), is to use the cash series to build the model, but take the trades using the individual contracts. This requires knowing the actual front month data and knowing the dates when the rollovers took place.

A fourth method creates a so-called perpetual or constant-expiration contract by taking a weighted average of all active contracts and using that as the price for a given day. The perpetual contract has no discontinuities, but has the disadvantage that not a single price in its historical data represents the price at which the commodity actually traded.

Still one more option, typically used with programs specifically designed to work with commodities, is for the program to know how to compute (or look up) the rollover date for each commodity, for the data for all active contracts to be stored, for the program to handle rollovers automatically, and to use the actual front month data for both testing and trading.

STOCK DATA

Stocks never expire, but they do split, pay dividends, and spin off or merge subsidiaries. Check with your data vendor to see how they handle stock splits and dividends. Every stock split or significant dividend must be reflected in the historical data before model development begins. The adjustment process works by multiplying all prior prices by the reciprocal of the percentage of the change. For example, a two-for-one split is adjusted by multiplying all historical prices by 0.50. Typically, stock splits or stock dividends of 10% or more will be adjusted – either by the data vendor or by the person who downloads that data. Smaller dividends will be unadjusted.

Recently, most stocks are paying small dividends, so the adjustment is small and is often ignored. But be aware of two issues.

One, adjusting historical prices causes the prices in the file to be different than the actual trading price. This causes the same difficulty as with commodity continuous contracts – indicators that rely on prices or ranges of prices are no longer accurate, and worse, will change when the next split occurs. After many splits, older data will show the price to be very much lower than it actually was. This would be very misleading for trading systems that rely on the characteristically different behavior of low-priced stocks.

Two, the price of the stock changes on the ex-dividend day by the amount of the dividend. For a stock that pays a significant quarterly dividend, there are four days a year when the price appears to drop. If a trading system is holding a long position on these days, and the prices are not adjusted for the dividend, the system is unfairly and inaccurately penalized.

Data revisions following mergers and spin-offs are almost never made. The cause for concern here is that the company is fundamentally different after the organizational change, and relying on historical data for earlier periods could be seriously misleading. Consider, for example, a manufacturing company which, after previously financing its own sales and earning most of its net revenue from its financing arm, spins off an independent financial services company. Or a company that goes into bankruptcy, reorganizes, and reemerges with the same company name and stock ticker.

OUTLIERS are valid data points, but the data is unusually high or low relative to nearby data. Should you remove outliers? Probably not. Outliers represent rare events that have significant consequences for the equity curve.

FOREX DATA

Foreign exchange (Forex) markets operate around the clock, around the globe, with the exception of one period each weekend when all the markets are closed. There are no traditional daily bars with open, high, low, and close. Trading the Forex markets is more akin to day trading than to swing or position trading.

There are some other issues related to trading the Forex markets.
- There is no central exchange and no central clearing agency.
- The data stream is usually provided by the broker.
- The broker is probably acting as a market maker.
- There may be no commission charged, but the individual trader is trading against the broker's bid-ask spread.

3

Trading System Overview

GENERAL

Emphasizing a few points about trading systems:
- The financial markets are non-stationary time series
- Trading systems are designed to recognize, then exploit, patterns that precede profitable trading opportunities
- As traders develop and trade models, inefficiencies their models identify are removed from the markets they trade
- Characteristics of the markets change over time, in part because trading systems make them more efficient
- Trading systems that once worked, but have failed, will probably never work again
- All trading systems eventually fail
- We will always be developing new trading models
- Trading systems we develop must pass tests of validity before they are traded

PSYCHOLOGY

There are many books that discuss the importance of psychology in successful trading. They go on at length about the need for the trader to understand herself, to trust the system, to enter the market when the buy signals appear, to set the stops at a comfortable level, to exit the trade at a loss when the money stop is hit, to exit the trade at a profit when the profit target is hit.

I believe that most of the reason that traders do not follow their system is that the system is not completely of their own making. We have very strong beliefs about the way the market and the systems we trade should act together. When we get signals from our systems to act and our feelings are in conflict with those beliefs, we second guess our system and delay actions.

Van Tharp, in his excellent *Trade your way to Financial Freedom,* talks about teaching people the mechanics of a trading system, and demonstrating its profitability, in the first few weeks of a college course. Then he needed the remainder of the semester to convince them to trade it. The system he described was a classical Donchian breakout – a system that is very easy to understand. It was designed in the 1960s before independent traders had computers, and is based on buying breakouts above previous highs and selling breakouts below previous lows. The length of the period used to establish the highs and lows was the primary parameter, and was often set to about 20 days. We will see this system in more detail in a later chapter.

I can understand why students would be reluctant to trade this system. One, it has a low percentage of winning trades. Two, it requires a large trading account because it needs to trade a portfolio of many markets to smooth out the equity curves from each market. Three, it no longer works.

Even if it passed the validation tests we will learn about later, I could not trade it personally because it relies on a small number of large profits from positions that are held for long periods. There are people who can trade breakout systems very well – particularly employees trading other people's money who just follow the rules and then go home, but not most independent traders trading their own accounts. My own bias is toward systems that have short holding periods, a high percentage of winning trades, and a smooth equity curve. The Donchian system and my own beliefs are in serious conflict.

My solution is not to convert myself to try to believe in a system someone else designed, but to design a trading system that is in agreement right from the beginning with my biases. For me, most of the psychological problems disappear when the trading system is truly my own.

SYSTEM DESIGN OUTLINE

I recommend a staged approach to system design. Start by designing a template of a trading system that includes the features most important to you – matching your personality with the personality of the system.

In the first stage, select the objective function, trading frequency, and order style. In the second, determine the amount of the trading account, type of positions, category of issues to trade, amount of leverage, and level of risk.

Then pause and review your choices. Imagine the best and worst scenarios. Be certain you are comfortable with these choices. In developing new trading systems, you will be able to start at this point and, in the third stage, add the entry conditions, exit conditions, divide the data into in-sample and out-of-sample periods, run the optimization, and test the validity. If the system passes the validity tests, it is ready to trade without further change.

FIRST STAGE OF DESIGN

SELECT AN OBJECTIVE FUNCTION. The objective function provides a measurement of the goodness of a trading system. It takes our preferences and biases into account and codifies them into a single numeric value. It is the single most important component of the trading system. A well designed objective function defines and identifies the trading personality of the trader using it. Objective function design is covered in the next chapter.

DECIDE ON THE FREQUENCY OF TRADING AND STYLE OF ORDERS. The decision on how often to trade will be determined, in part, by what else is going on in your life.

If you have a day job and plan to keep it, or are retired and like to pursue other activities, then your trading will be done in the evenings, after work, and on weekends. You will probably use daily market data, which is inexpensive and easy to work with. Daily data (end-of-day data) is collected once a day, after the markets close, and includes open, high, low, close, and volume, and open interest if the data is for a futures contract, but no intra-day detail.

If you prefer to work with weekly data on Saturday or Sunday, the daily open-high-low-close bars can be summarized into weekly OHLC bars on the fly by AmiBroker. Advantages of working with weekly data include the natural smoothing it provides, as well as the less frequent attention to the markets. Disadvantages include the greater exposure to sudden market moves during the week, and the increased difficulty of validation due to there being fewer trades possible in a given time period.

Daily bars are the comfort zone for most system designers. There are about 252 bars per year, giving ample opportunity to trade and making validation easier. Once the design of the system is complete, the data can be downloaded, the systems updated, and the new signals generated in the evening or early morning in only a few minutes. While we will briefly look into other time frames, most of this book will work with daily data and with techniques that can be used by part-time traders.

The natural time to make trades based on end-of-day analysis is at the open of the next day. AmiBroker makes it easy to design trading systems that accommodate market-on-open orders. If you wish to have transactions take place during the trading day, you can compute prices at which you want trades to take place, and place stop or limit orders with your broker for execution while you are away from your computer and market data. If you wish to trade at the close of the market on the next bar, you can place those market-on-close orders with your broker or mutual fund company for execution the following day.

Many, probably most, trading systems benefit from acting on the signal immediately. That is, trading on the signal generated by today's bar at the close of today's trading – market-on-close with no delay. There are two ways, without a crystal ball, to implement this. First, obtain market data near the close of trading, assume it is the closing price, enter it into the database, run the trading system to generate signals, and place orders before the close. Most of the time there will be no ambiguity. Some of the time the price will change between the time you generate your signals and the market actually closes, and the signal you acted upon will not be generated by the official data for that day – it will be a phantom signal. You will have to decide how to deal with that – probably close the position in after-market trading or at the next open; perhaps monitor the overnight trades to see if you are likely to get a legitimate signal. Second, precompute the price that will give you a signal and place a conditional order to trade market-on-close based on that price. Chapter 13 describes techniques for anticipating signals.

If you want to trade during the market day, you will need intra-day data, intra-day capability of your trading system platform, intra-day models, permission (from your boss) to follow the markets during the trading day, and the interest and patience to monitor your trading system and act on its signals during the trading day. AmiBroker has very powerful capabilities for working with intra-day models. Intra-day data is expensive and requires reliable communications. Watching the market closely during the day will become your new full-time job. It is difficult to overcome the high costs associated with intra-day trading. Although many of the examples that use end-of-day data can be applied to intra-day data, we will not devote much discussion to intra-day systems.

It is important to thoroughly examine your own preferences regarding the amount of time you want to spend working with trading system models, updating data, and monitoring the markets and managing your orders; your preferences regarding frequency and timing of trading; and your preferences for the type of orders you will use. These decisions will have a large influence on both the objective function you choose and the trading systems you design.

SECOND STAGE OF DESIGN

TRADING ACCOUNT. Decide how much money you will have in your brokerage accounts. This is the total amount you will have at risk; it is also the beginning balance you hope will grow. Your trading account should be a portion of your liquid assets, not all of them.

POSITIONS AND LEVERAGE. Decide whether you want to take only long positions, only short positions, or both. Long-only works best in rising markets. Do not rely on continuation of the super bull market that started in the 1980s to make your trading profitable. It is true that something is always going up, but test systems that take short positions for two reasons. One, so you will have systems that will be profitable in bear markets. Two, even if you will never take a short position, a system that is profitable on short trades can be used as a filter to exit existing long trades and block entries to new ones.

Also decide how many positions you want to hold at any one time and how much margin or leverage you will use.

ISSUE SELECTION. Decide which categories you want to trade – common stocks, exchange traded funds, mutual funds, commodities, options, currencies.

RISK ASSESSMENT. Decide what percentage of your trading account you are willing to risk on any single position. If you have a $50,000 trading account and are taking a $10,000 position which has a stop loss order set $500 below your entry, the risk on that one position is 1%. If you are using leverage, multiply the risk per trade by the leverage.

EXPECTED ANNUAL RETURN. Make a realistic estimate of the return you expect to achieve on your trading account. Stating this in advance will let you do some reality checks. It will also be useful as a standard for Monte Carlo runs. Monte Carlo is a technique used to examine the stability and sensitivity of a mathematical model, such as a trading system. Chapter 22 of this book discusses some aspects of Monte Carlo simulation. *Modeling Trading System Performance* expands the discuss with much more detail.

That completes the first two stages, and we have a template. An example might be:

Objective function:	rar / dd
Trading:	next open at the market
Account:	$50,000
Positions:	Long only
Tradable:	Common stocks and ETFs
Number positions:	5 at $10,000 each
Leverage:	None
Risk per position:	$1000 – 2% of account
Expected return:	15% per year

THIRD STAGE OF DESIGN

The most important work has been done. The decisions you have made in the first two stages almost guarantee that you will be comfortable with any trading system that complies with them. You have defined a template for your trading systems that incorporates your trading personality. Now you get to design the entries and the rest of the components.

ENTRY SIGNALS. Imagine, read about, or buy an idea that you will use to take an initial position in a market. Entry signals are the most discussed components of trading systems, but they are only one of several important components. We will expand on several entry methods in several later chapters.

EXIT SIGNALS. Your entry technique may have an exit associated with it. (For example, a moving average crossover.) Additionally, we will discuss stop loss, profit target, and other exits in later chapters. Good exits can salvage almost any trading system.

DATA. Data acquisition, data preparation, data normalization, division of the data into in-sample and out-of-sample data periods.

The in-sample period is used to investigate the ideas behind the trading system, either by trial and error or by an optimization process, looking for the best version. The best version is the version that has the highest value of the objective function. The out-of-sample period is reserved. It is not used during the optimizing process. After you are satisfied with the performance of the trading system in the in-sample period, the system is allowed to process the data for the out-of-sample period one time. It is the performance of your system on the out-of-sample data that determines whether it is likely to be profitable when you begin trading it with real money. Later chapters discuss optimization techniques.

OPTIMIZATION. After you have coded your idea into AmiBroker and run it over some data, you will think about ways to improve it. Whether you plan an automated search which changes the values of the variables in your trading system in an organized way, or just fiddle around changing things by trial and error, you are looking for a better system. That process is optimization.

In real-life system development, after searching the in-sample data exhaustively, and making one test on the out-of-sample data, you are rarely satisfied with the results. So the four steps of refining entry signals, trying other exits, dividing the data, and optimizing are repeated until you are satisfied with the results.

VALIDATION. In order for a trading system to be valid, it must make correct predictions in circumstances where the outcome is unknown to the system. Unfortunately, every time the out-of-sample data is processed, examined, evaluated, or even just peeked at, those results are invariably used to modify the trading system; and the out-of-sample data becomes less out-of-sample and more in-sample. It takes only a few peeks at the out-of-sample results to seriously compromise the ability to validate a trading system, because the outcome is known and the result it produces is no longer a prediction.

Eventually, you think you have a good system. Run it once more, this time over data that has not been used to develop the system. *Once! I am serious! Once!* If it fails to perform well, do not trade it. Perhaps, but with a small probability, the system is a good one, but the data in the validation period puts the system in a drawdown. Wait a few weeks or months, extend the validation data through the then current date, and attempt to revalidate it. If you decide to tweak it some more, make sure you have a *new* set of validation data. Read more about in-sample and out-of-sample data in Chapter 18. See Chapter 20 for a discussion of the walk forward technique which automates system development and helps to insulate it from compromising the out-of-sample data.

The market is going to test the validity of your trading system for you – whether you like it or not, whether you are ready or not. The best preparation for market validation is careful testing and avoiding contamination of the out-of-sample data by peeking into the future at that data.

COMMISSIONS AND SLIPPAGE. I recommend that your early investigations be done with commissions set to zero. Commissions have fallen considerably over the past few years, and commission cost may, in fact, be low enough to ignore. In any event, first study simply the accuracy of your system. If it passes all the validation tests and you are thinking about trading it, then set the commission rates to those your broker will charge you.

Slippage is a different matter. If you are using market-on-open or market-on-close orders, the prices you will pay will be close to those published in the historical data. You can use your own experience to adjust as necessary. Limit orders will be filled at your price, with no slippage. Stop orders will be filled at the price of the next trade after your stop price has been hit. That may be your price, or it may be worse – in some cases, considerably worse. By using intra-day bars of short length you may be able to estimate the slippage your system will experience. But be aware that the historical data may not show all of the trades and may not give an adequate indication of the size of the trades it does show. Data vendors sometimes omit trades in order to reduce the amount of data they store and transmit. Usually, the data omitted is at the same price as the data that precedes it, but not always.

POSITION SIZING. I have intentionally taken setting of position size out of the iterative loop. I recommend that you initially develop your system so that each new entry takes a standard sized position – such as one futures contract, 100 shares of stock, or $10,000 worth of whatever you are trading. Having a standard sized position during development makes it easier to carry out Monte Carlo analysis when it is used as part of the validation process. Chapter 22 of this book and *Modeling Trading System Performance* expand on position sizing in more detail. In fact, very ordinary trading systems become very profitable trading systems through use of intelligent position sizing.

Sensitivity and Monte Carlo analysis. The development of your trading system was done using a limited amount of data. Are you being fooled by one lucky draw, or have you found a reliable trading system? What would the results be if the sequence of trades was different? Or if a completely different set of trades resulted, even if they were drawn from the same statistical population in terms of average trade and standard deviation of trade? What would the results be if the input data was slightly different? Before beginning live trading, you might want to study the sensitivity of your model to the exact conditions that were present in your training data. Chapter 22 and *Modeling Trading System Performance* discuss some of these issues.

Live trading. After you have a trading system model that you have validated, and after you have worked through the materials on position sizing, begin trading the system.

Monitor performance. As long as the system performs well, keep trading it. Review the materials on position sizing and perhaps take advantage of some of the methods that make use of increased leverage. When the system begins to perform less well, analyze the data to decide whether the system is broken, or just in a period of weak performance. If it is clearly broken, stop trading it. If it is in a period of weak performance, review your position sizing and cut back on leverage.

More about optimization

Anything we do in the development of trading systems involves a search for a pattern that precedes a profitable trading opportunity. Any time we examine the results of alternative systems, we are involved in searching; and when we select the most promising of those alternatives, we are optimizing. Only a system based on truly random entries and exits would not be the result of some optimization. So the question of "should we optimize?" is moot – we have no choice but to optimize. Consequently, we should be aware of optimization techniques and apply them intelligently.

For the remainder of our discussion, optimization is defined as the organized, automated search for the best set of values for the arguments for a trading system. Optimization, and the resulting measure of goodness or fitness, is always with regard to a single-valued objective function. Given a tradable issue, a time period, and a model with parameters that can be changed, there is one single unambiguous value of the objective function associated with that set of arguments.

Aren't we just trying to find something that worked in the past? Yes. Isn't the likelihood of finding something that will work in the future higher if that thing worked in the past than if it did not?

When there is a single parameter that is being searched, the search is one-dimensional. We can imagine a horizontal line with values of the arguments from left to right and vertical bars representing by their height the associated values of the objective function. In an ideal situation, the profile of the bars is smooth, with a nicely defined plateau of high objective results surrounding a range of arguments. We would be happy to select one of the values near the center of the plateau as the value to use for that parameter in our trading system.

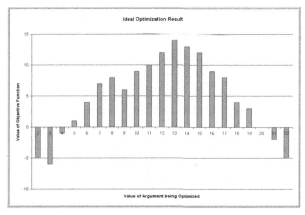

FIGURE 3.1 IDEAL OPTIMIZATION

We are seldom so fortunate. Often the highest objective value is a lonely peak surrounded by poor results. If there is a range of argument values that produces a smooth objective profile, even if it is less profitable, we will be safer to pick the smoother region.

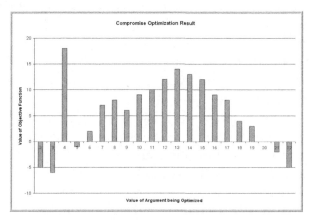

FIGURE 3.2 COMPROMISE OPTIMIZATION

If there is no region over which the objective profile is both smooth and profitable, that indicates that this parameter is not predictive, at least in these circumstances.

When optimizing, make some runs with very wide ranges to see what range for each variable should be tested in more detail. If changing a variable seems to have little effect, fix its value rather than optimize it.

When there are two arguments being searched, the search is two dimensional. We can imagine a table top with values for one of the arguments from left to right, values for the other argument from front to back, and vertical bars representing by their height the associated values of the objective function. In an ideal situation, there is a smooth hill of high objective results, and we would be happy to select a pair of values that are associated with the top of the hill.

When we are carrying out a traditional stepwise search in two dimensions, we have two alternative search methods. One is to search each parameter separately and sequentially, one after the other. The other is to search the two during the same optimization run.

Assume we are searching for the best values for two moving averages. One set of arguments ranges from 2 to 30 by steps of 2, the other ranges from 5 to 100 by steps of 5. There are 15 values for the first argument, 20 for the second.

To search them sequentially, we pick a likely value for the first argument, say 10, then vary the second argument from 5 to 100 in steps of 5, for a set of 20 iterations. When that is finished, we pick the best value for argument 2, say it was 45, then vary the first argument from 2 to 30 in steps of 2, for a set of 15 iterations. When that is finished, we pick the best value for argument 1, say it was 12. Using 12 for the first argument, we again search for the best value of the second argument. The process goes back and forth until we have found the best values for both. Industrial engineers call this process evolutionary operation. It essentially walks along a path up the hill, taking one dimension at a time. This procedure works whenever the contour of the objective function behaves nicely, as it often does in industrial processes. It can fail to find the best region, but it has the advantage that the search is in one dimension at a time. Unfortunately, financial time series are notoriously badly behaved, so this method might not work.

To search both moving average lengths during the same run, we let AmiBroker evaluate every combination of the two sets of values in what is called an exhaustive search. In this example there will be 300 of them – 15 times 20. At the expense of a longer computer run, we are sure we evaluate all possibilities.

When we have a more complex trading system with three or more parameters, we can extend the concept. The results are more difficult to visualize, but we have the same trade-offs – longer runs with assurance of evaluating all possibilities versus one or two dimensions at a time and a hill climbing approach.

There is a third, non-traditional, search method that finds near-optimum values without an exhaustive search. The method randomly selects a number of points in the parameter space, evaluates the system at those points, and chooses new points based on artificial intelligence techniques. AmiBroker supports non-exhaustive search methods—see Chapter 18 for more details.

DATA DIVISION. The literature on trading system development and optimization has two major points of view about the division of data into periods used for optimization and for validation.

One view optimizes using as much data as possible. The reason is to include as many market conditions as possible, hoping the resulting trading system will be able to respond well to whatever market conditions it will encounter in live trading.

The other view is that the underlying market being modeled by our trading system is very dynamic, and we should optimize using a much shorter amount of data in order to more accurately model the current conditions.

How short? Only one thing counts – the out-of-sample performance of this system. I am perfectly comfortable with a reoptimization period of one day, if that works. One of the potential difficulties with short reoptimization periods is handling trades that last longer than the reoptimization period. You might find that the parameters from the new optimization show you out of a trade that the old parameters had you in, and vice versa. Whatever length of time you choose, you will need to deal with the "edges" at the end of one period and start of the next. One approach is to exit trades that disappear, but wait for new signals to make new entries. Another approach is to exit trades that disappear, but enter trades that the system shows as open when the new period begins. The difference is whether the signals are treated as states or impulses. Arguments can be made for either point of view. If you are using very short reoptimization periods and you encounter a lot of trades that do not continue over the boundaries of the periods, that is an indication that the system may be unstable.

The market has so many dimensions that we cannot see them all, and we cannot know which are changing, and in what way. If conditions change within our in-sample period, that makes our model fit less well. The out-of-sample performance may still be acceptable, just not as good as it would have been without the condition change. If conditions change in the out-of-sample period, that drops our simulated or real profitability. My feeling is that a single trading strategy cannot cope with many changes. Trying to make it do so will require an increase in the number of parameters and the complexity of the model, which increases the likelihood of a curve-fit solution, which decreases the likelihood of profitable out-of-sample performance. (More about curve-fit models in a few paragraphs.) I prefer to make the in-sample and out-of-sample time periods shorter until the model fits fairly well throughout the period.

BioComp Dakota, a trading systems development program published by BioComp Systems, takes the artificial intelligence approach to optimization. Using techniques such as particle swarm optimization, it searches a subset of all possibilities in such a manner that it will probably find the best region without evaluating every possibility. Dakota reoptimizes essentially every bar, and all of its results are out-of-sample – they are the concatenation of a series of one-day out-of-sample results.

Another optimizer that efficiently searches very large spaces and performs automated walk forward analysis is Fred Tonetti's Intelligent Optimizer, which you can find at the AmiBroker web site, *finance.groups. yahoo.com/group/amibroker/files/*.

CURVE FITTING

A curve-fit, or over-fit, solution arises when the model has so many ways of adjusting to the data that one of the ways discovers a specific fit, but that specific fit is not a general fit. An over-fit model has learned the noise better than it has learned the signal.

Many books and articles that talk about the design of trading systems talk about the relationship between the number of data points examined, or the number of closed trades, in relationship to the number of parameters in the trading system. And they point out the necessity of having at least 30 closed trades to be able to statistically validate the results. If the only data period being studied is the in-sample period, then it is very easy to examine so many values for so many parameters that a profitable result is certain to be found. If a trading system uses two moving averages, the lengths of both averages vary from 1 to 50 in steps of 1, and 10 years of daily bars are used as the in-sample data, the system has essentially zero residual degrees of freedom. Ten years at 252 bars per year is 2520 bars. The trading system has used 2500 (50 times 50) values of the variables. So there might be a very good fit for the in-sample period, but the model fits well primarily due to the data mining that took place, not to the discovery of a fundamental relationship between the two moving averages and the underlying market.

The in-sample results always look good. The search process does not stop until they look good.

The higher the number of rules, conditions, and variables in the trading system, and the larger the range of values searched during the optimization, the more likely the resulting model will have been curve-fit, and the less likely the model will be profitable in out-of-sample tests.

It takes surprisingly few parameters to curve-fit a model to the in-sample data. Even if there are thousands of closed trades in the in-sample period, disregard those results and look at the out-of-sample results to evaluate the goodness of the model.

Unfortunately, some authors, many of whom should know better, and others who are intentionally misleading, devote articles, advertisements, and entire books to the analysis of in-sample data and draw very misleading conclusions. Examples include high gain equity curves, perfect buy and sell signals, portfolios constructed to minimize drawdowns, wild profits as result of position sizing algorithms, and on and on. Some of you have probably seen the advertisements, read the articles, and purchased the books.

SHOULD A TRADING SYSTEM WORK FOR A LARGE NUMBER OF TRADABLES?

Not necessarily. Many successful trading systems are designed for a single market, a single ticker – whether that market is S&P, TBonds, or Feeder Cattle. If the validation process passes, then there is no reason to insist that a model trade multiple markets. If a model trades feeder cattle well, it is probably worth trying it on hogs or pork bellies, but there is no reason to insist that it work on gold, oil, or orange juice. In common stocks, if a model works well for Wells Fargo and CitiCorp, it is probably worth trying it on other money center banks, insurance companies, and brokerages; but there is no reason to expect it to work for technology, utilities, or communications companies.

SYMBOL SPACE

The symbol space is very similar to the space defined by the numeric parameters. By symbol space, I mean the list of tickers that are used when the model is developed or tested.

If a system is based on a moving average crossover (buy when one moving average crosses up through the other, sell when it crosses down), and two lengths, each from 1 to 100 in steps of 1, are tested for the two moving averages, 10,000 combinations will have been tried. Some will be profitable, some not. Some areas of the space defined by the two length variables will be smooth and stable, others not. Similarly, given a model with the moving average lengths fixed, a search could be made of 10,000 tickers to determine for which tickers that model is profitable. Some will be very profitable, others not. If the tickers for which the model is profitable share some characteristic, such as belonging to the same industry group, that increases confidence that the model has validity. On the other hand, if the tickers are random, it may be that the optimization has simply searched the symbol space and gotten lucky.

NEVER WORK AGAIN?

When I say that trading systems that worked once, but stopped working, will probably never work again, people wonder what I mean and ask if I am serious. Yes, I am serious.

Trading systems work because they recognize inefficiencies in the markets they are trading, buy, sell, and make a profit. In so doing, they remove some of the inefficiency they recognized. A very profitable system recognizes a very large inefficiency. As long as the trading system is not well known and few traders are following its signals, it will continue to be profitable. When it becomes widely followed, and volume of trades based on its signals increase, the market becomes more efficient and profit using that system is more difficult to make. Eventually, most of the inefficiency is removed – those traders able to continue to make a profit are the earliest ones to recognize the signal and have the lowest frictional costs. As long as the signals generate some profit for some traders, the model continues to be followed and traded.

It is not necessarily the trading system that you, as an individual, are using to trade in small size that causes the system to no longer work. It is the fact that *some* trading method removed the inefficiency that your trading system recognized – maybe CitiCorp, maybe George Soros, maybe your system being traded by thousands of small traders after being published or posted.

As new people enter the business of trading system development, either on their own or as employees of trading companies, they acquire computers, data, and trading system development platforms. The whole package costs as little as $1000, total. To practice, they read about trading systems, see the associated equity curves, enter the code, and test the profitability. If a system is profitable, they trade it, and in so doing remove the inefficiency again.

My point is that there are so many people trying to make profitable trades, that every widely known profitable trading system is being monitored by someone hoping it will become profitable again.

For example, look ahead to Chapter 9 which has the code for a Donchian-style breakout system. Run it yourself on commodities data starting in the 1960s. It was very profitable on just about every commodity until the 1980s – about the time inexpensive personal computers became available.

A basic breakout or moving average system can be easily coded into a spreadsheet – VisiCalc, Lotus, or Excel work fine. Since historical data and trading system development platforms have become more widely available, and as commission rates have dropped, the profitability of the classical trading systems has declined to near zero.

Richard Donchian was trading his systems in the 1960s and writing about them in the 1970s. Richard Dennis and William Eckhardt started their famous group of Turtle traders in 1983 and made their most spectacular profits in the early years using Donchian-style systems.

4

Measuring Success

Recognizing goodness

An optimization is a search for a *best* trading system. The goodness of
a system is measured by the value of the objective function. The best
system is defined to be the one that has the highest objective function
value. Choosing the objective function is the most important, and the
most personal, task in designing a trading system.

An objective function assigns scores to each component or factor
that is used in its calculation and combines them into a single value. The
goal of the trading system is to maximize the objective function score
for every time period, especially the out-of-sample validation period.
If the objective function is properly designed, no other metric matters.
That is – if the objective function is properly defined, everything of importance is accounted for in the objective function, and in proportion
to its importance to you.

Only you can decide which trading systems are good and which are
not. Selection of the objective function is a management decision and
must be made prior to extensive model development. The objective function itself is not a candidate for optimization.

You already have subjective preferences regarding a trading system
and know what is important to you. Your preferences might be high
percentage annual gain, low drawdown, frequent trading, short holding periods, and so forth. Or you may not know exactly what statistics
are important, but you will recognize the equity curve that you prefer.
In that case, run an AmiBroker optimization (see Chapter 5 – AmiBro-

ker) and examine the results. AmiBroker will have calculated the metrics for each of the sets of arguments. Export the table of optimization results so it can be opened using a spreadsheet. Back in AmiBroker, set the variables to an assortment of argument values and plot the equity curve for each. Select those that are best in your judgment. Examine the values of the metrics that correspond to the equity curves you like. In essence, you are giving AmiBroker a problem you already know the solution to, and grading its performance.

You must have enough confidence in the definition of your objective function that you are always willing to accept the model at the top of the list. If you ever prefer a model below the top one, then the objective function does not accurately reflect your preference, and must be modified. Later, when you perform automated walk forward testing, the system development platform will be selecting the best model, testing that model's forward profitability, stepping ahead in time, and repeating the process, all without your active participation in decision making.

Benchmark

Before proceeding too far, decide what your benchmark is. Is beating one of the broad market averages, such as the Russell 2000, satisfactory? If the Russell 2000 is down ten percent in a year, does a system that is down only five percent qualify as a success? Or must there be an absolute gain? If necessary, the objective function should include a relative performance component.

If one of the metrics preprogrammed into AmiBroker is satisfactory, just use it. If not, then it will be necessary to program a custom metric. For AmiBroker, refer to the Appendix – Extending AmiBroker, and to the AmiBroker documentation explaining how to add custom metrics to the reports.

Metrics

The metrics preprogrammed into AmiBroker include:
- Net profit $. Profit in dollars for the entire period.
- Net profit %. Profit in percent for the entire period.
- Exposure %. Market exposure to the trading system calculated bar by bar.
- Net risk adjusted return in percent. Net profit percent / exposure in percent.

- Annual return % – CAR. Compounded Annual Return in percent.
- Risk adjusted return % – RAR. CAR / Exposure %.
- Average profit / loss. (profit of winners in dollars + loss of losers in dollars) / number of trades.
- Average profit / loss %. (percent profit of winners + % loss of losers) / number of trades.
- Average bars held. Sum of bars in trades / number of trades.
- Maximum trade drawdown. Largest peak to valley decline in dollars in any single trade.
- Maximum trade % drawdown. Largest peak to valley percentage decline in any single trade.
- Maximum system drawdown. Largest peak to valley decline in portfolio equity.
- Maximum system % drawdown. Largest peak to valley percentage decline in portfolio equity.
- Recovery factor. Net profit / maximum system drawdown.
- CAR / MaxDD. Compound annual percent return / maximum system percent drawdown.
- RAR / MaxDD. Risk adjusted return / maximum system percent drawdown.
- Profit factor. Profit of winners / loss of losers.
- Payoff ratio. Ratio of average win to average loss.
- Standard error. Standard error of the equity line.
- Risk-reward ratio. Slope of equity line as expected annual return / standard error of equity line.
- Ulcer index. Square root of sum of squared drawdowns / number of bars.
- Ulcer performance index. (annual return in percent – treasury note return in percent) / ulcer index.
- Sharpe ratio of trades. (annualized return in percent – risk free rate of return) / annualized standard deviation of returns.
- K-ratio. Linear regression slope of equity / standard error of equity, normalized.

EQUITY SMOOTHNESS is very important. Minimizing drawdowns allows optimal f, which is important in position sizing decisions, to be higher. Unexpected gains are nice, but predictability makes setting of profit targets easier. Given a sufficiently smooth equity curve with low drawdown, annual return for most tradables can be increased by increasing the leverage, up to the point of drawdown limitation.

Some of the metrics I find best for my personality are risk adjusted return, risk-reward ratio and K-ratio. In all cases, higher values are preferable.

OTHER METRICS that are useful include:

- Expectancy. (% winners * average profit) – (% losers * average loss).
- Sortino ratio. Computed in the same way as the Sharpe ratio, but does not penalize winning trades. Only losing trades are used to compute the downside deviation which is used in the denominator.
- Semi-deviation. An alternative to the variance in which only observations that fall below the mean, or below zero, are included in the calculation.
- Treynor ratio. A metric applied to portfolios that is similar to the Sharpe ratio. Computed as: (average return of the portfolio – risk free rate of return) / beta of portfolio.
- VAMI. Value Added Monthly Index. Computed as: Latest VAMI = previous VAMI * (1 + latest month percentage gain). Often used to compare performance of funds.
- Equity smoothness – Various measures. For example, correlation between day by day equity and linear regression of equity.
- Trading frequency – Number of trades per period. Long term traders prefer a lower number; models that look for infrequent but profitable situations prefer a lower number; high frequency traders prefer a higher number.
- Percent winners. Number of winners / number of trades.
- Win to loss ratio. Payoff ratio.
- Average profit per trade. Dollars per trade or percent per trade.
- Holding period. Average number of bars per trade.
- Pessimistic Return Ratio – PRR. Documented in Ralph Vince's books on money management, PRR adjusts the profit factor by increasing the weight given losing trades and decreasing the weight given winning trades.

$$PRR = \frac{\left(\#Wins - \sqrt{\#Wins}\right) * AvgWin}{\left(\#Losses + \sqrt{\#Losses}\right) * AvgLoss}$$

EXPECTANCY

Having gone through all the metrics that AmiBroker reports, there is one component that absolutely must be included in some form. That is expectancy. Think in terms of the trades made by a system over a long enough period that all the possible results have happened. It is best to measure the result from each trade as a percentage profit or loss. The expectancy of a trading system is the average profit per trade taken over all trades. If you separate trades into winning trades and losing trades, then expectancy is the percent of trades that are winning trades times the average percentage won per trade, plus the percent of trades that are losing trades times the average percentage lost per trade.

The expectancy of a trading system *must* be positive. No money management or position sizing technique will convert a system with a negative expectancy into a profitable one.

ANNUAL ACCOUNT GROWTH RATE

The average annual growth rate for a trading account depends on only two figures:
• expectancy
• trading frequency

Compute the geometric mean of expectancy per trade and express it as a decimal fraction. Call this e. For example, if a system has an average profit per trade of 0.8%, then e = 0.008.

Compute the average number of trades completed per year. Call this n. If that same system trades 12 times in a year, n = 12.

The final account equity at the end of the year will be some multiple of the account equity at the beginning of the year. Call this m.

$$m = (1 + e)^n$$

$$m = (1 + 0.008)^{12} = 1.1003$$

The annual account growth rate, g, is m - 1, or 10%.

The equity curves for two trading systems may look very different, but if they have the same values for both e and n, then they have the same annual growth rate.

Note the positive effect that compounding has. A system that trades once a week and averages a 1% profit, has an annual growth rate of 67%.

CASINO GAME

Just for interest, let's compute the expectancy and growth rate of a casino game. Take roulette, for example. In the United States, there are 38 slots the ball may fall into — 18 red, 18 black, 2 green. For the even money bets, such as red/black or odd/even, a win is a 100% profit, a loss is a 100% loss. Since green is neither even nor odd, red nor black, green is always a loss. On average, in every 38 plays, every slot will be hit once.

$$e = \frac{18 * (+1) + 20 * (-1)}{38} = \frac{-2}{38} = -0.0526$$

The expected return on every \$1.00 bet is \$.9474.

Playing once a minute for an hour gives 60 plays. The expected final value of every dollar after one hour is

$$(1 - 0.0562)^{60} = (0.9474)^{60} = 0.039 = 4 \text{ cents}$$

Since the expectancy is negative, no money management, position size, or betting sequence scheme can make roulette profitable for the player. Any trading system that has a negative expectancy is just as certain to go broke.

FURTHER DISCUSSION

Modeling Trading System Performance discusses expectancy and account growth in much more detail. It includes discussion of the distribution of results, both account growth and drawdown, that can be expected from a trading system.

CUSTOM METRICS

Calling on the object orientation of AmiBroker itself, it is possible to add custom metrics and have them reported in the Trade Report and the Optimization Report. Because of the advanced nature of the Ami-Broker Formula Language (AFL) code required to implement custom metrics, discussion of them is postponed until the Appendix – Extending AmiBroker.

5

AmiBroker

WHY USE AMIBROKER?

One of my goals was that every reader should be able to test for him
or herself the methods I describe. In order to do that, the method must
be coded as an indicator or program in the language of some trading
system development platform, then executed using historical data. In
early drafts of this book, I coded examples in several languages, including AmiBroker, TradeStation, MetaStock, Dakota, WealthLab, and
Excel. Several problems became apparent.

- The book has about 80 examples written as code. Increasing the
  number of languages increases the page count of the book by
  some factor of 80 for each additional language.
- With the exception of one example, everything could be coded and
  executed in AmiBroker. No other trading system development
  platform came even close to being able handle everything. Enhancements made to AmiBroker between the first and second edition of this book have removed that one exception, and everything
  can now be done in AmiBroker.
- AmiBroker code is both easy to understand and concise. Most of
  the other trading system development platforms require several
  times the number of lines of code to do the same tasks when compared with AmiBroker.
- My editors found that using multiple languages was confusing
  and recommended I pick one and use it exclusively.
- Selecting a single trading system development platform allows me

to use its name as shorthand for "a trading system development platform of your choice."

- AmiBroker is powerful and inexpensive, and is easily a peer to other trading system development platforms available to retail-level developers.

While I did not set out to write "an AmiBroker book," AmiBroker turned out to be an ideal choice. If *Quantitative Trading Systems* is seen as an AmiBroker book, no apology is necessary—it is that good.

MODELING TRADING SYSTEM PERFORMANCE

Throughout this book, you will see references to *Modeling Trading System Performance* (MTSP). MTSP was published after the first edition of *Quantitative Trading Systems*, and before the second edition. It is a sequel to this book. It discusses expectancy, trading frequency, holding period, Monte Carlo simulation, estimation of profit potential and drawdown, position sizing, and how to tell whether a system is working or broken. You can learn more about it at its website: *www.modelingtradingsystemperformance.com.*

FEATURES AND FUNCTIONS

TO SUMMARIZE SOME OF AMIBROKER'S FEATURES. It was chosen to develop, test, and illustrate the quantitative concepts described in this book because:
- It has all the features necessary, including:
  - Ease of use
  - High speed execution
  - Ability to use data from a variety of sources
  - Ability to use intra-day data as well as end of day data
  - Fast optimizer
  - Flexible back-tester
  - Equity curve analysis
  - Automated trading
- It is very fast
- It is inexpensive
- It is extremely well supported
- It uses the AFL programming language
- It has a large library of indicators and systems

- It can be extended
- It operates on portfolios as well as individual series
- It can model rotational trading systems
- It can model position sizing
- Its models can use multiple data streams
- It has a large user base with excellent discussion groups
- It is a stable program with years of history

AmiBroker comes in two editions – Standard and Professional. Both have excellent functionality including:
- 32 bit version
- End-of-day processing, including:
  - Charting
  - Backtesting
  - Scanning
- Intra-day processing, resolution of 1 minute bars on up, including:
  - Charting
  - Backtesting
  - Scanning
- Automatic updating of real time charts
- Data feed functionality covering any exchange in the world and with almost any data source
- Database for an unlimited number of symbols and unlimited number of quotes.
- Supports multiple databases
- Automatic accumulation of ticks into minute bars up to end-of-day bars
- Companion AmiQuote downloader program works with many sources of free end-of-day data
- Streaming real-time quote handling for many real-time data sources
- Automated trading interface for many on-line brokerages
- Portfolio level testing and optimization
- Walk forward validation
- Ability to trade a basket of equities on a single signal
- Create spreads and trading signals for spreads
- Position sizing
- Currency conversion
- Portfolio management

THE PROFESSIONAL EDITION ADDS:

- 32 bit version
- Tick charts
  - Charting
  - Backtesting
  - Scanning
- 5 second and 15 second bars
  - Charting
  - Backtesting
  - Scanning
- Maximum adverse and favorable excursion reports and charts
- Unlimited time and sales window
- Get extended real time data

BOTH VERSIONS OF AMIBROKER also have these operational features:
- Charting includes over 70 built in indicators that can be applied by drag-and-drop and object oriented drawing tools such as trend lines, regression channels, cycles.
- Time frames can be changed on the fly, multiple time frame charts can be easily displayed, and multiple time frame trading systems are easily created.
- The windows and chart panes are completely customizable.
- AmiBroker Formula Language (AFL) allows creation and application of custom indicators and trading systems. Over 200 built-in AFL functions including statistics, data manipulation, looping, conditional branching, and signal generation, are provided as building blocks.
- AFL code is stored in clear text files and can be edited using the built-in editor or an editor of your choice. AFL language can be extended via custom written DLL modules.
- Screening automatically scans the database for current buy and sell signals, or signals over any defined period of time.
- Exploration searches the database for symbols matching user defined criteria and creates reports showing values of indicators, past performance, etcetera.
- Backtesting and optimizing operate on either individual issues or portfolios over any period of time desired, computing and reporting about twenty built-in metrics. Custom metrics can be defined. Equity curves are automatically generated and can be used to filter trades.

VERSUS OTHER SOFTWARE

The programs listed here are the primary competition for AmiBroker as of the time this chapter is being written. An Internet search for "trading system development platforms" will bring up new or additional entries. The monthly magazine, *Technical Analysis of Stocks and Commodities* (TASC), has a regular column, Trader's Tips. Each month, one of the articles in TASC is coded into a directly usable indicator or trading system for several trading system platforms. Checking the most recent issues will give an idea of what software is being actively supported. The code listings provide a comparison of the programming languages each uses. The AmiBroker code is regularly both the fewest lines and the easiest to understand.

METASTOCK

Reuters Corporation owns MetaStock, which has been one of the major platforms for many years. It comes in two distinct versions – end-of-day (about $500) and real-time (about $1400 to $1700). Reuters is also a supplier of market data that can be used with the MetaStock program, as well as most other platforms, including AmiBroker.

MetaStock's capabilities for systems design, programming, backtesting, and optimization have lagged the other platforms. They recently changed from a "fill in the box" system development methodology to a more modern programming language.

TRADESTATION

For many years, TradeStation was a standalone trading system development platform distributed by Omega Research, Inc. In about 2001 it became a publicly traded company, symbol TRAD, and changed its orientation to that of a combination system development platform and brokerage. As of this writing, it is in the process of being acquired by Monex, a Tokyo-based brokerage.

TradeStation's current emphasis is on real-time trading systems and their brokerage. Their development language, EasyLanguage, is a procedural language with special functions for trading, and is integrated with their trading platform. There are extensive libraries of code to compute and display indicators and trading signals, and an active users community. Traders who trade actively through TradeStation brokerage get the TradeStation program at fees ranging from free to $100 per month. Monthly fees for subscribers who use other brokerages begin at about $250. Although support for the final standalone version, TradeStation 5.0, aka 2000i, was closed in 2003, copies can still be found for about $2500.

WEALTH-LAB PRO

Wealth-Lab was acquired by Fidelity Investments a few years ago. Before that time, the program was available for license for a fee. It is now free to active traders in the United States who make at least 120 trades per year through Fidelity brokerage.

ESIGNAL

eSignal is both a trading system development platform and real-time data provider. It is priced at $115 to $200 per month, plus exchange fees. Of the alternatives to AmiBroker listed here, eSignal's programming language is the most inconvenient to use. What might be a 30 line AmiBroker program could well be 200 lines in eSignal. Consider, for example, the September 2006 Trader's Tips describing an Adaptive Price Zone indicator and trading system. The AmiBroker code is listed in Chapter 10, Figure 10.5.

AMIBROKER – RECAP

Both the Standard ($199) and Professional ($279) versions of AmiBroker support both end-of-day and real-time data and trading systems based on that data. The license fee for AmiBroker gives the purchaser the right to use the programs forever at no additional cost. Yahoo hosts several users groups where the exchange of ideas related to AmiBroker from over 11,000 registered members produces dozens of messages a day. The AmiBroker web site has a library of indicators and trading systems ready to copy and paste. Some of these have been provided by AmiBroker, others by users. AmiBroker works with just about any source of data, end-of-day or real-time, covering just about every market in the world, from just about any data vendor. AmiBroker works with many automated order entry systems.

Persons just starting development of trading systems and trading can get AmiBroker Standard for $199 and use Yahoo or msn end-of-day data at no cost. AmiBroker is highly recommended.

A<small>MI</small>B<small>ROKER</small> SETUP

AmiBroker can be downloaded from *www.amibroker.com*. The setup file
is about 8 MB, and includes both 32 and 64 bit versions. Double click the
program's icon and accept all the defaults. A small database, consisting
of about eighteen month's data for each of the 30 stocks in the Dow Jones
Industrial Average, is automatically installed, as are files which provide
the context-sensitive help. Until a license has been purchased, the program runs in demo mode – everything works, but nothing can be saved.

The User's Guide, a 1000+ page printable version of the help files, is
both included in the 8 MB AmiBroker setup and available as a separate
6 MB download.

A<small>MI</small>Q<small>UOTE</small>

AmiQuote is a separate program, but is included in the AmiBroker download file and is integrated into AmiBroker. The AmiBroker Help system
has detailed instructions for setting up a database and using AmiQuote
to retrieve data from any of several data services. I recommend using
AmiQuote and free end-of-day data from Yahoo or msn while learning
AmiBroker.

D<small>ATA</small> SERVICES

Both the AmiBroker Help system and the User's Guide contain detailed
instructions for setting up AmiBroker with the data subscription service of your choice.

AmiBroker supports end-of-day services, including Norgate, Quotes
Plus, TC2000, FastTrack, MetaStock, CSI, Quote.com, msn, Yahoo, ASCII,
and any DDE source. It also supports real-time and delayed services including eSignal, DTN IQFeed, QuoteTracker, and Interactive Brokers.
AmiBroker manages backfilling real-time databases.

G<small>ETTING</small> STARTED

AmiBroker has tutorials in its Help system, and in its User's Guide.
When you are on-line, there are excellent video tutorials. While this
book is not intending to be a comprehensive instruction guide to Ami-
Broker, a few basic techniques will be described, particularly those
that will help lay the foundation for discussions related to quantitative
trading later in the book.

DISPLAY A PRICE SERIES

There is always a primary data series. To choose a new series, on the **Symbol** menu, click the desired symbol.

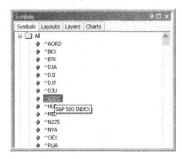

FIGURE 5.1 DISPLAY DATA SERIES

Once a symbol has been selected, the up and down arrows will select the symbol earlier or later in the list.

DISPLAY A CHART

The AmiBroker Charts tab shows a list of all the indicators and systems. Some of them are complete, in that they will show the price series along with some indicators and can be displayed on their own. Others are only indicators and must be applied to a price series to be meaningful. To display a chart in its own Window Pane, on the **Charts** menu, right-click, select **Insert**, left-click.

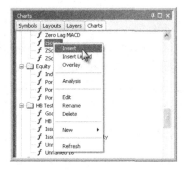

FIGURE 5.2 DISPLAY CHART

This chart shows an indicator called z-score applied to a price series, and can be displayed on its own.

FIGURE 5.3 CHART DISPLAYED

ADD AN INDICATOR

Other charts contain only indicators and are intended to be applied to a price series that is already displayed. To add an indicator to an existing chart:

- On the **Charts** menu, select the indicator to be applied.
- Left-click and drag-and-drop it onto the series to be used as the base.

The example shows the DEMA moving average being applied to a price series.

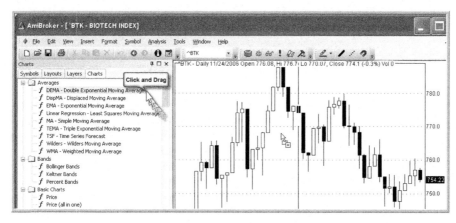

FIGURE 5.4 DRAG AND DROP AN INDICATOR

Figure 5.5 shows the result.

FIGURE 5.5 DRAG AND DROP RESULT

WRITE IN THE COMMENTARY WINDOW

During the development of a program, it is useful to have debugging information output. Two ways to do that easily and quickly are:
* Compute something and plot it.
* Write something to the Commentary Window.

When a program is finished and being used for trading, the Commentary Window is a good place to review information about the issue, the indicators, and the signals.

Any string that is not assigned to a program variable is automatically written to the Commentary Window.

```
//   CommentaryWindow.afl
//
//   An example of using the Commentary Window.
//
//   Perform whatever calculations are needed.

FMA = MA(C,3);
SMA = MA(C,20);
Diff = FMA - SMA;

//   Write debugging information to the Commentary Window.
"The values of the two moving averages are: ";
WriteVal (FMA, 1.4);
WriteVal (SMA, 1.4);
```

```
//   Combining text with variables.
"The difference between them is: " + WriteVal(Diff,1.4);
```

FIGURE 5.6 COMMENTARY WINDOW

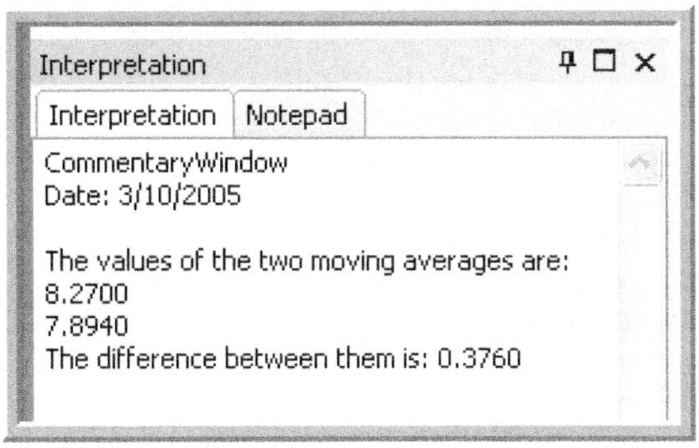

FIGURE 5.7 COMMENTARY OUTPUT

TEST A TRADING SYSTEM

Write a trading system, complete with Buy and Sell signals, and save it.

- From the **Analysis** menu, select **Formula Editor**.
- It will open with a blank screen. Type in, or use copy and paste, whatever AFL program you want to use. The code in Figure 5.8, for example.
- When you are done typing, save the program.
- On the **File** menu, select **Save As**.
- Navigate to the directory you want to use for your custom functions, indicators, and systems. AmiBroker will probably suggest C:\Program Files\AmiBroker\Formulas\Custom.
- Name the file something meaningful.
- Let AmiBroker add the .afl extension.
- Click **Save**.

```
//   ExampleTradingSystem.afl
//
//   Very simple trading system

FMA = MA(C,3);
SMA = MA(C,20);

Buy = Cross (FMA, SMA);
Sell = Cross (SMA, FMA);
```

FIGURE 5.8 EXAMPLE TRADING SYSTEM

To select the issue to be traded, on the **Symbols** menu, double-click the desired symbol.

FIGURE 5.9 SYMBOL SELECT

To select the trading system to be used, on the **Analysis** menu, select **Automatic Analysis**. Click **Pick**, select ExampleTradingSystem, click **Open**.

To set the data range and other settings, from the main **Automatic Analysis** window, select **Current Symbol**, set the **from** and **to** dates.

FIGURE 5.10 AUTOMATIC ANALYSIS SETTINGS

Click **Settings**, select the **General** tab. Set **Positions** to Long. Set **Initial Equity** to the starting amount in the account.

FIGURE 5.11 BACKTESTER SETTINGS - GENERAL

Click the **Trades** tab. Set the **Buy price** and **Sell price** as you wish them. Choosing *Close* instructs AmiBroker to trade at the close of trading using a Market on Close order. The Buy delay and Sell delay setting specify how many bars to wait after the signal before the action. Setting Buy price to Close and Buy delay to zero means trade at the close of the bar that triggers the signal. To trade at tomorrow's open, set Buy price to Open and Buy delay to 1.

FIGURE 5.12 BACKTESTER SETTINGS - TRADES

Click the **Reports** tab. Set the **Result List** to **Trade List**.

FIGURE 5.13 BACKTESTER SETTINGS - REPORT

Click **OK** back to the Automatic Analysis window. Click **BackTest**. The trade by trade list will appear in the window.

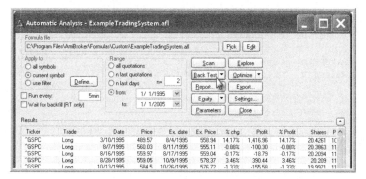

FIGURE 5.14 BACKTEST TRADE LISTING

Click **Report**, and the Backtest Report will open. There is a lot more to the report than is shown here.

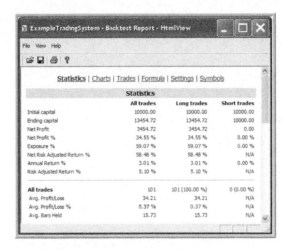

FIGURE 5.15 BACKTEST REPORT

OPTIMIZE A TRADING SYSTEM

To search for the best values for the parameters in a trading system, use AmiBroker's optimization features. Modify the trading system so that the variables to be searched are set as Optimize. Save the new version.

```
//    ExampleTradingSystemOptimize.afl
//
//    Very simple trading system
//    set up to optimize.

MA1Length = Optimize("MA1Length",3,1,20,1);
MA2Length = Optimize("MA2Length",20,5,50,5);

FMA = MA(C,MA1Length);
SMA = MA(C,MA2Length);

Buy = Cross (FMA, SMA);
Sell = Cross (SMA, FMA);
```

FIGURE 5.16 EXAMPLE TRADING SYSTEM OPTIMIZE

Pick the system to be optimized (the one saved in the last step), click **Optimize**.

FIGURE 5.17 OPTIMIZING EXAMPLE

AmiBroker will evaluate each of the combinations of parameters and report the metrics for each combination in a list.

By default, the results are sorted in descending order by net profit. Clicking the heading of any column will sort the results based on that column.

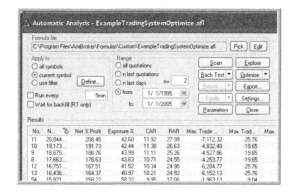

FIGURE 5.18 OPTIMIZING RESULTS, LEFT SIDE

Scroll over to the right to see the values of the parameters associated with each line in the report.

FIGURE 5.19 OPTIMIZING RESULTS, RIGHT SIDE

OTHER FEATURES AND CAPABILITIES of AmiBroker will be introduced as they arise in the discussion.

RESOURCES

AmiBroker has a very large support community. Whether you are just evaluating the program or are an active user of it, join the Yahoo Ami-Broker Group. There are over 5000 members – some just lurk and listen, some post and answer questions, others volunteer ideas.

The User Guide is excellent, including tutorials as well as specific descriptions of individual features. It prints out at over 600 pages.

The AmiBroker Help command opens a hyperlinked version of the User Guide. From it, examples of AFL code can be copied and pasted into the program you are working on.

TASC's monthly column entitled Trader's Tips provides the code for one of its articles each month for each of several development platforms. There is an on-line version of this column as well at *www.traders.com*. The article is often written by a principal developer of the platform company. AmiBroker is featured in almost every issue, with many of the programs written by AmiBroker's president and chief designer, Tomasz Janeczko.

6

Issue Selection

THE IDEAL ISSUE TO TRADE has several characteristics.

1. There is enough data to allow us to model its behavior.
2. The price is reasonable throughout its history.
3. There is sufficient liquidity over the recent period.
4. The length and amplitude of its typical cycle matches the holding period and drawdown of our comfort level.
5. It offers enough profit potential.
6. We can discover one or more quantitative trading systems that work with it.

Too often, modelers start with point 6 – looking for trading systems that work. A few simple filters can be run first to select a group of issues that meet points 1 through 5, then begin system development and testing. You may have other criteria that are important to you.

We can address points 1, 2, and 3 with a simple AmiBroker program that will run as an Exploration.

When AmiBroker was set up, it came with a small database. You can use that database to practice the techniques described in this chapter, but to get the full advantages, a more complete database should be installed.

Assume we want:
- Ten years of historical data.
- The lowest price over the last ten years to be at least $2.00.

- The average daily liquidity (dollar volume) over the past year to be at least $1,000,000.

On the **Analysis** menu, select **Formula Editor**, and enter the following:

```
// IssueSelectionFilter1.afl
//
// This AmiBroker program uses filters to help
//      with issue selection.
//
// To use this filter,
// 1. Analysis >> Automatic Analysis
// 2. "Pick", then select this file, and Open it
// 3. "Explore"
//
// With the results of any exploration,
// you can sort the result of any column
// by clicking on that column's header.
//
// Assume we are working with stocks and using daily bars.

// There are about 252 trading days in a year.
// See if there is a closing price for the date 10 years ago.
PriceYearsAgo = Ref(C,-2520);
HistoryExists = PriceYearsAgo!=0;

// Find the lowest closing price for the past 10 years.
LowestClose = LLV(C,2520);
PriceReasonable = LowestClose > 2.00;

// Compute the average daily Liquidity
// (Closing Price times Volume) for the past Year.
Liquidity = MA(C*V,252);
LiquidityOK = Liquidity > 1000000;

// "Comment Out" the "Filter = " statement that
//      you do not want to use,
// leaving the other active.
// Allow all issues to pass the filter.
Filter = 1;
// Set the filter to block issues that do not
//      meet our criteria.
// Filter = HistoryExists AND PriceReasonable AND LiquidityOK;

// Add columns to report the items of interest.
AddColumn(C,"Close",4.2);
AddColumn(PriceYearsAgo,"PriceYearsAgo",4.2);
AddColumn(LowestClose,"LowestClose",4.2);
AddColumn(Liquidity,"Liquidity",4.0);
```

FIGURE 6.1 ISSUE SELECTION FILTER

Using a small nine issue Watch List, here are the results:

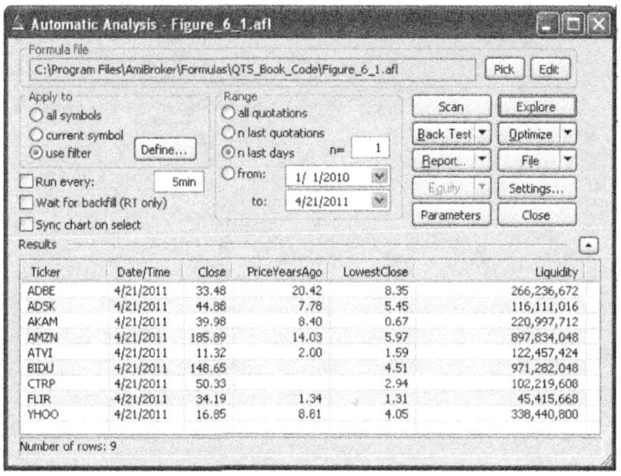

Ticker	Date/Time	Close	PriceYearsAgo	LowestClose	Liquidity
ADBE	4/21/2011	33.48	20.42	8.35	266,236,672
ADSK	4/21/2011	44.88	7.78	5.45	116,111,016
AKAM	4/21/2011	39.98	8.40	0.67	220,997,712
AMZN	4/21/2011	185.89	14.03	5.97	897,834,048
ATVI	4/21/2011	11.32	2.00	1.59	122,457,424
BIDU	4/21/2011	148.65		4.51	971,282,048
CTRP	4/21/2011	50.33		2.94	102,219,608
FLIR	4/21/2011	34.19	1.34	1.31	45,415,668
YHOO	4/21/2011	16.85	8.81	4.05	338,440,800

Figure 6.2 Issue Selection Results

We see that two of the issues do not have ten years of history, three have a lowest close below $2.00, and all nine pass the liquidity test.

Criterion 2 specifies that the lowest daily closing price during the last ten years be $2.00 or higher. Be aware that most historical data series are adjusted for splits. The adjustment process gives the appearance of low prices in the early portion of the data series, when in fact they were not. Whenever there is a stock split, the historical prices for dates before the split are adjusted. Say the closing price for some stock on August 1 is $40.00 and a 2 for 1 split is effective August 2. After the split, all stockholders will have twice as many shares, each priced at $20.00. To avoid the discontinuity of the price change from $40.00 to $20.00, all prices (Open, High, Low, and Close) for August 1 and all earlier dates are divided by two and all volumes are multiplied by two. If a stock has had a large split or several splits, the accumulated effect is to lower the apparent price of the shares several years ago. Look at FLIR Systems, ticker FLIR, for example. When this exploration was run, it was $34.19. The historical data shows that it was as low as $1.31 in April, 2001. But FLIR stock split 2-for-1 three times—on 5/30/2003, 2/3/2005, and 12/11/2007. The actual lowest price in 2001 was $10.55. The split adjustments caused the earlier data to appear to be lower, and applying the filter in criterion 2 excludes it from the group of issues you want to work with.

After running the Exploration, click the heading at the top of one of the columns and AmiBroker will sort the report using that column as the key. For example, sorting on LowestClose gives this result:

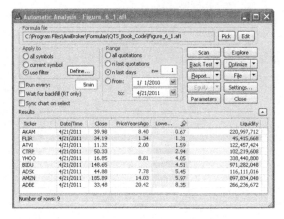

FIGURE 6.3 SORTED LOWEST CLOSE

If you wish to have AmiBroker filter out all those issues that fail to meet your criteria, un-comment the line:

```
Filter = HistoryExists AND PriceReasonable AND LiquidityOK;
```

And rerun the Exploration. The code looks like this:

```
// IssueSelectionFilter2.afl
//
// This AmiBroker program uses filters to help
//      with issue selection.
//
// To use this filter,
// 1. Analysis >> Automatic Analysis
// 2. "Pick", then select this file, and Open it
// 3. "Explore"
//
// With the results of any exploration,
// you can sort the result of any column
// by clicking on that column's header.
//
// Assume we are working with stocks and using daily bars.

// There are about 252 trading days in a year.
// See if there is a closing price for the date 10 years ago.
PriceYearsAgo = Ref(C,-2520);
HistoryExists = PriceYearsAgo!=0;

// Find the lowest closing price for the past 10 years.
LowestClose = LLV(C,2520);
PriceReasonable = LowestClose > 2.00;

// Compute the average daily Liquidity
// (Closing Price times Volume) for the past Year.
Liquidity = MA(C*V,252);
LiquidityOK = Liquidity > 1000000;
```

```
// "Comment Out" the "Filter = " statement that
//      you do not want to use,
// leaving the other active.
// Allow all issues to pass the filter.
// Filter = 1;
// Set the filter to block issues that do not
//      meet our criteria.
Filter = HistoryExists AND PriceReasonable AND LiquidityOK;

// Add columns to report the items of interest.
AddColumn(C,"Close",4.2);
AddColumn(PriceYearsAgo,"PriceYearsAgo",4.2);
AddColumn(LowestClose,"LowestClose",4.2);
AddColumn(Liquidity,"Liquidity",4.0);
```

FIGURE 6.4 ISSUE SELECTION FILTER

This is the result you will see:

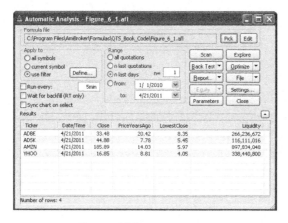

FIGURE 6.5 FILTERED ISSUES

There are several ways to create a Watch List with the tickers that satisfy the criteria.

The first, and most straight forward, uses the menu that comes up when you click any line of the results of an Exploration. Right-click, then select **Add all results to watch list**. The **Select Watch List** menu comes up, and you can select the list you wish to use. See Figure 6.8.

Before you add those tickers, you might want to do two things:

- be sure that watch list is empty,
- give the watch list a meaningful name.

To see if the watch list is empty, just click the "+" sign next to **Watch lists** on the **Symbol** menu. There is a switch that lets you control whether to display all watch lists or only those that are empty. Right-click in Watch-

List area to set it. In Figure 6.6, List 22 is empty and has not been renamed.

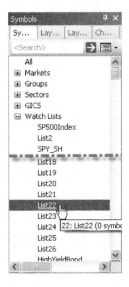

FIGURE 6.6 WATCH LISTS

To change the name of a watch list to be Filtered Tickers use the following sequence of commands:

1. On the **Symbol** menu, select **Categories**, then **Watch Lists**
2. Select the list to use, click **Edit Name**, type in the new name, such as Filtered Tickers
3. Click **OK**

Like this:

FIGURE 6.7 EDIT WATCH LIST NAME

Now go ahead and **Add all results to watch list** — the watch list named Filtered Tickers.

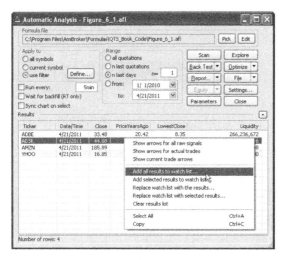

FIGURE 6.8 ADD ALL RESULTS TO WATCH LIST

You may want to analyze test results outside AmiBroker, for example in a spreadsheet. On the **Automatic Analysis** menu, use the drop-down menu next to the **File** button, then click **Export**. A **Save As** menu will open, allow you to browse to the directory when you want to save the file, and save the data as a comma-separated-value (CSV) file.

From the spreadsheet, or any other source, a text (TXT) file with a list of tickers you want to use in AmiBroker can be imported into a watch list. To do that:

On the **Symbol** menu, select **Watch List,** then **Import**

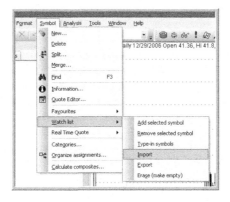

FIGURE 6.9 WATCH LIST IMPORT

Select the Watch List named Filtered Tickers
Click **OK**.

FIGURE 6.10 SELECT WATCH LIST

Select the text file you just created, then **Open**. This copies the symbols
into the Watch List named Filtered Tickers.

If there are other issues that you want included in this Watch List,
you can add them using the **Watch List** option on the **Symbols** menu,
and either type them in manually or import them from another file. For
example, add FLIR back in, since its actual price was not less than our
filter criterion. You might want to add them to the FilteredTickers.tls list
as well, so AmiQuote will include them when you update quotes.

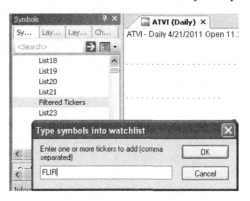

FIGURE 6.11 ADD SYMBOL TO WATCH LIST

Be sure to review Chapter 2, Data, before finalizing your Filtered Tickers and before proceeding with the next section of this chapter. If your
data has unadjusted splits, distributions, or dividends, or other serious
data inconsistencies, the results will be misleading. Be aware of extreme
price changes that are not splits – issues that often have extreme prices
changes can be difficult to model.

That takes care of points 1, 2, and 3. Points 4 and 5 are important to prevent us from wasting our time developing trading systems that cannot provide the profit we need, or that have cycle lengths that do not match our own trading style.

The primary criterion for the goodness of a trading system for many traders is drawdown. Assume for a minute that you are an investor who holds positions for months or years, and you have a long position in a stock or fund. Your entry price was $25.00 per share and your initial investment was $10,000.00. If the price never rose significantly, what percentage loss would cause you to sell? We all have perfect hindsight and can see in the historical chart instances where one particular 10% drop was temporary, but where other 10% drops were the first 10% of a 30% or 50% drop. When there is no way to see the next bars on the chart, what is your drawdown tolerance?

For discussion, say the tolerance is 10%. That means that, in addition to exit signals that come from the trading system, any drop in price of 10% from the highest price of the open long position will cause a sell. In AmiBroker, this can be implemented by using a trailing stop set to 10 percent.

Assume all transactions take place at the close using daily bars. (It is easy to modify AmiBroker code to trade at the Open, or to recognize high and low prices.) Using perfect hindsight, we can analyze the historical prices of any issue we are considering. We will do the analysis in AmiBroker using the ZigZag function, which accepts two parameters – the series being analyzed and percentage. Since we are trading on the close, our series is the Close. Since our drawdown tolerance is 10%, we will set the percentage to 10. The ZigZag function connects closing prices such that there is no "correction" of more than 10% in any uptrend or downtrend. That is, the ZigZag indicator can give perfect buy and sell signals so that there is never a drawdown of 10% or more in any long or short position.

Figure 6.12 shows a 10% ZigZag applied to Adobe Corporation (ticker ADBE) daily bars with buy arrows at the low points and sell arrows at the high points. If we had a trading system capable of generating these buy and sell signals, our exits would always come from exit signals – we would never sell because our drawdown tolerance was exceeded. But, if we set the ZigZag percentage to 15%, or even to 11%, then there could be, and probably would be, trades where the 10% drawdown would cause an exit before the trade continued to its profitable trading system-generated exit.

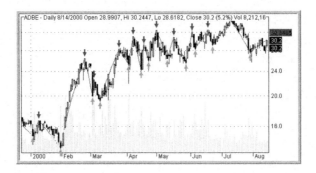

FIGURE 6.12 ZIGZAG INDICATOR

By setting the ZigZag percentage to some value, buying at the low, selling at the high, and analyzing the trades, we can tell several things:

1. The cycle length associated with the given percentage, and the consistency of the cycle length.
2. The typical holding period for long positions, and for short positions, and their consistency.
3. The profit potential.

Use the following AmiBroker code for the ZigZag System, which gives perfect buy and sell signals.

```
// ZigZag.afl
//
// This AmiBroker program uses the ZigZag function
// to give perfect buy and sell signals
// to help analyze the appropriateness of an
// issue.
//
// To use this system,
// 1. Analysis >> Automatic Analysis
// 2. Pick >> select ZigZag.afl >> Open
// 3. Other Settings as desired
// 4. Backtest >> Individual Backtest
//

// Analyze using the Closing price
PricePoint = C;

// Set the ZigZag Percentage
Percentage = 10;

Z = Zig(PricePoint,Percentage);

Buy = Z<=Ref(Z,1) AND Z<=Ref(Z,-1);
```

```
Sell = Z>=Ref(Z,1) AND Z>=Ref(Z,-1);
Short = Sell;
Cover = Buy;

Plot(C,"C",colorBlack,styleCandle);
Plot(Z,"Z",colorRed,styleLine);
PlotShapes(shapeUpArrow*Buy,colorBrightGreen);
PlotShapes(shapeDownArrow*Sell,colorRed);
```

FIGURE 6.13 ZIGZAG

Set the percentage to the drawdown tolerance you want to test. Pick one of the issues that passed your filters and plot it – this makes it the Current Symbol. To examine the profitability of long positions for this issue, use these menus and settings:

On the **Analysis** menu, select **Automatic Analysis**
Click **Pick**, select ZigZag.afl, click **Open**
Under **Apply to**, choose **current symbol**
Set **Range** to **n last quotations** with a value of **2520**
(or specific **from** and **to** dates)
Click **Settings**, on the **General tab**, set **Positions** to **Long**,
under **Commission & rates**, set **Percent** to **0**
under **Commission & rates**, set **Annual interest rate** to **0**
under **Commission & rates**, set **Account margin** to **100**
on the **Trades** tab, set **Buy Price** (and all Prices) to **Close**
set **Buy Delay** (and all Delays) to 0
on the **Stops** tab, choose **Disabled** for all choices
on the **Report tab**, for **Result list shows**, select **Trade List**
Click **OK**
Pull down the **Back Test** menu and click **Individual Backtest**

When you click Individual Backtest, AmiBroker will apply the system to the data file and produce a list of all trades. It is very interesting to look at the columns entitled "% Profit" and "# bars." Click on the column heading to sort the entire report using that column as a sort key. Scroll down to about the middle of the listing and note that the median gain is about 20% and the median time in a long position is about 13 days, depending on which issue you selected.

Using the File button and Export command, you can save this data to a file in comma separated format to be further analyzed to show the mean, range, distribution, standard deviation, etcetera of all metrics of interest. An analysis of the exported detailed data using a spreadsheet might show the average gain is 28.33% and the average time in a long position is 21 bars.

Run this same back test after making the following changes:
    Click **Settings**, on the **Report** tab choose **Summary**
    Click **OK**
    Click **Back Test**

The results are now a single line and it shows the average gain to be 28.33% and the average holding period 21 bars, confirming the spreadsheet. It will usually be the case that the average is higher than the median for these two statistics.

To analyze all of the issues that passed the filters. Make just one change:
    Under **Apply to**, choose **use filter**. Click **Define**
This opens the Filter Settings screen:
    On the **Include** tab, pull down the **Watchlist** menu
    Select **Filtered Tickers**
    Click **OK**

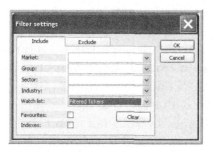

FIGURE 6.14 FILTER SETTINGS

Now run the backtest on the entire list:
    Pull down the **Back Test** menu, click **Individual Backtest**

The results are now one line for each ticker. Either sort them by clicking on the column header or export the data to a spreadsheet. Look for issues whose trades indicate that you are probably not interesting in trading them. Remove those issues from both FilterTickers.tls and the Filtered Tickers Watch List.

Spend some time working with the ZigZag system. Try different values for the percentage. Analyze the results for short positions. Pick a few issues that appeal to you and compare the detailed trade listing for long positions and short positions. Some issues have price patterns that are quite regular, uniform, and symmetrical, others lack regularity. Issues with regular price patterns lend themselves to profitable quantitative trading systems.

Caution

The ZigZag function looks into the future. It is very useful as a research tool, but is unusable in a trading system. Read the section about future leaks in Chapter 7.

7

Entries and Exits

ORDER TYPES

In part, the entry and exit options for your trading system are limited by those of the exchange on which the order will be executed and the broker with whom it will be placed.

Interactive Brokers (*www.interactivebrokers.com*), to use a specific example, supports over forty order types. The most common of these are explained below. The term asset is used to mean any tradable item – stock, bond, commodity, option, future, fund, or other asset.

- Market   A market order is an order to buy or sell an asset at the current bid or offer price.
- Stop   A stop order becomes a market order to buy or sell assets once the specified stop price is attained or penetrated.
- Stop-Limit   A stop-limit order becomes a limit order once the specified stop price is attained or penetrated.
- Trailing Stop   A trailing stop for a sell order sets the stop price at a fixed amount below the market price. If the market price rises, the stop loss price rises by this amount, but if the stock price falls, the stop loss price remains the same. Reverse this for a buy trailing stop order.
- Market-if-Touched (MIT) A market-if-touched order is an order to buy (or sell) an asset below (or above) the market. This order is held in the system until the trigger price is touched, and is then submitted as a market order.

- Market-on-Close (MOC)   A market-on-close order is an order submitted to execute as close to the closing price as possible.
- Market-on-Open (MOO)   A market-on-open order is executed at the opening of trading at the market price.
- Limit   A limit order is an order to buy or sell at a specified price or better.
- Limit-if-Touched (LIT)   A limit-if-touched order is an order to buy (or sell) an asset below (or above) the market. This order is held in the system until the trigger price is touched, and is then submitted as a limit order.
- Limit-on-Close (LOC)   A limit-on-close order is a limit order that executes at the closing price if the closing price is at or better than the submitted limit price, according to the rules of the specific exchange. Otherwise the order will be canceled.
- Limit-on-Open (LOO)   A limit-on-open order is a limit order executed at the market's open if the opening price is equal to or better than the limit price.
- One-Cancels-All (OCA)   All remaining orders in a one-cancels-all group of orders will be canceled when any one of the orders is executed.

MOO AND MOC ORDERS

If you use market-on-open or market-on-close orders, your backtesting results will closely approximate execution prices that would have been received. The New York Stock Exchange, the American Stock Exchange, and the NASDAQ Stock Market all match orders placed before the opening of trading and before the close of trading, then execute those orders at a single price (or a narrow range of prices). That price is the one quoted by the data distribution services and newspapers as the open or close, respectively.

STOP ORDERS

An order to buy at the market when a certain price has been touched will guarantee your order is filled. But in rapidly moving markets, your fill price could be different than your stop price. That difference is almost always to your disadvantage and is called slippage.

LIMIT ORDERS

An order to buy that is placed below the best offer, or an offer to sell that is placed above the best bid, hopes to improve the execution price relative to a market order. When your order is filled, it will be at your price or better – that is, no slippage. If your trading system issues a buy signal and you enter a limit order in hopes of purchasing at a lower price than the market, your limit order may not be filled if the market rises. But, if the market falls, your limit order will be filled. When using a limit order to enter a position, you are guaranteed to be filled on all your losing trades, but not on all your potentially winning trades.

STOP AND REVERSE SYSTEMS

If a system identifies tops and bottoms accurately, exits from long positions can be treated as entries to short positions, and exits from short positions as entries to long positions. In equities, long trades tend to have a longer duration than short trades, but the slope of the short trades is steeper. Applying the zigzag indicator to the daily bars helps identify that. Assume a moving average crossover trading system is used to give buy and sell signals to trade the zigzag line – just for purposes of illustration. There is a lag associated with any moving average, as there is with most indicators. That lag means that the peak will be identified only after it has passed. If long trades average 14 days, short trades average 6 days, and the lag is 2 days (all reasonable assumptions), then the first two days of each trade are lost and each trade is held two days too long. A long trade is entered on day 3 instead of day 1. A profit will still be made on long trades, but little or none on the short trades – unless the parameters for the signal that reverses long to short are changed. The parameter values for the long entry and the long exit do not need to be the same, but the additional parameters increase the likelihood that the trading system will be curve-fit and out-of-sample performance will be poor.

Beware of long-only systems, particularly those that keep trying to buy in a declining market. A person might never take a short position. But having a trading system that is profitable for short trades will act as a filter to keep long-only systems safe.

ENTRIES IN AMIBROKER

MARKET ORDERS

If your trading system generates a Buy signal, but does not compute and explicitly specify the price for the entry, then the entry will take place at the Market price. In AmiBroker, the default Market price is set on the **Automatic Analysis** menu, using the **Settings** and **Trades** window. Use the dropdown box to select either Open or Close. (Use High or Low with care; the backtest results may be unrealistic.) In the Delay box, enter 0 (zero) to trade the same day as the signal is generated, or 1 to trade the following day.

- If you are anticipating a signal near the close of trading and planning to place an order for execution Market-on-Close on the day of the signal, then choose Close with a Delay of 0.
- If you will download the actual closing data in the evening, and place the order for execution Market-on-Open the day following the signal, then choose Open with a Delay of 1.
- If you will download the actual closing data in the evening, and place the order for execution Market-On-Close that day following the signal (as some mutual funds might require), then choose Close with a Delay of 1.

You can override the Delay settings with your AFL code. The statement is:

```
SetTradeDelays(BuyDelay,SellDelay,ShortDelay,CoverDelay);
```

You can also override the BuyPrice and SellPrice settings with your AFL code. The statement to change the BuyPrice is:

```
BuyPrice = (price);
```

Where **price** is set within your AFL code.

For example, to be certain that your trading system will be buying at the close of the bar that generates the signal, the code to override whatever is set in the settings is:

```
SetTradeDelays(0,0,0,0);
BuyPrice = C;
```

Figure 7.1 has the code for a trading system that enters at the market.

```
//   EnterAtMarket.afl
//
//   Entry at the Market
//
//   This example uses a simple moving average crossover to
//   illustrate entering a long position at the market
//
//   The delay between the signal and the entry is
//   controlled either by the Settings window or the AFL code
//
//   The following code will insure that trades will be made
//   on the Close of the same bar that generates the Buy or
//   Sell signal.
SetTradeDelays(0,0,0,0);
BuyPrice = C;
SellPrice = C;

//   The trading system is a simple moving average crossover
MA1 = MA(C,5);
MA2 = MA(C,25);

//   The Buy signal is generated on the bar when MA1 crosses
//   from below MA2 to above MA2.
Buy = Cross(MA1,MA2);
Sell = Cross(MA2,MA1);
```

FIGURE 7.1 ENTER AT MARKET

LIMIT ORDERS

If you hope to get a better price on the entry, you might try a limit order. Say you get a Buy signal at today's close and you want to enter a long position tomorrow at 1% below today's close, with the order good for the day. You get complete control over the entry with the following code in Figure 7.2.

```
//   EnterAtLimit.afl
//
//   Entry using a Limit Order.
//   Try to get a better price than the Market Order would give.
//
//   This example uses a simple moving average crossover to
//   illustrate entering a long position at the market.
//
//   The delay between the signal and the entry is
//   controlled either by the Settings window or the AFL code.
//
//   For market orders, enter and exit Market On Close
//        with no delay
SetTradeDelays(0,0,0,0);
```

```
BuyPrice = C;
SellPrice = C;

//   The trading system is a simple moving average crossover
MA1 = MA(C,5);
MA2 = MA(C,25);

//   The signal is generated on the bar when MA1
//       crosses above MA2
BuySig = Cross(MA1,MA2);

//   If we can get in at 1% below the Close on the
//   day the signal was generated, we will enter,
//   otherwise pass on this signal.
Buy = (Ref(BuySig,-1)==1) AND (L<0.99*Ref(C,-1));
BuyPrice = 0.99*Ref(C,-1);

//   When the sell signal comes, use a Market On Close order.
Sell = Cross(MA2,MA1);
```

FIGURE 7.2 ENTER ON LIMIT

STOP ORDERS

Trading systems that watch for prices to break out to new highs, then enter long positions, use Buy Stop orders. They use Sell Stop orders to take short positions when prices break to new lows.

```
//   EnterAtStop.afl
//
//   Entry using a Stop Order.
//
//   When the price today breaks out above the highest
//   price of the previous 20 days,
//   buy at that breakout price.
//
//   Sell on a Stop on a breakout below the 10 Day Lowest Low.
//
SetTradeDelays(0,0,0,0);

Buy = H>Ref(HHV(H,20),-1);
BuyPrice = Ref(HHV(H,20),-1);
Sell = L<Ref(LLV(L,10),-1);
SellPrice = Ref(LLV(L,10),-1);

//   ExRem removes the extra signals that occur between
//   the buy that enters a position and the sell that exits it.
//   Comment out the ExRem to see the extra buy signals.
//   Since the system is already in a long position,
//   and the system is set by default to take only one position,
//   the extra buy signals do not do anything.
Buy = ExRem(Buy,Sell);
Sell = ExRem(Sell,Buy);
```

FIGURE 7.3 ENTER AT STOP

FORCE AN ENTRY

For testing purposes, it can be useful to force a long or short entry on a particular date.

```
//   EnterOnSpecificDate.afl
//
//   Entry on a specific date.
//
//   Used to force an entry so that the operation of
//   a trading system or indicator can be checked.
//
//   For market orders, enter and exit Market On Close
//       with no delay
SetTradeDelays(0,0,0,0);
BuyPrice = C;
SellPrice = C;

//   Enter on June 23, 1995
Buy = IIf(DateNum()==950623,1,0);
//   or Buy = Datenum()==950623;

//   Exit on September 12, 2002
Sell = IIf(DateNum()==1020912,1,0);
//   or Sell = Datenum()==1020912;
```

FIGURE 7.4 ENTER ON SPECIFIC DATE

RANDOM ENTRY

Using a random entry, it is possible to isolate the effects of the exit from the entry.

```
//   EnterAtRandom.afl
//
//   Entry a position at the close of a random bar.
//
//   A random entry for use as a benchmark.
//
//   Expect this entry to mirror the buy and hold.
//   It cannot be profitable taking long positions in
//   a declining market, or taking short positions
//   in a rising market.
//
//   This code just waits a fixed number of bars to exit.
//   It can be used to test any of the exit systems.
//
//   For market orders, enter and exit Market On Close
//       with no delay
SetTradeDelays(0,0,0,0);
BuyPrice = C;
SellPrice = C;
```

```
//   Frequency is the number of entries per year.
Frequency = Param("Entries per Year",12,1,100,1);

//   Repeatable is a switch.
//   True (1): the sequence of random numbers will be repeated.
//   False (0): each sequence is random.
Repeatable = Param("Repeatable",0,0,1,1);

//   Seed is the number used to start the random sequence
//   when repeatable sequences are desired.
Seed = Param("Seed",13331,1,99999,1);

//   Generate a fraction, uniformly distributed
//   between 0.00000 AND 0.99999.
NextRandom = IIf(Repeatable,Random(Seed),Random());

Buy = IIf(NextRandom<Frequency/252,1,0);

//   The code for the exit being tested starts here.
//
//   HoldBars is the number of bars to wait for exit.
HoldBars = Param("HoldBars",3,1,100,1);

Sell = BarsSince(Buy)>=HoldBars;
//   The code for the exit being tested ends here.

//   Remove extra Buy and Sell signals.
Buy = ExRem(Buy,Sell);
Sell = ExRem(Sell,Buy);
```

FIGURE 7.5 ENTER AT RANDOM

An alternative is to enter a position at a fixed interval – say every six days.

```
//   EntryAtFixedInterval.afl
//
//   Use fixed interval to enter long positions.
//
SetTradeDelays(0,0,0,0);
BuyPrice = C;

//   Enter every fixed number of bars.
//   Setting EntryInterval to 6 enters every sixth bar.
//
EntryInterval = Param("EntryInterval",6,4,100,1);

Buy = (BarIndex() % EntryInterval) == 0;

HoldDays = Param("HoldDays",3,1,100,1);

Sell = BarsSince(Buy) >=HoldDays;

Sell = ExRem(Sell,Buy);
```

```
e = Equity();

Plot(C,"C",colorBlack,styleCandle);
shape = Buy * shapeUpArrow + Sell * shapeDownArrow;
PlotShapes( shape, IIf( Buy, colorGreen, colorRed ),
                    0, IIf( Buy, Low, High ) );
GraphXSpace = 5;

Plot(e,"Equity",colorRed,styleLine|styleOwnScale);
```

FIGURE 7.6 ENTRY AT FIXED INTERVAL

SCALING INTO A POSITION

The sigScaleIn option informs the backtester to add to an existing position. This can be used to scale into, or pyramid, a position as profits in an open position grow, or as additional buy signals are generated.

```
//   ScaleIn.afl
//
//   Example of adding to an open position.
//
//   Buy at the Close of the bar when the High
//   of that bar breaks out above the highest high
//   of the previous five bars.
//   The initial position is 25% of available equity.
//   Every time there is a new five day high,
//   add another 25% to the position.
//
//   Sell the entire position at the Close of the
//   bar when the Low of that bar breaks out below
//   the Lowest Low of the previous twenty bars.
//
//   Note:  sigScaleIn does not work when the test
//   is run under Old Backtester.
//
//   In order to see the scaling in trades,
//   select settings > report > detailed log.
//
//   The logic is probably foolish,
//   but the code illustrates the concept clearly.
//
SetTradeDelays(0,0,0,0);
BuyPrice = C;
SellPrice = C;

//   Each Buy is allocated 25% of available equity.
PositionSize = -25;

Buy = IIf(H>Ref(HHV(H,5),-1),sigScaleIn,0);

Sell = IIf(L<Ref(LLV(L,20),-1),1,0);
```

```
//   Remove the extra Sell signals,
//   but NOT the extra Buy signals.
Sell = ExRem(Sell,Buy);
```

FIGURE 7.7 SCALE IN

AMIBROKER'S BUILT-IN EXITS

There are two ways to exit a position.

One is to have the trading system generate the exit signal from its own logic. For example, a moving average crossover system has a statement like:

```
Sell = Cross(MA2,MA1);
```

The second is to have the price trigger an exit before the exit signal is generated.

When a long position is entered, the trader expects the price to rise.

The price could drop without ever having a significant profit in the position. A maximum loss stop is placed some percentage or number of points below the entry price to keep the loss from becoming too large. Once set, it is not adjusted during the trade. A stop loss order at a given price is not a guarantee that the exiting trade will be executed at that price – it could be worse, and will seldom be better. This stop is enabled and the amount of the stop is set on the **Settings** menu, **Stops** tab.

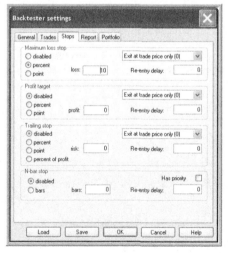

FIGURE 7.8 MAXIMUM LOSS STOP

The price could rise enough to give a good profit, then drop back. A trailing stop follows the price up, and protects some of the profit when the price drops back. Whenever a new high price is reached, the trailing stop moves up so that it is always the same amount below the highest price reached. If the price declines, the trailing stop stays at its last level. This stop is enabled and the amount of the stop is set on **Automatic Analysis** menu, **Settings** menu, **Stops** window.

The price could rise far enough to satisfy the trader and trigger a profit target exit. The target is set some percentage or number of points above the entry price, and remains at that level for the duration of the trade. If the price rises above the level of the profit target, the entire position is sold at that price. This order will be entered with your broker as a limit order. This exit is enabled and the amount of the profit target is set on the **Settings** menu, **Stops** window.

The price could stay between the stops and the profit target for longer than expected. A maximum holding period, or n-bar, exit ends the trade when the trade has been open for a specified number of bars. This exit need not be a stop order. This exit is enabled and the number of bars is set on the **Settings** menu, **Stops** window.

All of these exits can also be set within the model's AFL code. The statements corresponding to the four stops described above are:

```
ApplyStop(stopTypeLoss,stopModePercent,10,True );
ApplyStop(stopTypeTrailing,stopModePoint,3*ATR(14));
ApplyStop(stopTypeNBar,stopModeBars,5);
ApplyStop(stopTypeProfit,stopModePercent,5);
```

If these built-in exits satisfy your needs, use them. If not, you can program your own custom stops in the AFL language, using the looping construction if necessary.

CUSTOM EXITS

PROFIT TARGET

The code that follows in Figure 7.9 illustrates a custom profit target that exits the entire position when the desired price is reached.

```
//   ProfitTarget.afl
//
//   Illustration of looping code to implement a profit target.
//
//   If you code this and run it,
//        the results look great at first blush.
```

```
//   None of the closed trades are losers.
//   When you look more closely,
//       you will see that there is no exit
//       other than the profit target.
//   So each and every trade either
//   exits at a profit or is still being held
//   waiting for the price to eventually recover.
//   The drawdowns are very high.
//
//   Since you will be setting the values of
//       SellPrice yourself, this code overrides
//       SetTradeDelays and SellPrice for the exit.
//   But those settings will still apply to the entry.
SetTradeDelays(0,0,0,0);
BuyPrice = C;
SellPrice = C;

//   Use a simple moving average crossover for the entry.
Buy = Cross(MA(C,5),MA(C,25));

//   Load all the Sell array elements with value of 0.
//   The looping code that follows will reset them as necessary.
Sell = 0;

//   Set the profit target value --
//       a percentage in this example.
ProfitTargetPercent = 10;

//   EntryPrice is used to both indicate that a trade
//       is active, and to give the price at which the
//       entering transaction took place.
//   EntryPrice is a scalar.
EntryPrice = 0;

//   Loop through all the bars.
//   There are BarCount bars, indexed from 0 to BarCount-1.
for (i=0; i<BarCount; i++)
{
    //   Check for being flat and entering a new trade.
    if (EntryPrice == 0 AND Buy[i] == 1)
    {
        EntryPrice = BuyPrice[i];
    }
    else
        //   Check for being in a trade
        //       and having the profit target hit.
        if (EntryPrice > 0 AND
            H[i] > EntryPrice * (1.0 + 0.01*ProfitTargetPercent))
        {
            Sell[i] = 1;
            SellPrice[i] = EntryPrice
                * (1.0 + 0.01*ProfitTargetPercent);
            EntryPrice = 0;
        }
}
```

```
//  When the loop has completed,
//      every bar has been checked for trade entry (Buy).
//  Once the trade is active,
//      every bar has been checked to determine whether
//      the profit target was reached.
//      If it was, the Sell array and SellPrice array
//      have been set to properly reflect the exit.

Buy = ExRem(Buy,Sell);
Sell = ExRem(Sell,Buy);
```

FIGURE 7.9 PROFIT TARGET

SCALING OUT OF A POSITION

In order to take partial profits at several prices levels, use the sigScale-Out option to the Buy command.

```
//  ScaleOut.afl
//
//  Sells part of holdings at one profit target,
//  sells remainder of holding at second profit target,
//  sells entire holding on trailing stop.
//
//  This example patterned after one in the
//      AmiBroker User's Guide.
//
SetTradeDelays(0,0,0,0);
BuyPrice = C;
SellPrice = C;

//  Use a moving average crossover to enter long positions
Buy = Cross(MA(C,5),MA(C,25));
Sell = 0;

//  Targets are in percentages.
FirstProfitTarget = 10;
SecondProfitTarget = 20;
TrailingStop = 10;

//  Scalars to keep track of prices while in trade.
PriceAtBuy=0;
HighSinceBuy = 0;
Exit = 0;


//  Loop through all the bars.
for( i = 0; i < BarCount; i++ )
{
    if (PriceAtBuy==0 AND Buy[i]==1)
    {
        PriceAtBuy = BuyPrice[i];
    }
    else
```

```
if(PriceAtBuy > 0 )
{
    HighSinceBuy = Max(High[i],HighSinceBuy);
    if (exit==0 AND
        High[i] >= (1 + FirstProfitTarget*0.01)
            * PriceAtBuy)
    {
        // first profit target hit - scale-out
        Exit = 1;
        Buy[i] = sigScaleOut;
        BuyPrice[i] = (1 + FirstProfitTarget*0.01)
            * PriceAtBuy;
    }
    if(Exit==1 AND
        High[i] >= (1 + SecondProfitTarget*0.01)
            * PriceAtBuy)
    {
        // second profit target hit - exit
        Exit = 2;
        SellPrice[i] = Max(Open[i],
            (1 + SecondProfitTarget*0.01) * PriceAtBuy);
    }
    if (Low[i] <= (1 - TrailingStop*0.01) * HighSinceBuy)
    {
        // trailing stop hit - exit
        Exit = 3;
        SellPrice[i] = Min(Open[i],
            (1 - TrailingStop*0.01) * HighSinceBuy);
    }
    if (Exit >= 2)
    {
        Buy[i] = 0;
        Sell[i] = Exit + 1; // mark appropriate exit code
        Exit = 0;
        PriceAtBuy = 0;
        HighSinceBuy = 0;
    }
    }
}

SetPositionSize( 50, spsPercentOfEquity );
// scale out 50% of position
SetPositionSize( 50, spsPercentOfPosition * ( Buy==sigScaleOut) );

//Buy = ExRem(Buy,Sell);
//Sell = ExRem(Sell,Buy);
```

FIGURE 7.10 SCALE OUT

PARABOLIC TRAILING STOP

The Parabolic Trailing Stop rises according to a formula. One version of it is a component of the SAR indicator that is built-in to AmiBroker. To see how it looks, open any price chart, and apply the SAR indicator — on the **Charts** Tab, **Indicators** section, **SAR**. Left click SAR, drag it, and drop it on the price series. The red dots above and below the price series show how the parabolic indicator starts below a long trade, moves up slowly at first, then accelerates. It may slow its rise at some points, but it never drops back. When the price hits the stop, or the stop hits the price, the long position exits and a short position is established – hence the name Stop And Reverse (SAR). There are many other ways to implement a stop and reverse trading system, but the name SAR is commonly associated with the parabolic trailing stop. The code that follows uses looping to implement the adjustment of the stop price as the trade continues, and exits when the stop price is hit. The reentry is left to some other code – no reversal is coded, although it could be.

```
// ParabolicStop.afl
//
//   This implementation is for a long position.
//
//   The parabolic trailing stop is set below the
//   entry point on the first day of long position,
//   and rises according to a formula as the price rises.
//   Unlike the traditional trailing stop, the
//   parabolic stop continues to rise even as the
//   price holds steady or drops.  Eventually, the
//   price and the parabolic stop meet, which triggers
//   an exit.
//
SetTradeDelays(0,0,0,0);

//   Trading system entry logic goes here.
//   Exit will be made by the parabolic stop.

//   For example, use moving average crossover entry.
MALen1 =     Optimize("MALen1",30,1,31,1);
MAvg = AMA(C,2/(MALen1+1));

MALen2 =Optimize("MALen2",15,1,31,2);
Pass = C>=MA(C,MALen2);

Buy = pass AND Cross(C,MAvg);

//   The code for the Parabolic Trailing Stop begins here.
//
//   Assume that entry will be made at the close of the day the
//        buy signal is generated.
//
//   Setting TradeAtStop to 1 assumes that there is a stop
//        in place and the trade exits intraday at the stop price.
//   Setting TradeAtStop to 0 assumes that intraday exit
//        cannot take place (as in mutual fund end-of-day
//        trading) and the trade takes place at the close
//        of the signal day.

TradeAtStop = Param("TradeAtStop",0,0,1,1);
```

```
//   Set the initial stop level.
//   For this example, it is set at the Lowest Low
//        for some number of days.

LBDays = Optimize("LBDays",1,0,10,1);

//   Set the Acceleration factor and Maximum Acceleration.

IAF = Param("IAF",0.02,0.001,0.1,0.001);      // acceleration factor
MaxAF = Param("MaxAF",0.2,0.001,1.0,0.001); // max acceleration

Psar = Close;          // initialize
mp = 0;                // flat initial conditions
Sell = 0;              // clear sell signals
af = IAF;              // initial acceleration factor
hp = High [ 0 ];
lp = Low [ 0 ];
Lp = LLV(Low,LBDays);

//   Loop through all the bars.

for( i = 2; i < BarCount; i++ )
{
    //   Check for exit from long position

    if (  (mp == 1) AND (Low[i] < Psar[i-1])  )
    {
        Sell[i] = 1;
        if (TradeAtStop)
        {
            SellPrice[i] = Psar[i-1];
        }
        else
        {
            SellPrice[i] = Close[i];
        }
        mp = 0;
    }

    //   Continuation of long position -- adjust stop

    if ( mp == 1 )
    {
        if (High[i] > Hp)
        {
            Hp = High[i];
            af = af + IAF;
            if (af > MaxAF) af = MaxAF;
        }
        psar [ i ] = psar [ i-1 ] + af * ( hp - psar [ i-1 ] );
    }
    else
```

```
{
    //  not in a long position.
    //  value of psar is not important.
    //  set the psar level so it will plot
    //      on the price graph.

    psar[i] = Close[BarCount-1];
}

//  Check for new long position

if ( (mp == 0) AND (Buy[i]) )
{
    BuyPrice[i] = Close[i];
    Psar[i] = Lp[i];
    Hp = High[i];
    af = IAF;
    mp = 1;
}
}

//  The code for the Parabolic Trailing Stop ends here.


Plot( Close, "Price", colorBlack, styleCandle );
Plot( MAvg, "MAvg", colorBlue,styleLine);
Plot( psar, "SAR", colorRed,
        styleDots | styleNoLine | styleThick );

Buy = ExRem(Buy,Sell);
Sell = ExRem(Sell,Buy);
```

FIGURE 7.11 PARABOLIC STOP - LOOPING CODE

CHANDELIER STOP

The Chandelier Stop is a trailing stop based on price volatility, as measured by Average True Range (ATR), and either the highest high or highest close at any point in an open trade.

```
//  ChandelierStop.afl
//
//  The Chandelier Stop is a trailing stop that rises
//  as the price rises, with the distance between the
//  price and the stop determined by the volatility
//  of the price.
//  Volatility is measured by Average True Range.
//  The chandelier is "hung" below either the highest
//  high or the highest close.
//
SetTradeDelays(0,0,0,0);
BuyPrice = C;
SellPrice = C;
```

```
//  Use a moving average crossover to generate the Buy signals.
MA1 = MA(C,5);
MA2 = MA(C,25);
Buy = Cross(MA1,MA2);

//  ATRRange is the number of bars used in the
//      calculation of the ATR.
ATRRange = 10; //Optimize("ATRRange",5,1,30,1);

//  ATRMult is the number of ATRRanges below
//      the highest value to place the stop.
ATRMult = 3.0; //Optimize("ATRMult",2,0.5,5,0.25);

//  Trail the exit from the highest High
//      -- it could be the highest Close.
TrailPrice = H;

//  Compute this bar's Chandelier Exit Price.
ThisBarsExitPrice = TrailPrice - ATRMult*ATR(ATRRange);

//  The trade's exit price is the highest
//      of the bar's exit prices.
TradeExitPrice = HighestSince(Buy,ThisBarsExitPrice,1);

//  Sell when the price drops to the CurrentChandExit.
//  If there is a Stop Order in place during the day,
//      use L as the triggering price.
//  If there is not an intraday stop,
//      use C as the triggering price.
TriggerPrice = L;
Sell = TriggerPrice <= TradeExitPrice;

Buy = ExRem(Buy,Sell);
Sell = ExRem(Sell,Buy);


shape = Buy * shapeUpArrow + Sell * shapeDownArrow;
Plot( Close, "Price", colorBlack, styleCandle );
Plot(TradeExitPrice,"Chand",colorRed,styleLine);
PlotShapes( shape, IIf( Buy, colorGreen, colorRed ),
        0, IIf( Buy, Low, High ) );
GraphXSpace = 5;
```

FIGURE 7.12 CHANDELIER STOP

Now that all the detail about the Chandelier Stop has been explained, here is a one line implementation of it in AFL using the ApplyStop function.

```
ApplyStop(stopTypeTrailing,stopModePoint,3*ATR(14),True,True );
```

FIGURE 7.13 CHANDELIER STOP IN ONE LINE

DESIGNING ENTRIES

Assume a promising entry signal has been discovered. When coded into a trading system, there are profitable trades that this signal fails to notice and trades taken that are not profitable. Both are errors, but of different types.

Statisticians define the two types of errors as Type I and Type II. Given a hypothesis, Type I errors consist of those cases where the hypothesis was rejected when it should have been accepted, and Type II errors consist of those cases where the hypothesis was accepted when it should have been rejected. One type represents lost opportunities, the other represents losing trades – which is which depends on how the hypothesis is stated.

Trades not taken because the signal does not appear are lost opportunities. They can be reduced by being in the market a higher percentage of the time. A buy and hold position never misses an opportunity. But, the longer the holding period, the higher the drawdown, since, on average, the drawdown increases in proportion to the square root of the holding period.

Losing trades taken because the signal was not correct lose actual money. They can be reduced by being more selective – by requiring a higher quality signal and being in the market a lower percentage of the time. This type of error can be eliminated completely by not taking any positions.

If the accuracy of a signal is related to the numeric strength of the signal, then the signal can be made more selective simply by requiring a higher value to initiate a trade. But if the increase in selectivity comes from the addition of rules and conditions, each added condition causes the model to become less general. The increase in complexity of the signal comes at a cost of loss of degrees of freedom, and the system is more likely to become curve-fit.

For a given amount of data, decreasing one type of error increases the other. Tending toward buy and hold will decrease missed opportunities, increase market exposure, and increase drawdowns. Tending toward selectivity will increase missed opportunities, decrease market exposure, and decrease drawdowns. If there are only a few opportunities, it is important to take them all. If there are lots of opportunities, the trader can be more selective. Fortunately, there are thousands of opportunities to trade every day. Refer to Chapter 19, Statistical Tests, for further discussion.

QUALITY OF ENTRY SIGNALS

The competition for the entry signal being designed is the random entry.

One method, probably the traditional method, of designing or discovering entry signals is to pick an entry indicator and analyze the trade that would have resulted. If the entry is for a long position, then test the profitability after some fixed number of days. The trade should show a profit after some small number of days. If it does not show a profit soon after signaling an entry, but does show a profit after a longer time in the trade, then the entry was premature. Since it is very easy to delay entry, and usually very easy to cause a signal to be generated later, this situation is easy to solve. If most of the trades show losses, try inverting the signal and see if that creates a profitable entry.

The AmiBroker code to evaluate profit after a fixed holding period for a moving average crossover system follows. You will want to substitute entry methods of your own.

```
//    EntryIdentificationI.afl
//
//    First method of analyzing entries.
//    Pick an entry method, analyze profit
//    after a few days.
//
SetTradeDelays(0,0,0,0);
BuyPrice = C;
SellPrice = C;

//    Moving average crossover
MALength1 = Param("MALength1",3,1,50,1);
MALength2 = Param("MALength2",16,1,50,1);

MA1 = MA(C, MALength1);
MA2 = MA(C, MALength2);

Buy = Cross(MA1, MA2);

HoldDays = Param("HoldDays",6,1,60,1);

Sell = BarsSince(Buy) >= HoldDays;

Buy = ExRem(Buy, Sell);
Sell = ExRem(Sell, Buy);

e = Equity();

Plot(C, "C", colorBlack, styleCandle);
Plot(MA1, "MA1", colorGreen, styleLine);
Plot(MA2, "MA2", colorBlue, styleLine);
```

```
shape = Buy * shapeUpArrow + Sell * shapeDownArrow;
PlotShapes( shape, IIf( Buy, colorGreen, colorRed ),
        0, IIf( Buy, Low, High ) );
GraphXSpace = 5;

Plot(e, "Equity", colorRed, styleLine|styleOwnScale);
```

FIGURE 7.14 ENTRY IDENTIFICATION I

The system variables are set as parameters using AmiBroker's Param construction. With the system applied to some tradable data series, change the parameters and observe the effect they have. Watch the performance of the system in rising markets versus declining markets.

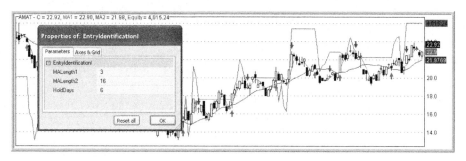

FIGURE 7.15 ENTRY IDENTIFICATION I CHART

Another method is to identify trades that fit your trading preferences in terms of holding time, profit, drawdown, and so forth. Then look for indicators that reliably precede the entry points.

The AmiBroker code to do this follows.

```
//   EntryIdentificationII.afl
//
//   Second method of analyzing entries.
//   Identify ideal entries, adjust indicators to
//   find a good match.
//
SetTradeDelays(0,0,0,0);
BuyPrice = C;
SellPrice = C;

//   This code looks into the future to compute
//   potential gain and potential loss from the present.
//   Gain is computed from Close of entry day
//   to Close of exit day.
//   Risk is computed from Close of entry day
//   to lowest Low while in trade.
```

```
DaysAhead = Param("DaysAhead",5,1,20,1);
GainAhead = 100.0 * (Ref(C,DaysAhead) - C) / C;
RiskAhead = 100.0 * (C - LLV(Ref(L,DaysAhead),DaysAhead)) / C;

DesiredProfit = Param("DesiredProfit",5,0.5,10,0.5);
MaximumRisk = Param("MaximumRisk",3,0.5,10,0.5);

IdealEntry = (GainAhead >= DesiredProfit)
                    AND (RiskAhead <= MaximumRisk);

HoldDays = Param("HoldDays",3,1,60,1);

IdealExit = BarsSince(IdealEntry) >= HoldDays;

//   Remove extra exits, but show all entries.
IdealExit = ExRem(IdealExit, IdealEntry);

IdealShape = IdealEntry * shapeHollowUpTriangle
                + IdealExit * shapeHollowDownTriangle;
IdealColor = IIf(IdealEntry,colorPaleGreen,colorPink);
IdealPosition = IIf(IdealEntry,Low,High);
PlotShapes(IdealShape,IdealColor,0,IdealPosition);

//   The ideal part is above -- the candidate indicator is below

//   Moving average crossover
MALength1 = Param("MALength1",5,1,50,1);
MALength2 = Param("MALength2",20,1,50,1);

MA1 = MA(C, MALength1);
MA2 = MA(C, MALength2);

IndicatorBuy = Cross(MA1, MA2);
IndicatorShape = IndicatorBuy * shapeUpArrow;
IndicatorColor = colorGreen;
IndicatorPosition = IIf(IndicatorBuy,Low,High);
PlotShapes(IndicatorShape,IndicatorColor,0,IndicatorPosition);

Plot(C, "C", colorBlack, styleCandle);
Plot(MA1, "MA1", colorGreen, styleLine);
Plot(MA2, "MA2", colorBlue, styleLine);
GraphXSpace = 5;
```

FIGURE 7.16 ENTRY IDENTIFICATION II

The resulting chart follows.

FIGURE 7.17 ENTRY IDENTIFICATION II CHART

If the indicator buy (green up-arrows) coincides with the ideal entry (hollow up-triangles), then the entry is worth considering. Unmatched green up-arrows indicate losing trades. Unmatched hollow up-triangles indicate missed opportunities.

If desired, AmiBroker's AddColumn() statements can be added to the code to give tabular results that can be analyzed using a spreadsheet.

In either case, the random entry gives a standard for comparison – either an informal comparison or test of statistical significance. If statistical tests are performed, be sure to use results that have come from the out-of-sample portion of the data. For the in-sample period, the candidate indicator or signal is certain to be better than the random entry. Read the sections on validation for more details about in-sample and out-of-sample testing. Do not be surprised if most of the candidates for entry signals do not beat a random entry.

CHECK FOR FUTURE LEAKS

Everyone wants to read tomorrow's newspaper before they place today's trade.

During backtesting and optimization, it is possible for the program to look ahead and make decisions based on information that would not be available in real time.

It can be useful to look ahead in some circumstances, such as developing entry or exit strategies, and most development platforms permit this. But when a trading system uses information it should not know, the resulting trades are impossible to make. This condition is a future leak.

AmiBroker's Ref statement is used to refer to data from bars other than the current bar. Usually, the reference is to earlier bars. For example, the two day percentage rate of change of the closing price can be coded as:

```
Chg = (C - Ref(C,-2))/C;
```

The -2 specifies the closing price 2 bars earlier. If a coding error omits the minus sign, the line becomes:

```
Chg = (C - Ref(C,2))/C;
```

The 2 now specifies the close 2 bars into the future.

Hidden deep within a long and complex program, future leaks can be difficult to detect. While everyone would catch the difference between those two lines, others are more subtle, such as:

```
Lookback = Optimize("LB",-2,-5,2,1);
//   Many lines of code
Chg = (C - Ref(C,Lookback))/C;
```

The first sign of a future leak is backtest results that are spectacular. Be suspicious of great results! The second sign is that signals appear and disappear as new bars of data are added to the series.

Figure 7.18 lists a program with an intentional future leak. When it is run as a backtest, there is no evidence that a future leak exists, other than high profitability and a high percentage of winning trades.

```
//   FutureLeak.afl
//
//   Program with a known future leak
//
Buy = (Ref(C,2) - C)/C > 0.01;
Sell = BarsSince(Buy) >=2;
shape = Buy * shapeUpArrow + Sell * shapeDownArrow;
Plot( Close, "Price", colorBlack, styleCandle );
PlotShapes( shape, IIf( Buy, colorGreen, colorRed ), 0,
        IIf( Buy, Low, High ) );
GraphXSpace = 5;
```

FIGURE 7.18 PROGRAM WITH A FUTURE LEAK

AmiBroker can check your program and inform you if there is a future leak. With the program open in the Formula Editor, click the down arrow along side the Analysis icon, the exclamation point. From the drop-down menu, click Check.

FIGURE 7.19 TESTING FOR A FUTURE LEAK

A message will appear, telling you whether your program has a future leak in the AFL code. In the example above, there is future leak. Passing the Check is not a guarantee that the code has no future leak. There may still be undetected future leaks in looping code, in a plugin, or in a script.

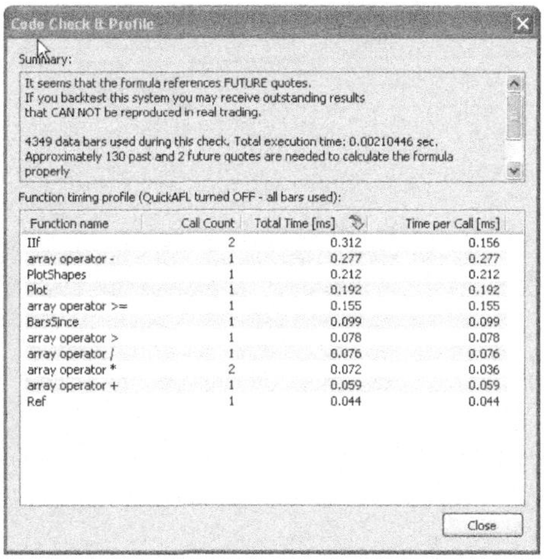

FIGURE 7.20 FUTURE LEAK WARNING

8

Functions and Indicators

FUNCTIONS

Functions are logical or mathematical expressions that take input values, perform some comparisons or calculations using the inputs, and produce an output value. The calculations required are encapsulated within the function, hiding the details, and allowing easy use and reuse of the code, by using the function name. AmiBroker has an extensive library of functions available for use simply by calling them. Here is a partial list, organized by category. The AmiBroker Help system has detailed information about each, many of which include examples which can be copied and pasted into your own custom functions and indicators.

BASIC PRICE PATTERN DETECTION

- Fast Fourier Transform
- GapDown - gap down
- GapUp - gap up
- Inside - inside day
- Outside - outside bar
- Peak - peak
- PeakBars - bars since peak
- Trough - trough
- TroughBars - bars since trough
- Zig - zig-zag indicator

COMPOSITES

- AddToComposite - add value to composite ticker
- ADLine - advance/decline line
- AdvIssues - advancing issues
- AdvVolume - advancing issues volume
- DecIssues - declining issues
- DecVolume - declining issues volume
- Trin - traders (Arms) index
- UncIssues - unchanged issues
- UncVolume - unchanged issues volume

DATE/TIME

- BarIndex - get zero-based bar number
- BeginValue - Value of the array at the beginning of the range
- Date - date
- DateNum - date number
- DateTime - retrieves encoded date time
- DateTimeConvert - format conversions
- DateTimeDiff - difference in seconds
- Day - day of month
- DayOfWeek - day of week
- DayOfYear - get ordinal number of day in a year
- DaysSince1900 - number of days since January 1, 1900
- EndValue - value of the array at the end of the selected range
- Hour - get current bar's hour
- Interval - get bar interval (in seconds)
- Minute - get current bar's minute
- Month - month
- Now - gets current system date/time
- Second - get current bar's second
- TimeNum - get current bar time
- Year - year

INDICATORS

- AccDist - accumulation/distribution
- ADX - average directional movement index
- ATR - average true range

- BBandBot - bottom Bollinger band
- BBandTop - top Bollinger band
- CCI - commodity channel index
- Chaikin - Chaikin oscillator
- ColorBlend - blends two colors
- GetChartBkColor - get color of chart background
- GetCursorMouseButtons - get current state of mouse buttons
- GetCursorXPosition - get current X position of mouse pointer
- GetCursorYPosition - get current Y position of mouse pointer
- HighestVisibleValue - get the highest value visible on the chart
- LowestVisibleValue - get the lowest value visible on the chart
- MACD - moving average convergence/divergence
- MDI - minus directional movement indicator (-DI)
- MFI - money flow index
- NVI - negative volume index
- OBV - on balance volume
- OscP - price oscillator
- OscV - volume oscillator
- PDI - plus directional movement indicator (+DI)
- PlotText - write text on the chart
- PlotVAPOverlayA - plot Volume-At-Price chart
- PVI - positive volume index
- RequestTimedRefresh - force periodic refresh of indicator pane
- RMI - relative momentum index
- ROC - percentage rate of change
- RSI - relative strength index
- RWI - random walk index
- RWIHi - random walk index of highs
- RWILo - random walk index of lows
- SAR - parabolic stop-and-reverse
- SetBarFillColor - set background color of chart
- SetChartBkColor - set color of chart background
- SetChartBkGradientFill - enable gradient color fill in indicators
- Signal - macd signal line
- StochD - stochastic slow %D
- StochK - stochastic slow %K
- Trix - triple exponential smoothed price
- Ultimate - ultimate oscillator

Information / Categories

- CategoryAddSymbol - adds a symbol to a category
- CategoryFind - search for category by name
- CategoryGetName - get the name of a category
- CategoryGetSymbols - retrieves list of symbols belonging to given category
- CategoryRemoveSymbol - remove a symbol from a category
- CategorySetName - set the name of the category
- FullName - full name of the symbol
- GetCategorySymbols - retrieves list of symbols belonging to given category
- GetDatabaseName - retrieves folder name of current database
- GetFnData - get fundamental data
- GroupId - get group ID/name
- IndustryId - get industry ID / name
- InWatchList - watch list membership test by number
- InWatchListName - watch list membership test by name
- IsContinuous - checks 'continuous quotations' flag state
- IsFavorite - check if current symbol belongs to favorites
- IsIndex - check if current symbol is an index
- MarketId - market ID / name
- Name - ticker symbol
- SectorId - get sector ID / name

Lowest/Highest

- HHV - highest high value
- HHVBars - bars since highest high
- Highest - highest value
- HighestBars - bars since highest value
- HighestSince - highest value since condition met
- HighestSinceBars - bars since highest value since condition met
- LLV - lowest low value
- LLVBars - bars since lowest low
- Lowest - lowest value
- LowestBars - bars since lowest
- LowestSince - lowest value since condition met
- LowestSinceBars – bars since lowest value since condition met

MATH FUNCTIONS

- abs - absolute value
- acos - arccosine
- AlmostEqual - rounding error comparison
- asin - arcsine
- atan - arctangent
- atan2 - arctangent of y/x
- ceil - ceil value
- cos - cosine
- cosh - hyperbolic cosine function
- exp - exponential function
- floor - floor value
- frac - fractional part
- int - integer part
- log - natural logarithm
- log10 - decimal logarithm
- max - maximum value of two numbers / arrays
- min - minimum value of two numbers / arrays
- prec - adjust number of decimal points of floating point number
- round - round number to nearest integer
- sign - returns the sign of the number/array
- sin - sine function
- sinh - hyperbolic sine
- sqrt - square root
- tan - tangent
- tanh - hyperbolic tangent

MISCELLANEOUS FUNCTIONS

- #include - preprocessor include command
- #include_once - preprocessor include (once) command
- #pragma - sets AFL pre-processor option
- ClipboardGet - retrieves current contents of Windows clipboard
- ClipboardSet - copies the text to the Windows clipboard
- ColorHSB - specify color using Hue-Saturation-Brightness
- ColorRGB - specify color using Red-Green-Blue components
- CreateObject - create COM object
- CreateStaticObject - create static COM object
- EnableScript - enable scripting engine

- EnableTextOuput - enables/disables text output in the Chart Commentary window
- GetExtraData - get extra data from external data source
- GetPerformanceCounter - retrieve value of performance counter
- GetRTData - retrieves the real-time data fields
- GetRTDataForeign - retrieves the real-time data fields (for specified symbol)
- GetScriptObject - get access to script COM object
- IsEmpty - empty value check
- IsFinite - check if value is not infinite
- IsNan - checks for NaN (not a number)
- IsNull - check for Null (empty) value
- IsTrue - true value (non-empty and non-zero) check
- NoteGet - retrieves the text of the note
- NoteSet - sets text of the note
- Nz - Null (Null/Nan/Infinity) to zero
- Prefs - retrieve preferences settings
- Say - speaks provided text
- SetBarsRequired - set number of previous and future bars needed for script/DLL to properly execute
- StaticVarCount - get total number of static variables in memory
- StaticVarGet - gets the value of static variable
- StaticVarGetText - gets the value of static variable as string
- StaticVarRemove - remove static variable
- StaticVarSet - sets the value of static variable
- StaticVarSetText - sets the value of static string variable.
- Status - get run-time AFL status information
- Study - reference hand-drawn study
- VarGet - gets the value of dynamic variable
- VarGetText - gets the text value of dynamic variable
- VarSet - sets the value of dynamic variable
- VarSetText - sets dynamic variable of string type
- Version - get version info
- _TRACE - print text to system debug viewer

Moving averages, summation

- AMA - adaptive moving average
- AMA2 - adaptive moving average
- Cum - cumulative sum

- DEMA - double exponential moving average
- EMA - exponential moving average
- MA - simple moving average
- Sum - sum data over specified number of bars
- TEMA - triple exponential moving average
- Wilders - Wilder's smoothing
- WMA - weighted moving average

STATISTICAL FUNCTIONS

- Correlation - correlation
- LinearReg - linear regression end-point
- LinRegIntercept – linear regression intercept
- LinRegSlope - linear regression slope
- Median - calculate median (middle element)
- mtRandom - Mersenne Twister random number generator
- mtRandomA - Mersenne Twister random number generator (array)
- Percentile - calculate percentile
- Random - random number
- StdErr - standard error
- StDev - standard deviation
- TSF - time series forecast

STRING MANIPULATION

- Asc - get ASCII code of character
- DateTimeToStr - convert datetime to string
- NumToStr - convert number to string
- printf - print formatted output to the output window
- StrCount - count occurrences of substring
- StrExtract - extracts substring from comma-separated string
- StrFind - find substring in a string
- StrFormat - write formatted output to the string
- StrLeft - extracts the leftmost part
- StrLen - string length
- StrMid - extracts part of the string
- StrReplace - string replace
- StrRight - extracts the rightmost part of the string

- StrToDateTime - convert string to datetime
- StrToLower - convert to lowercase
- StrToNum - convert string to number
- StrToUpper - convert to uppercase

TRADING SYSTEM TOOLBOX

- AlertIf - trigger alerts
- ApplyStop - apply built-in stop
- BarsSince - bars since
- Cross - crossover check
- EnableRotationalTrading - Turns on rotational-trading mode of the backtester
- Equity - calculate equity line
- ExRem - remove excessive signals
- ExRemSpan - remove excessive signals spanning given number of bars
- Flip – flip flop signal
- GetBacktesterObject - get access to backtester object
- GetOption - gets the value of option in automatic analysis settings
- GetTradingInterface - retrieves OLE automation object to automatic trading interface
- Hold - hold the alert signal
- IIF - immediate IF function
- LastValue - last value of the array
- Optimize - define optimization variable
- OptimizerSetEngine - select external optimizer engine
- OptimizerSetOption - set the value of optimizer parameter
- Ref - reference past/future values of the array
- SetBacktestMode - Set working mode of backtester
- SetCustomBacktestProc - define custom backtest procedure file
- SetFormulaName - set the name of the formula
- SetOption - sets options in automatic analysis settings
- SetPositionSize - set trade size
- SetTradeDelays - control trade delays applied by the backtester
- ValueWhen - get value of the array when condition met

EXPLORATION / INDICATORS

- AddColumn - add numeric exploration column

- AddSummaryRows - add summary rows to exploration output
- AddTextColumn - add text exploration column
- EncodeColor - encodes color for indicator title
- GetCchartID - get current chart ID
- GetPriceStyle - get current price chart style
- LineArray - generate trend-line array
- Param - add user user-definable numeric parameter
- ParamColor - add user user-definable color parameter
- ParamDate - add user user-definable date parameter
- ParamField - creates price field parameter
- ParamList - creates the parameter that consist of the list of choices
- ParamStr - add user user-definable string parameter
- ParamStyle - select styles applied to the plot
- ParamTime - add user user-definable time parameter
- ParamToggle - create Yes/No parameter
- ParamTrigger - creates a trigger (button) in the parameter dialog
- Plot - plot indicator graph
- PlotGrid - plot horizontal grid line
- PlotOHLC - plot custom OHLC chart
- PlotShapes - plots arrows and other shapes
- PlotVAPOverlay - plot Volume-At-Price overlay chart
- SelectedValue - retrieves value of the array at currently selected date/time point
- SetChartOptions - set/clear/overwrite defaults for chart options
- SetSortColumns - set columns used for sorting AA window
- WriteIf - commentary conditional text output
- WriteVal - write number or value of the array
- _DEFAULT_NAME - retrive default name of the plot
- _N - no text output
- _PARAM_VALUES - retrieve param values string
- _SECTION_BEGIN - section begin marker
- _SECTION_END - section end marker
- _SECTION_NAME - retrieve current section name

FILE INPUT/OUTPUT FUNCTIONS

- fclose - close a file
- fdelete - deletes a file
- feof - test for end-of-file
- fgets - get a string from a file

- fgetstatus - retrieve file status
- fmkdir - creates (makes) a directory
- fopen - open a file
- fputs - write a string to a file
- frmdir - removes a directory

LOW-LEVEL GRAPHICS

- GfxArc - draw an arc
- GfxChord - draw a chord
- GfxCircle - draw a circle
- GfxDrawText - draw a text
- GfxEllipse - draw an ellipse
- GfxGradientRect - draw a rectangle with gradient fill
- GfxLineTo - draw a line to specified point
- GfxMoveTo - move graphic cursor to new position
- GfxPie - draw a pie
- GfxPolygon - draw a polygon
- GfxPolyline - draw a polyline
- GfxRectangle - draw a rectangle
- GfxRoundRect - draw a rectangle with rounded corners
- GfxSelectFont - create / select graphic font
- GfxSelectPen - create / select graphic pen
- GfxSelectSolidBrush - create / select graphic brush
- GfxSetBkColor - set graphic background color
- GfxSetBkMode - set graphic background mode
- GfxSetOverlayMode - set low-level graphic overlay mode
- GfxSetPixel - set pixel at specified position to specified color
- GfxSetTextAlign - set text alignment
- GfxSetTextColor - set graphic text color
- GfxTextOut - writes text at the specified location

REFERENCING OTHER SYMBOL DATA

- Foreign - access foreign security data
- GetBaseIndex - retrieves symbol of relative strength base index
- PlotForeign - plot foreign security data
- RelStrength - comparative relative strength
- RestorePriceArrays - restore price arrays to original symbol
- SetForeign - replace current price arrays with foreign security

TIME FRAME FUNCTIONS

- TimeFrameCompress - compress single array to given time frame
- TimeFrameExpand - expand time frame compressed array
- TimeFrameGetPrice - retrieve O, H, L, C, V values from other time frame
- TimeFrameMode - switch time frame compression mode
- TimeFrameRestore - restores price arrays to original time frame
- TimeFrameSet - switch price arrays to a different time frame

CUSTOM FUNCTIONS

If the function that you want to use is not among the functions built in to AmiBroker, you can write it yourself using the AFL language.

Functions must be defined before they are called. Functions are either placed at the beginning of the AFL file that will call them, or saved in a directory and referenced by the *#include* directive.

The function definition consists of two parts – the function statement and the function body.

The function statement always begins with the keyword *function*, is followed by the function's name, which is followed by the parameter list enclosed in parentheses. The function's name should be meaningful and should not be the same as any of AFL's keywords or functions (AFL will complain if there is a conflict). The parameter list can be any number of parameters, including none. The parameters are the names used by the function as it is compiled. When the function is called, the values of the actual arguments will be used to evaluate the function.

The body of the function is enclosed in a set of curly braces. Within the body, variables can be defined, storage allocated, and comparisons and calculations performed, and a final single value computed. That value is associated with the function's name, and is returned by the function to the routine that called it.

The example that follows in Figure 8.1 creates a second order smoothing function. It is taken from the AmiBroker User's Guide.

```
// IIR2.afl
//
// Documentation to describe what the function does.
// Second order smoother
// the function statement
function IIR2( input, f0, f1, f2 )
// the function body
{
result[ 0 ] = input[ 0 ];
result[ 1 ] = input[ 1 ];
for( i = 2; i < BarCount; i++ )
{
result[i] = f0 * input[i] + f1 * result[i-1] + f2 * result[i-2];
}
// the function returns a single value and exits.
return result;
}
// The routine that calls the function.
SmoothedClose = IIR2(Close, 0.2, 1.4, -0.6 );
Plot( Close, "Price", colorBlack, styleCandle );
Plot( SmoothedClose, "function example", colorRed );
```

FIGURE 8.1 IIR2

To add this function to your own library of AmiBroker indicators, and to apply it to a price series, refer to the steps described in Chapter 5, AmiBroker.

Figure 8.2 illustrates IIR2 applied to a price series.

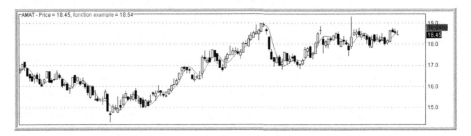

FIGURE 8.2 IIR2 APPLIED

There are a few limitations to functions and indicators created in AFL. They cannot be used without including the source code for them in the routine that is calling them, cannot be used recursively (they cannot call themselves), the AFL code takes longer to execute than equivalent code written in a lower level language, and the logic behind the indicator can be seen by anyone who opens the AFL file. If any of these limitations are a problem, you can overcome all of them by writing the function in a compiled language and creating a DLL version of the function. Please refer to the Appendix, Extending AmiBroker, which contains an example.

INDICATORS

Indicators are a special type of function designed to be applied to financial time series to help identify characteristics that lead to profitable trades. Indicators are often plotted, either in the same window as the price series, or in a separate window, but with the time scales aligned. Both the standard and professional versions of AmiBroker have an extensive library of indicators. Any of these can be applied to any series by using the drag-and-drop, which does not require writing any code.

- ABI – Absolute Breadth Index
- AccDist - Accumulation/Distribution
- AD Price – Williams Advance Decline of Price
- AD Ratio – Advance Decline Ratio
- ADLine – Advance Decline Line
- ADX – Directional Movement Index
- ASI – Accumulation Swing Index
- Beta – compare ROC with base series
- Breadth Thrust – advancing issues / (advancing + declining issues)
- CCI – Commodity Channel Index
- Chaikin – Chaikin Oscillator
- DPO – Detrended Price Oscillator
- DVI – Daily Volume Indicator
- EOM – Ease of Movement
- HPI – Herrick Payoff Index
- MACD – Moving Average Convergence Divergence
- Market Facilitation Index – (H-L) / V
- Mass Index – Double moving average of H-L
- MFI – Money Flow Index
- Momentum – price – previous price
- NVI – Negative Volume Index
- OBV – On Balance Volume
- OSCP – Price Oscillator
- OSCV – Volume Oscillator
- PVI – Positive Volume Index
- PVT – Price Volume Trend

- RMI – Relative Momentum Index
- ROC – Rate of Change (%)
- RS – Comparative Relative Strength
- RSI – Relative Strength Index
- RSIa – Relative Strength Index (custom array)
- RWI – Random Walk Index
- RWIHI – Random Walk Index of Highs
- RWILO – Random Walk Index of Lows
- SAR – Parabolic Stop and Reverse
- STIX – EMA of advance decline ratio
- Stochastic %D – slow stochastic
- Stochastic %K – fast stochastic
- Stochastic Momentum
- TRIN – Traders Index
- TRIX – Triple Exponential
- TVI – Trade Volume Index
- Ultimate – Ultimate Oscillator
- Volatility (Chaikin)
- Volatility (Wilder)
- Volume Oscillator
- Williams %R – faster stochastic
- ZIG – Zig-zag indicator

CREATING YOUR OWN INDICATORS

If the indicator you want to use is not already built in to AmiBroker, you can create it yourself using the AmiBroker Formula Language, AFL. The steps outlined in Figure 8.3 below create a custom indicator that uses a different moving average to compute a variation on the classical MACD.

```
//   MACDDemaIndicator.afl
//
// The classic MACD,
//   rewritten using Double Exponential Moving Averages
//
//   Set up the lengths for the MACD components
Length1 = Param("Length1",10,2,40,2);
Length2 = Param("Length2",20,1,39,2);
Length3 = Param("Length3",9,1,20,1);
//   The Moving Average Convergence Divergence calculations
MACD1 = 100 * (DEMA(C,Length1)-DEMA(C,Length2))/C;
MACD2 = DEMA(MACD1,Length3);
MACD3 = MACD1-MACD2;
Plot( Close, "Price", colorBlack, styleCandle );
GraphXSpace = 5;
```

```
//   Plot the MACD lines.
Plot(MACD1,"MACD1",colorGreen,styleLine|styleLeftAxisScale,-1,1);
Plot(MACD2,"MACD2",colorBlue,styleLine|styleLeftAxisScale,-1,1);
Plot(MACD3,"MACD3",colorRed,styleLine|styleLeftAxisScale,-1,1);
Plot(0,"",colorRed,styleLine|styleLeftAxisScale,-1,1);
```

FIGURE 8.3 MACD DEMA INDICATOR

Figure 8.4 shows the application of the MACDDema indicator to a price series.

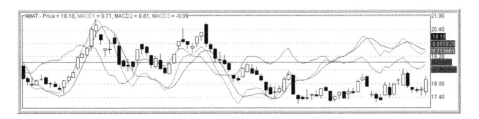

FIGURE 8.4 MACD DEMA INDICATOR APPLIED

PIVOT POINTS EXAMPLE

We often hear market analysts or experienced traders talking about an equity price nearing a certain support or resistance level. And they say that is important because those are levels at which major price movements are expected to occur.

One of the methods of determining support and resistance levels is pivot points. There are several different methods for calculating pivot points, the most common of which is the five-point system. This system uses the bar's high, low, and close to derive the pivot point, two support levels, and two resistance levels. Here is the code to compute the five points, and display them.

```
//   PivotPoints.afl
//
//   Traditional pivot points.
//   Thought by some to indicate levels of support
//   and resistance.
//R2 = P + (H - L) = P + (R1 - S1)
//R1 = (P x 2) - L
//P = (H + L + C) / 3
//S1 = (P x 2) - H
//S2 = P - (H - L) = P - (R1 - S1)
P = (H + L + C) / 3;
R1 = (P * 2) - L;
S1 = (P * 2) - H;
R2 = P + (R1 - S1); // P + (H - L)
S2 = P - (R1 - S1); // P - (H - L)
Plot(C,"C",colorBlack,styleCandle);
```

```
//   Displace the plot of the pivot points one bar
//   to the right.
//   Pivot points are based on the current bar,
//   but are thought to provide indication of
//   support and resistance for the next bar.
//
Displace=1;
Plot(R2,"R2",colorRed,styleLine,0,0,Displace);
Plot(R1,"R1",colorPink,styleLine,0,0,Displace);
Plot(P,"P",colorBlue,styleLine,0,0,Displace);
Plot(S1,"S1",colorPaleGreen,styleLine,0,0,Displace);
Plot(S2,"S2",colorGreen,styleLine,0,0,Displace);
```

FIGURE 8.5 PIVOT POINTS

Figure 8.6 shows the PivotPoints indicator applied to a chart of Alcoa's stock prices. Note the pivot point and the support and resistance levels have all been displaced one bar to the right so the bar that would be traded relative to the pivot points and the pivot points themselves are aligned. At the right side of the chart, the pivot points extend into the future for one bar, showing the trading levels for the next bar.

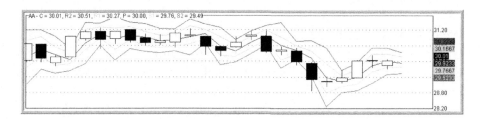

FIGURE 8.6 PIVOT POINTS APPLIED

9

Trending Systems

TREND FOLLOWING SYSTEMS are based on the premise that prices often continue to move in one direction for a long enough period of time so that a trader can recognize that a trend has begun, take a position in the direction of the trend, and make a profit by following the trend. Two of the most classical trend following systems are Moving Average Crossover and Breakout.

MOVING AVERAGE CROSSOVER SYSTEMS

The moving average system takes a long position when a fast moving average, one that averages only the most recent bars, crosses from below to above a slow moving average, one that averages a much longer number of bars.

This section of the book does three things:
1. Gives a step-by-step introduction to model testing and optimization.
2. Tests the moving average crossover trading system.
3. Demonstrates that the conventional wisdom is very wrong about simple moving averages.

Figure 9.1 has the code to create a moving average crossover trading system.

```
//   MACrossSystem.afl
//
//   The classic Moving Average crossover
//   using simple Moving Averages
//

//   Set up the lengths for the moving averages
Length1 = Param("Length1",6,1,81,2);
Length2 = Param("Length2",35,2,200,2);

//   The Moving Average calculations
MA1 = MA(C,Length1);
MA2 = MA(C,Length2);

//   The Buy and Sell logic
//   Buy when MA1 crosses from below MA2 to above MA2.
Buy = Cross(MA1,MA2);
Sell = Cross(MA2,MA1);

//   Compute the equity for the single ticker
e = Equity();
Maxe = LastValue(Highest(e));
Plot( Close, "Price", colorBlack, styleCandle );

//   Plot the MA lines.
Plot(MA1,"MA1",colorGreen,styleLine);
Plot(MA2,"MA2",colorBlue,styleLine);

//   Plot the Buy and Sell arrows.
shape = Buy * shapeUpArrow + Sell * shapeDownArrow;
PlotShapes(shape, IIf(Buy,colorGreen,colorRed), 0, IIf(Buy,Low,High));

//   Plot the equity curve
Plot(e,"Equity",colorBlue,styleLine|styleOwnScale,0,Maxe);
Plot(10000,"",colorBlue,styleLine|styleOwnScale,0,Maxe);
GraphXSpace = 5;
```

FIGURE 9.1 MA CROSS SYSTEM

If you have the data for it, load the daily OHLC bars for Louisiana Pacific (LPX) from 1994 through current.

Click the small m on the AmiBroker toolbar to have the data displayed as monthly.

FIGURE 9.2 LPX MONTHLY

LPX closed at 18.62 on January 3, 1995 and closed at 25.01 on January 3, 2005. It had several years of trading range, a substantial decline, and a substantial rise. An advantage of having the opening and closing price approximately the same is that there is very little overall bias toward either long or short positions. Ten years of daily data is about 2520 bars. So we should be able to make some meaningful tests and observations.

On the **Charts** tab, right-click MACrossSystem, select **Insert**, left-click.

This will open a new pane and load the MACrossSystem into it. Switch back to daily data and zoom in or out until you see about 15 months of daily data, including all of 2003.

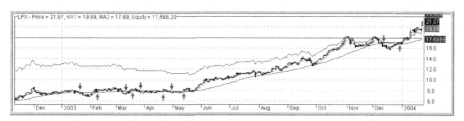

FIGURE 9.3 LPX 2003

The moving average lengths are set to arbitrary but typical values of 6 and 35. You will recognize the black candle stick bars for the daily open, high, low, close. The 6 day moving average is the green line (on your monitor) that follows the daily bars closely, the 35 day moving average runs through the data until late May, then stays below the candles for the six month rise. The green arrows below the candles mark the Buy signals, the red arrows above the candles mark the Sell signals. The ragged line, blue on your monitor, above the candles is the equity – the balance in the account from trades that take the buy and sell signals. The equity line follows the price while in a long position, and changes to a straight horizontal line when not in a position. The blue line going straight across is the starting equity — $10,000.

The conventional wisdom tells us that it is good to have a long data series – the system will be exposed to several different conditions and learn to adjust to all of them. Using the scroll bar, move the window back and forth to show the early part of the data and the end. The system gains a total of $484, before commissions, from 1/1/1995 through 1/1/2005. There are some good runs, but a lot of whipsaws. The trading system has been programmed using the Param feature, so that you can adjust the lengths of the moving averages from the chart – you do not have to go back to the formula editor. Position the window so that January 2005 is at the right side of the window. Right-click in the window with the LPX data and the MACrossSystem, select **Parameters**, then left-click.

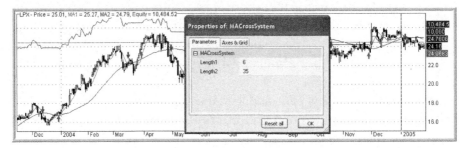

FIGURE 9.4 LPX MA CROSS PARAMETERS

Left-click the white area to the right of the 35. A slider will appear. Adjust it until Length2 is 200. Adjust Length1 to 1. A moving average of length 1 is just the close itself.

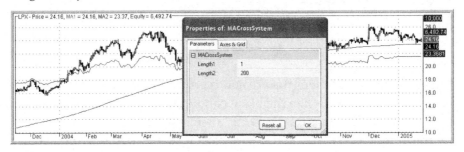

FIGURE 9.5 LPX MA PARAMETERS

Click **OK** and then use the scroll to look at the buy and sell signals for the ten years. This setting corresponds to the guru advice that the stock is a buy whenever the closing price is above its 200 day moving average. Over the ten years, this strategy lost $3508 from a $10,000 account. The equity had gotten as low as $2000 – a loss of 80% – in 2003.

Try the cross of the close (1 day average) with the 50 day average, another combination widely recommended. The equity drops from the start and the account never has a profit.

Open the AFL code in the formula editor and change the two instances of Param to Optimize, and save the file. That is the only change needed. The next figure shows that section of code.

```
// MACrossSystem.afl
//
// The classic Moving Average crossover
// using simple Moving Averages
//

// Set up the lengths for the moving averages
Length1 = Optimize("Length1",6,1,81,2);
Length2 = Optimize("Length2",35,2,200,2);
```

FIGURE 9.6 MA CROSS OPTIMIZE

From the **Analysis** menu, select **Automatic Analysis**, then **Pick**, select MACrossSystem.afl, click **Open**.

The next few screens prepare to perform an optimization to find the best moving average lengths.

On the **Settings** menu, on the **Report** tab, click **Summary**.

FIGURE 9.7 MA CROSS SETTINGS - REPORT

On the **Settings** menu, on the **Trades** tab, be sure that all Prices are set to *Close* and all Delays are set to 0 (zero).

On the **Settings** menu, on the **General** tab, set Initial Equity to 10,000, Positions to Long, Periodicity to Daily.

Click **OK** to close the settings window.

On the **Automatic Analysis** screen:
• Select **Current Symbol**.
• Set date Range from 1/1/1995 to 1/1/2005.
• The Formula File should still show MACrossSystem.afl, if it does not, use **Pick** to find it again.
• Click **Optimize** to begin the optimization.

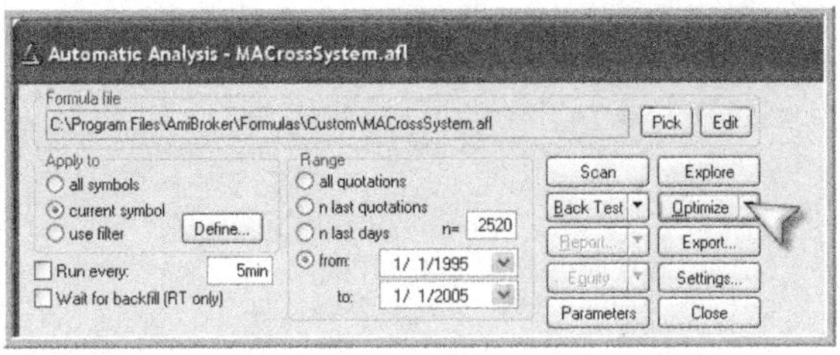

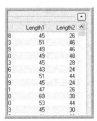

FIGURE 9.8 MA CROSS START OPTIMIZE

AmiBroker will evaluate all 4100 of the tests you have requested. Length1 has 41 different values (1 to 81 in steps of 2), Length2 has 100 different values (2 to 200 in steps of 2). The results of the tests are sorted with the best at the top. Each cell contains an entry – the column is the metric, the row is the test run. Click on any column heading to sort by that objective function. In the example, the results were sorted by RAR/MDD (high values are preferred) – choose whatever objective function you decided on. Scroll over to the right hand side to see what the best values for the lengths are.

	Length1	Length2
8	45	26
3	51	46
9	49	46
0	49	48
3	45	28
6	43	24
0	51	44
9	45	24
1	47	26
0	69	38
0	53	44
3	45	30

FIGURE 9.9 MA CROSS OPTIMIZATION RESULTS

The best combination is Length1 of 45 days, Length2 of 26 days. The top 74 entries all have Length1 greater than Length2. Edit the program again and change the values for the Length1 and Length2 to 45 and 26, respectively. The Optimize part of each statement has just been made a comment, so the program can easily be returned to optimizing.

```
//  MACrossSystem.afl
//
//  The classic Moving Average crossover
//  using simple Moving Averages
//

//  Set up the lengths for the moving averages
Length1 = 45; //Optimize("Length1",6,1,81,2);
Length2 = 26; //Optimize("Length2",35,2,200,2);
```

FIGURE 9.10 MA CROSS FIXED LENGTHS

Click the **Save** Icon, then the **Apply Indicator** Icon. Look at the moving average lines and the trades. The system takes a long position when the fast moving average falls below the slow moving average – just the opposite of conventional wisdom.

FIGURE 9.11 MA CROSS 45 26

My conclusion is that we would not want to trade a simple moving average crossover system on equities. The fact that the moving averages are "upside-down" means that the trading system is not acting as a trend following system, but an anti-trend, or mean reversion, system. If the system not only exited from long positions on a sell signal, but went short as well, it would be short during the long rises in price, and the trade statistics for short trades would show large loses. We'll return to mean reversion systems in the next chapter, but it seems clear that a simple moving average system is not a trustworthy trend following system.

BREAKOUT SYSTEMS

There are still people who are, or say they are, making money with breakout systems. If so, they are probably trading many different tradables and reporting the results from the portfolio. Breakout systems have a low percentage of winning trades – 30% is not unusual. They keep taking every signal, look for a few large winners, but get stopped out of most trades with a loss. Many people cannot keep taking trades that are predominantly losers. A lot of the success of a breakout system comes from retaining most of the profit from large winners. Trailing stop loss orders are helpful here, but profit targets do not work well. Setting profit targets that are often hit means giving up the big gains; setting profit targets that are seldom hit means creating a curve-fit system. Breakout systems often enter on stop orders, with the slippage associated with stop orders. If a breakout system is rewritten to use limit orders, the system is guaranteed to have its orders filled on all the losing trades, but is not guaranteed to have its orders filled on all the winning trades – in fact, it will miss some of the best trades.

When breakout methodologies work, they work best to trade commodities, but do not work well on common stocks.

In my opinion, there is a good reason why breakout systems do not work any more. Prices move from one level to another for fundamental reasons. In the early days of system trading, breakout systems noticed a breakout, took a position, and stayed with the position until the new price level was reached. As more and more companies and individuals began using computerized trading systems, breakout systems were profitable and easy to code. More money followed each system which accentuated the size of the breakout moves and increased slippage. The price became choppier, triggering counter-trend trades and stop-loss exits from trend-following positions. The larger trends were broken up.

In general, I believe that systems that were once profitable will eventually fail as they are discovered by more traders. Every profitable trade removes inefficiency from an inefficient market. Once a trading system has been published and coded, it will be tested periodically by many traders. When it returns to profitability, traders will trade it and again make it unprofitable. It may be coincidental, but breakout systems stopped working well shortly after the "turtle" systems became widely known and programmed.

FOR ANOTHER EXAMPLE, in the 1980s a profitable TBond system held just overnight. Figure 9.12 has the AFL. The system computed the daily change (Close minus Open) for the TBonds. Just before the close of trading, it took a position in the same direction as that change. At the next open, it exited the position. That was a clear market inefficiency. Once identified, profitable trades removed the inefficiency to the point that frictional costs now exceed the overnight continuation move.

```
//    TBondOvernight.afl
//
//    Buy the Close if Close is higher than Open,
//    Short the Close if Close is lower than Open
//    Exit next morning
//
SetTradeDelays(0,0,0,0);
BuyPrice = Close;
SellPrice = Open;
ShortPrice = Close;
CoverPrice = Open;
```

```
PositionSize = MarginDeposit = 1;

Buy = C>0;
Sell = Ref(Buy,-1)==1;
Short = C<0;
Cover = Ref(Short,-1)==1;
```

FIGURE 9.12 TBOND OVERNIGHT

Another trend-following breakout system buys as the price rises through the upper Bollinger Band, and exits when the priced drops back into the Bollinger Band. Code is shown in Figure 9.13.

```
//    BBandBreakout.afl
//
//    A trend-following breakout system
//    based on the Bollinger Bands.
//
//    Buy when the closing price rises through the
//    upper Bollinger Band, Sell when the price
//    drops back into the Bollinger Bands.
BBLookback = Optimize("BBLookback",12,2,30,2);
BBWidth = Optimize("BBWidth",2.8,1,3,0.1);
BBT = BBandTop(C,BBLookback,BBWidth);
BBB = BBandBot(C,BBLookback,BBWidth);
Buy = Cross(C,BBT);
Sell = Cross(BBT,C);
Short = Cross(BBB,C);
Cover = Cross(C,BBB);
e = Equity();
Plot(e,"Equity",colorBlack,styleLine);
```

FIGURE 9.13 BOLLINGER BAND BREAKOUT

Like so many trend following system, this one is marginal for stocks and works for some commodities.

DONCHIAN-STYLE BREAKOUT

The breakout system attributed to Richard Donchian buys strength and shorts weakness. It buys on the intra-day bar when the high rises above the previous high of the last 20 trading days, and sells when the low drops below the previous low of the last 10 trading days. Volatility, as measured by the average true range, is used as a maximum loss stop.

This system was expanded by Richard Dennis and William Eckhardt when they established the famous Turtle group of traders in 1983. Among other enhancements, Dennis and Eckhardt included a trade filter that only entered after the previous trade was, or would have been, a loser. They added a second system that took long positions on a breakout of 55 day highs and took short positions on a breakout of 55 day lows, without regard to the previous trade. And they added to winning positions by scaling in. The Turtles traded only very liquid futures contracts.

```
//    DonchianBreakout.afl
//
//    Simplified version of breakout system
//    attributed to Richard Donchian and used
//    by Richard Dennis and the Turtles.
//
//    Buy an upside breakout of 20 day highs,
//    set a maximum loss stop based on volatility,
//    sell a downside breakout of 10 days lows.
//
//    Short a downside breakout of 20 day lows,
//    set a maximum loss stop based on volatility,
//    cover an upside breakout of 10 day highs.

//    Usually used on futures contracts.
//    To set up for a "points only" test,
//    uncomment the following line and set
//    Futures Mode to True on the Setting Menu.
//PositionSize = MarginDeposit = 1;

StopPoints = 2*ATR(20);

Buy = H > Ref(HHV(H,20),-1);
BuyPrice = Ref(HHV(H,20),-1);
Sell = L < Ref(LLV(L,10),-1);
SellPrice = Ref(LLV(L,10),-1);

Buy = ExRem(Buy,Sell);
Sell = ExRem(Sell,Buy);

Short = L < Ref(LLV(L,20),-1);
ShortPrice = Ref(LLV(L,20),-1);
Cover = H > Ref(HHV(H,10),-1);
CoverPrice = Ref(HHV(H,10),-1);

Short = ExRem(Short,Cover);
Cover = ExRem(Cover,Short);

ApplyStop(stopTypeLoss,stopModePoint,StopPoints,
          1,False);
```

FIGURE 9.14 DONCHIAN BREAKOUT

SECOND EDITION

After reading this chapter in the first edition, several people inquired about the commonly held views that the 50 day and 200 day moving averages were important. Television commentators and writers suggest that each of these conditions are bullish:

- The price is above the 50 day average – take a long position at the close of the day the closing price rises through the 50 day simple moving average of closing prices; exit and go flat at the close of the day when the closing price fall through the simple 50 day moving average.
- The price is above the 200 day average – be long when the closing price is above the 200 day simple moving average; be flat when it is below.
- The 50 day average is above the 200 day average – be long when the 50 day simple moving average is above the 200 day simple moving average; be flat when it is below.
- Prices have broken out to make new 20 day highs – take a long position when the intra-day price rises above the highest high price of the previous 20 days; exit and go flat when the intra-day price falls below the lowest low value of the previous 10 days; use a trailing stop 2 times the 20 day average true range as an alternate exit.

For the second edition, we test those ideas.

The first task is remove confusion between a rising market and a system that is profitable for long positions. The broad US markets had a long steady increase from 1982 through 2000. Essentially any technique that took long positions during that time was successful. Many people doubt that those conditions will return, and suggest that systems should be evaluated for their performance independent of the broad trend. Measured by the S&P 500 or NASDAQ 100, the markets as of May 2011 are at approximately the same price level as they were early 1999, giving a 12 year period with little overall price change. The component stocks of the S&P 100 were examined individually and those whose price was little changed over the 12 years were selected for testing. Several ETFs were also chosen.

The initial account was $100,000, and each succeeding position was taken using all available funds. The starting date was 1/1/1999 and the ending date was 4/30/2011. These results are for long positions, going flat when the averages cross downward.

Two metrics were measured:

- Compound Annual Rate of Return, CAR.
- Maximum System Drawdown, MaxDD.

The ratio of CAR to MaxDD is a commonly used metric known as MAR – the Managed Account Report metric.

Figure 9.15 shows the tabular results for each of the four systems.

Ticker	50 day average		200 day average		50 and 200 crossing		breakout new highs	
	CAR	Max DD	CAR	Max DD	CAR	Max DD	CAR	Max DD
AEP	3.3	-33.5	1.2	-34.6	2.7	-33.3	0.2	-35.6
ALL	-5.6	-63.3	4.6	-35.2	9.0	-35.4	3.9	-31.9
BAC	-2.0	-72.8	-9.1	-71.1	0.2	-43.6	-0.8	-59.8
BK	-18.7	-93.5	-9.9	-76.1	-4.8	-47.5	-12.0	-81.9
CMCSA	-10.3	-84.3	-1.8	-62.6	2.6	-46.4	-6.3	-70.3
COF	-3.0	-73.5	-4.4	-66.3	-1.7	-74.8	3.0	-65.0
CSCO	-7.9	-82.3	2.1	-46.7	1.1	-37.1	-6.3	-68.8
DD	-2.3	-64.8	-2.2	-69.3	-2.6	-70.0	-1.5	-55.2
DELL	-11.1	-81.0	-9.7	-78.9	-12.1	-86.7	-7.8	-78.0
DIS	-3.8	-69.1	0.7	-52.1	2.1	-41.4	-0.1	-43.7
EWJ	2.6	-32.8	-0.7	-34.5	2.5	-23.6	2.5	-26.9
F	1.9	-78.2	5.8	-53.5	1.4	-62.6	2.9	-49.8
GE	-2.1	-59.8	0.2	-31.0	-0.1	-28.8	5.5	-26.2
HD	-1.6	-66.2	-2.4	-69.3	-3.8	-58.9	2.3	-38.0
HNZ	-3.3	-47.5	-0.4	-40.9	-1.4	-44.6	-2.4	-38.1
INTC	-2.3	-79.8	3.1	-58.6	3.6	-43.8	-1.6	-58.8
IVV	0.9	-36.6	3.9	-19.3	5.9	-16.0	2.3	-19.5
KO	-1.6	-49.5	-1.4	-58.4	-0.7	-49.7	-1.3	-40.8
MRK	-2.3	-51.2	-1.9	-53.8	-1.0	-44.4	0.4	-41.2
MS	-6.4	-67.0	-1.3	-67.4	5.0	-42.5	-5.1	-69.8
MSFT	-3.6	-67.4	-4.4	-66.3	-6.7	-62.0	5.5	-30.0
PFE	-5.1	-74.4	-5.7	-61.4	-3.0	-52.4	-5.4	-66.0
QQQ	7.9	-38.7	1.8	-45.2	4.8	-26.1	2.1	-43.9
RTN	-0.3	-53.2	7.0	-33.0	2.2	-45.2	4.7	-33.1
SMH	-8.3	-76.3	0.7	-44.8	3.3	-34.3	-11.2	-79.8
SPY	-0.4	-40.5	2.0	-24.5	5.4	-16.1	0.2	-30.3
T	-5.9	-65.0	-1.5	-47.8	0.7	-49.1	-5.5	-55.8
TWX	-6.2	-78.1	-5.6	-74.0	-2.8	-60.8	-2.3	-62.4
VZ	-7.7	-71.2	-2.5	-56.2	-3.8	-47.7	-4.9	-52.6
WY	-4.1	-72.4	0.4	-34.2	-0.7	-51.8	-3.3	-66.1
XLU	0.4	-34.7	2.9	-22.7	5.4	-24.4	-3.9	-42.7
XLV	-1.2	-43.4	-3.3	-55.0	-1.3	-44.8	-4.2	-52.3

FIGURE 9.15 TREND FOLLOWING RESULTS

Encouraging results would show an acceptably large (5% or higher) positive value for CAR, combined with a small (20% or smaller) negative value for Max DD. Out of the 128 test runs, there are only two of those—IVV and SPY—both of which track the S&P 500 index.

Figure 9.16 shows the plot of CAR versus Max DD. Note that the drawdown exceeds 40% in 94 of the cases tested, which we assume would have caused the trader to exit his position. The CAR exceeds 5% in only 8 of the 34 cases where the drawdown remained below 40%. Only 8 had an MAR ratio greater than 0.20.

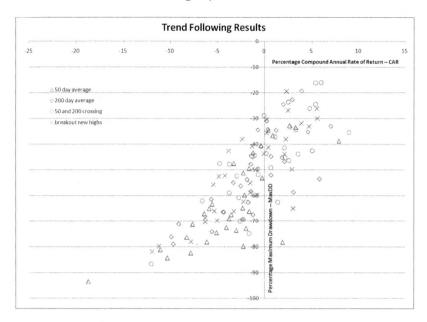

FIGURE 9.16 TREND FOLLOWING SCATTER PLOT

Results for SPY were among the best. The next few figures show the running equity balance and drawdown for the combinations as tested using SPY. In each figure, the upper horizontal line is $100,000, which represents the initial equity, and the upper moving line is the running equity balance. The lower horizontal line is $0, which represents the initial drawdown, and the lower moving line is the drawdown in dollars from highest equity. The first three figures are for long positions; the second three are for short positions.

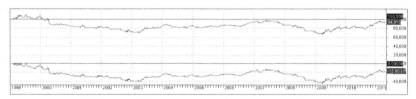

FIGURE 9.17 SPY LONG CROSS 1 WITH 50

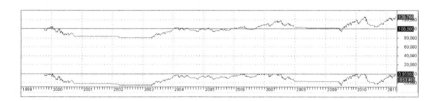

FIGURE 9.18 SPY LONG CROSS 1 WITH 200

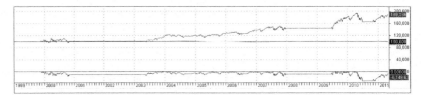

FIGURE 9.19 SPY Long cross 50 with 200

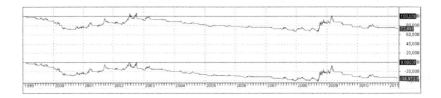

FIGURE 9.20 SPY Short cross 1 with 50

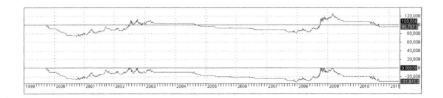

FIGURE 9.21 SPY Short cross 1 with 200

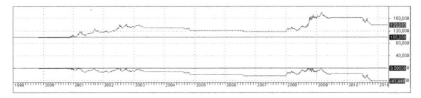

FIGURE 9.22 SPY Short cross 50 with 200

When the short positions of a trading system are not profitable, that means that not only will there be losses if short, but there would have been profits if long and therefore lost opportunity. The crossover of the 50 day and 200 day moving averages is the best combination for SPY for this time period.

Although these results are disappointing and cast doubt on the generic guidelines, might there be some other pair of moving average lengths that can be used to signal when to be long and when to be flat? Ideally that pair would work for most issues, but even finding specific values for each issue would be valuable.

Using the entire 12 years as an in-sample test period, a search was made for the best pair of lengths for each issue. Lengths for the "fast" and "slow" moving averages were allowed to range from 1 to 81 and 2 to 400, respectively. A buy was signaled when the fast moving average crossed up through the slow moving average; a sell to go flat was signaled on the downward cross. The pair that produced the highest MAR is reported. Figure 9.23 shows the results in tabular format, including the lengths of the two moving averages, CAR, MaxDD, and MAR. Note that there is no pattern among the lengths. Also note that for about half of the issues, the best MAR came when the "fast" moving average was longer than the "slow" moving average, resulting in a mean reverting system rather than a trend following system.

Ticker	Custom CAR	Max DD	MAR	Fast Len	Slow Len
AEP	5.9	-22.3	0.27	19	122
ALL	13.6	-36.1	0.38	3	2
BAC	12.4	-80.4	0.15	15	14
BK	28.7	-37.5	0.77	3	2
CMCSA	17.5	-40.7	0.43	3	2
COF	17.3	-58.2	0.30	19	22
CSCO	12.7	-46.2	0.28	69	70
DD	10.6	-44.3	0.24	61	56
DELL	8.3	-65.5	0.13	37	34
DIS	12.3	-22.0	0.56	63	88
EWJ	6.4	-23.7	0.27	63	70
F	11.3	-31.7	0.36	79	214
GE	6.0	-30.6	0.20	79	190
HD	9.2	-36.8	0.25	19	20
HNZ	7.1	-24.3	0.29	5	4
INTC	18.1	-39.9	0.45	3	2
IVV	6.7	-13.3	0.50	45	164
KO	9.6	-26.8	0.36	25	24
MRK	3.8	-29.9	0.13	67	92
MS	32.2	-75.2	0.43	11	4
MSFT	9.7	-33.0	0.29	17	18
PFE	16.1	-31.8	0.51	5	2
QQQ	16.1	-48.0	0.34	3	2
RTN	7.6	-26.1	0.29	13	122
SMH	14.8	-25.0	0.59	73	78
SPY	5.4	-12.0	0.45	13	174
T	11.1	-34.6	0.32	47	46
TWX	7.2	-47.4	0.15	33	34
VZ	7.7	-29.6	0.26	5	2
WY	12.7	-44.4	0.29	55	52
XLU	6.7	-15.6	0.43	81	312
XLV	10.0	-22.0	0.46	3	2

FIGURE 9.23 CUSTOM MOVING AVERAGE LENGTHS

In the event that a strong multi-year bull market returns, traditional trend following techniques might be profitable for long positions. If the markets continue to move sideways or fall, neither any of the four generic trend following systems, nor the system custom fit to each individual issue, produced satisfactory trend following results, even for the in-sample data. Although not reported here, tests were also run using in-sample periods shorter than 12 years, still without useful results.

You can replicate this study using the code found in Figures 9.1 and 9.14.

10

Mean Reversion Systems

MEAN REVERSION SYSTEMS are based on the premise that prices tend to oscillate above and below some level of equilibrium with some degree of regularity. When prices are extended too far from equilibrium, take a position that will profit by return to equilibrium. Almost any indicator that swings between high and low levels can be used to create a mean reversion trading system.

CENTER OF GRAVITY OSCILLATOR SYSTEM

John Ehlers describes an indicator he calls the Center of Gravity Oscillator in *Cybernetic Analysis for Stocks and Futures,* published by Wiley in 2004. The code to compute that oscillator and use it in a trading system follows in Figure 10.1. This example shows only the calculation of the entry signal, and some very simple exits. It is not a complete trading system.

```
//   CenterOfGravity.afl
//
//   Trading system based on John Ehlers'
//   Center of Gravity Oscillator.
//   Cybernetic Analysis for Stocks and Futures,
//   Wiley, 2004.
//
SetTradeDelays(0,0,0,0);
BuyPrice = C;
SellPrice = C;
SetBarsRequired(200, 0);
```

```
function CGOscillator(Price, Length)
{
    Result = 0;
    for (i=length; i< BarCount; i++)
    {
        Num = 0;
        Denom = 0;
        for (j=0; j<Length; j++)
        {
            Num = Num + (1 + j) * Price[i-j];
            Denom = Denom + Price[i-j];
        }
        if (Denom != 0) Result[i]
                = 100.0 * ((-Num / Denom) + (Length + 1)/2);
}
return Result;
}

Price = (H + L) / 2;
CGOLength = Param("CGOLength", 13, 1, 250, 10);
CGO = CGOscillator(Price, CGOLength);
SmLength = Param("SmLength", 2, 1, 20, 2);
CGOSmoothed = DEMA(CGO,SmLength);

Buy = Cross(CGO,CGOSmoothed);

HoldDays = Param("HoldDays",6,1,10,1);

Sell = Cross(CGOSmoothed, CGO)
            OR (BarsSince(Buy) >= HoldDays);

Sell = ExRem (Sell,Buy);

e = Equity();
shape = Buy * shapeUpArrow + Sell * shapeDownArrow;
Plot( Close, "Price", colorBlack, styleCandle );
PlotShapes( shape, IIf( Buy, colorGreen, colorRed ),
            0, IIf( Buy, Low, High ) );
GraphXSpace = 5;

Plot(e,"Equity",colorRed,styleLine|styleOwnScale);
Plot(CGO, "CG Oscillator", colorRed,
        styleLine|styleLeftAxisScale);
Plot(CGOSmoothed, "CGO Smoothed", colorBlue,
        styleLine|styleLeftAxisScale);
```

FIGURE 10.1 CENTER OF GRAVITY

Figure 10.2 shows it being applied to a common stock.

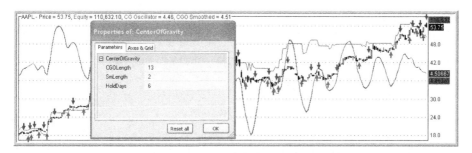

FIGURE 10.2 CENTER OF GRAVITY ON AAPL

Any series, whether naturally occurring, such as the day of the month or phase of the moon, or calculated, such as the RSI or stochastic oscillator, can be used in a mean reversion system. If the series is not already a series that oscillates, it can easily be transformed into one that is.

One technique is to subtract a moving average of the series from itself, resulting in a series that oscillates about zero and having a period about the length of the moving average.

Another technique is to compute a position-in-range statistic for the series, resulting in a series that oscillates between zero and one. Williams R and fast stochastic oscillator are both position-in-range transformations and both are functions that are built-in to AmiBroker.

Oscillator systems get their signals from any of several techniques.

One is zero crossing. Buy when the value of the oscillator crosses from below zero to above zero. Sell when the oscillator crosses from above zero to below zero. If the buy and sell signals seem to be reversed, multiply the oscillator by minus one before looking for the zero crossing.

A second is crossing of the series with another series. The second series is a delayed or smoothed copy of the original series. The CenterOfGravity.afl example uses a smoothed version of the COG – Dr. Ehlers' book uses a delayed version.

A third is the crossing of the oscillator with a level. The stochastic oscillator, call it Sto, is bounded by 0.00 and 1.00. Buy when Sto crosses from below 0.20 to above 0.20, and sell when Sto crosses from above 0.80 to below 0.80.

STOCHASTIC OF THE RSI

Another oscillator that works well as a component of a mean reversion trading system is the Stochastic of the RSI. The AFL code and the chart showing it applied to a common stock follows.

```
//   StochasticOfTheRSI.afl
//
//   A Mean Reversion trading system.
//
//   Use this as it is, or make it part of a more
//   complete and complex trading system.
//
SetTradeDelays(0,0,0,0);
BuyPrice = C;
SellPrice = C;

RSILength = Optimize("RSILength",10,2,20,1);
PIRLookback = Optimize("PIRLookback",20,4,40,2);
TriggerSmoother = Optimize("TriggerSmoother",3,2,10,1);

r = RSIa(C,RSILength);

pir = (r-LLV(r,PIRLookback))/(HHV(r,PIRLookback)
              -LLV(r,PIRLookback));
trigger = DEMA(pir,TriggerSmoother);

Buy = Cross(pir,trigger);
Sell = Cross(trigger,pir);

e = Equity();

Plot(C,"C",colorBlack,styleCandle);
PlotShapes(shapeUpArrow*Buy,colorBrightGreen);
PlotShapes(shapeDownArrow*Sell,colorRed);

Plot(pir, "pir", colorRed,styleLine|styleLeftAxisScale);
Plot(trigger, "trigger", colorBlue,styleLine|styleLeftAxisScale);

Plot(e,"e",colorBlue,styleLine|styleOwnScale);
```

FIGURE 10.3 STOCHASTIC OF THE RSI

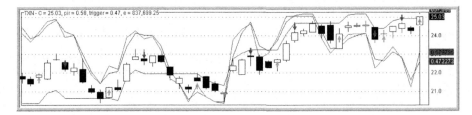

FIGURE 10.4 STOCHASTIC OF THE RSI ON TXN

ADAPTIVE PRICE ZONE

The efficiency of coding in AmiBroker was mentioned in Chapter 5, and reference was made to an article from the September 2006 issue of TASC. Figure 10.5 shows the code and explanation provided by Tomasz Janeczko, president of AmiBroker.

> In "Trading With An Adaptive Price Zone," author Lee Leibfarth presents a trading technique that uses adaptive bands based on the double-smoothed exponential moving average and the classic ADX indicator.
>
> Implementing the adaptive price zone technique using AmiBroker Formula Language is easy and straightforward. Listing 1 shows ready-to-use code. The formula is for both the indicator and the trading system. (A sample chart is shown in the TASC article.)

```
// Adaptive Price Zone Indicator & system
/////////////////////////////
function DblSmoothEMA( price, Length )
{
    period = IIf( Length < 0, 1, sqrt( Length ) );
    smooth = 2 / ( period + 1 );
    return AMA( AMA( price, smooth ), smooth );
}
price = ParamField("Price");
period = Param("period", 20, 2, 100 );
BandPct = Param("width[%]", 1.4, 0.1, 4, 0.1 );
DsEMA = DblSmoothEMA( price, period );
RangeDsEMA = DblSmoothEMA( H - L, period );
UpBand = BandPct * RangeDsEMA + DsEMA;
DnBand = DsEMA - BandPct * RangeDsEMA ;
Plot( C, "Price", colorBlack, styleBar );
Plot( UpBand , "UpBand", colorLightGrey );
Plot( DnBand , "DownBand", colorLightGrey );
// you may uncomment lines below to get 'cloud' chart
// if you are using version 4.80 or higher
// PlotOHLC( UpBand, UpBand, DnBand, DnBand, "Band",
// ColorRGB( 245,245,255), styleCloud );
SetTradeDelays( 1, 1, 1, 1 );
ADXThshold = 30;
ADXValue = ADX( 14 );
Buy = ADXValue <= ADXThshold AND Low <= DnBand;
Short = ADXValue <= ADXThshold AND High >= UpBand;
Sell = Cover = ADXValue > ADXThshold;
if( Status("action") == actionIndicator )
{
 Equity(2);
 PlotShapes( Buy * shapeUpArrow, colorGreen, 0,
        DnBand, -24 );
```

```
PlotShapes( Sell * shapeDownArrow, colorRed, 0,
        UpBand, -24 );
PlotShapes( Short * shapeHollowDownArrow, colorRed, 0,
        UpBand, -24 );
PlotShapes( Cover * shapeHollowUpArrow, colorGreen, 0,
        DnBand, -24 );
}
```

--Tomasz Janeczko, AmiBroker.com
www.amibroker.com

FIGURE 10.5 TASC ARTICLE - LISTING 1

The code has been changed a little so it is similar in style to that of the rest of the book, and applied to a stock. Figure 10.6 shows the AFL code, Figure 10.7 shows the price with Bollinger Bands, Buy and Sell arrows, and equity line.

```
// AdaptivePriceZone.afl
//
function DblSmoothEMA( price, Length )
{
    period = IIf( Length < 0, 1, sqrt( Length ) );
    smooth = 2 / ( period + 1 );
    return AMA( AMA( price, smooth ), smooth );
}
SetTradeDelays( 0,0,0,0 );
BuyPrice = C;
SellPrice = C;

price = C;
period = 50; //Optimize("period", 50, 2, 100, 2 );
BandPct = 2; //Optimize("width[%]", 2, 0.1, 4, 0.1 );

DsEMA = DblSmoothEMA( price, period );
RangeDsEMA = DblSmoothEMA( H - L, period );

UpBand = BandPct * RangeDsEMA + DsEMA;
DnBand = DsEMA - BandPct * RangeDsEMA ;

ADXThshold = 30; //Optimize("ADXThshold",30,1,50,1);
ADXLength = 14; //Optimize("ADXLength",14,2,40,2);
ADXValue = ADX( ADXLength );

Buy = ADXValue <= ADXThshold AND Low <= DnBand;
Sell = ADXValue > ADXThshold;

Buy = ExRem(Buy,Sell);
Sell = ExRem(Sell,Buy);

Plot( C, "Price", colorBlack, styleBar );
```

```
Plot( UpBand , "UpBand", colorLightGrey );
Plot( DnBand , "DownBand", colorLightGrey );
PlotShapes( Buy * shapeUpArrow, colorGreen, 0, DnBand, -24 );
PlotShapes( Sell * shapeDownArrow, colorRed, 0, UpBand, -24 );

e = Equity();
Plot(e,"Equity",colorGreen,styleLine|styleOwnScale);
```

FIGURE 10.6 ADAPTIVE PRICE ZONE

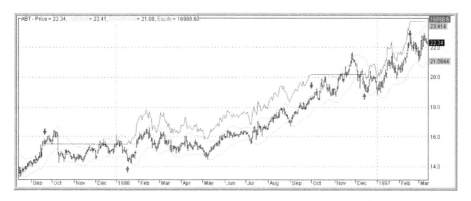

FIGURE 10.7 ADAPTIVE PRICE ZONE RESULT

CONVERT A DATA SERIES INTO AN OSCILLATOR

Almost any well behaved series can be converted into an oscillator, which can then be used as an indicator in a mean reversion system. To illustrate, Figure 10.8 shows the AFL to detrend a price series by subtracting a long term moving average forming an oscillator. The oscillator is used to compute buy and sell signals. Note that there are both Param and Optimize statements in the code, one of which is commented out. If you want to plot the oscillator and adjust it visually, use the Param statements. If you want to have AmiBroker search for the best parameters, use the Optimize statements.

```
//   DetrendedPriceOscillator.afl
//
//   Using any price series as input,
//   compute an oscillator by subtracting
//   a moving average of the series from
//   the series itself.
//   Then use that series to compute
//   Buy and Sell signals.
//
SetTradeDelays(0,0,0,0);
```

```
BuyPrice = C;
SellPrice = C;

//   The series to be detrended
Price = C;

//   The length of the moving average to remove
MALength = Param("MALength",30,2,200,1);
//MALength = Optimize("MALength",30,2,200,1);

//   Subtract the moving average, leaving
//   an oscillator
MovingAverage = MA(Price, MALength);
Oscillator = Price - MovingAverage;

//   Smooth the oscillator once to smooth it
OscSmoothLength = Param("OscSmLen",10,1,50,1);
//OscSmoothLength = Optimize("OscSmLen",10,1,50,1);
SmOsc = DEMA(Oscillator,OscSmoothLength);

//   Smooth again to create a trigger line
Trigger = DEMA(SmOsc,3);

Buy = Cross(SmOsc, Trigger);
Sell = Cross(Trigger, SmOsc);

e = Equity();

Plot(C,"C",colorBlack,styleCandle);
Plot(MovingAverage,"MA",colorRed,styleLine);
PlotShapes(Buy*shapeUpArrow+Sell*shapeDownArrow,
        IIf(Buy,colorGreen,colorRed));
Plot(e,"Equity",colorRed,styleLine|styleOwnScale);
Plot(Oscillator,"Osc",colorBlue,styleLine|styleLeftAxisScale);
Plot(SmOsc,"SmOsc",colorGreen,styleLine|styleLeftAxisScale);
Plot(Trigger,"Trigger",colorRed,styleLine|styleLeftAxisScale);
GraphXSpace = 5;
```

FIGURE 10.8 DETRENDED PRICE OSCILLATOR

Figure 10.9 shows the chart resulting from the Plot statements. It is pretty busy, so you might want to comment out some of the lines after you understand how they work.

FIGURE 10.9 DETRENDED PRICE OSCILLATOR CHART

OTHER EXAMPLES

There are several other examples of mean reversion systems in this book. Look at:
- Figure 8.3, MACD using DEMA.
- Figure 16.2, A Moving Average Crossover.
- Figure 17.11, Advance - Decline Diffusion Index.
- Figure 17.13, Z-Score Diffusion Index.
- Figure 20.2, CMO Oscillator.

PROS AND CONS

The price of any tradable issue at any given time is categorized as being in either a trend or a trading range. Mean reversion systems work well when the tradable is in a trading range. They fail badly when it is in a trend – because they are designed to take positions against the trend. To be used as a trading system with real money, a mean reversion system must have a method for identifying that it is wrong and exiting. The system might include a stop, or it might rely on a separate filter to identify the mode as being either trending or trading range. Filters are discussed in Chapter 17.

SECOND EDITION

In the previous chapter, we saw that when the lengths of two moving averages used to signal long or flat positions were allowed to vary without restriction, the best pair often resulted in the system being mean reverting rather than trend following. SPY is one of the series where that is true. Figures 10.10 and 10.11 show the equity and drawdown for SPY for long and short positions, respectively, using moving average lengths of 3 and 2.

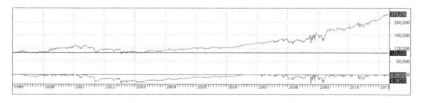

FIGURE 10.10 SPY LONG CROSS 3 WITH 2

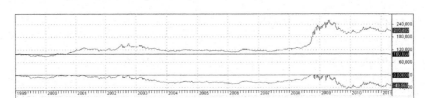

FIGURE 10.11 SPY SHORT CROSS 3 WITH 2

11

Seasonality Systems

COMMODITY TRADERS are often solicited to subscribe to services that base trades on seasonality. For example, buy August Feeder Cattle on May 31 and sell on July 22. The advertisement documents that that trade has been profitable in 87% of years from 1985 to 1999. The historical record probably confirms that. The question is whether the trade described is profitable for some reason, even an unknown reason, and likely to continue, or is simply a result of data mining. Since there are so many combinations of contract, buy date, sell date, and historical period, and so little opportunity to test out-of-sample, seasonality trades like these are difficult to validate using statistical methods.

But there are possible seasonal trades that we might be able to validate. These are "seasonal" periods that happen more frequently and apply to a larger population of tradable issues. For example, many people believe that stocks exhibit seasonality related to:
- The end of one month and the beginning of the next.
- Options expiration.
- New moon or full moon.

If reliable seasonality is found, it could be used to:
- Trade individual stocks that show profitable seasonality using the seasonal pattern as a trading system.
- Model all 100 of the NASDAQ 100 stocks, then trade the QQQ based on the composite results.
- Create a filter that favors long positions or short positions accord-

ing to the seasonality cycles and use that filter to allow or block signals from a different trading system.

SEASONALITY PROCEDURE

Dividing data into in-sample and out-of-sample periods was introduced in Chapter 3 and will be discussed in more detail in Chapter 18. Please refer back to Chapter 5, to the sections describing how to test a trading system and how to optimize a trading system for details about running the AmiBroker backtester and optimizer.

The steps that are taken to evaluate each of the possible seasonal patterns are:

1. Design and code a test program that will determine the profit or loss from some specific condition to be tested.
2. Set the data range to the in-sample period.
3. Use a single issue and the backtester to verify that the program works as it should.
4. Add the code necessary so that the optimizer can be used to cycle through all the possible values or conditions.
5. Still using a single issue, make an optimizer run and verify that the program works as intended and gathers the results desired.
6. Set up a watchlist containing the list of tickers to be tested.
7. Set the filter so that the runs will process all the tickers in that watchlist.
8. Run the Old Optimizer, which has the effect of running the optimizer on each ticker individually, and accumulating the results for all tickers for each value of the index of optimization.
9. Analyze the output report from the optimizer in whatever ways are helpful – sort, graph, compute, et cetera.
10. Based solely on the results of the test runs made on the in-sample data, draw tentative conclusions about the profitability of the conditions.
11. Design a trading system based on the conclusions.
12. Apply the trading system to an individual ticker and verify that the logic is as intended.
13. Apply the trading system to the entire list, and analyze and record the results. The results will always be good – this is the in-sample data.
14. Set the data range to the out-of-sample period.
15. Test the tickers in the list and determine whether the conditions continue to be profitable out-of-sample.

Throughout this chapter, the in-sample period is 1/1/1995 through 1/1/2005. The out-of-sample period is the two years immediately following – 1/1/2005 through 1/1/2007. The list consists of 513 stocks, each actively traded, each with price history from 1995 through the present.

The list of stocks you select will affect the results. For example, if you plan to use the results of your own study to trade SPY, the exchange traded fund that tracks the S&P 500, then an analysis of the stocks that make up that index would be a good choice.

During testing, commission is set to zero. The tests are looking for conditions and patterns that may be traded as individual rules, that may be grouped together into a larger rule, or that may be used as filters to allow or prohibit specific actions. The time to allow for commission is after the conditions and patterns have been evaluated, the trading system designed, and the realistic profitability evaluated.

On the charts that follow, do not focus on the profit figures themselves. They depend very much on the stocks and the time period being analyzed. Instead, focus on the relative heights of the profit bars and the periods of profitability or loss.

END OF THE MONTH

If there is a pattern around the end of the month, it will show up if we look at the gain or loss from one-day trades, summarized by the day of the month on the day of entry.

The program is very simple. For a specific day of the month, buy on the close, hold one day, and sell on the next close. For the testing runs, it is only necessary to take long positions. A loss for a long position for a particular day shows that a short position would be profitable.

```
//   SeasonalityDayOfMonth_Testing.afl
//
//   Test for seasonality based on the day of the month.
//   This version does the day-by-day testing.
//
SetTradeDelays(0,0,0,0);
BuyPrice = Close;
SellPrice = Close;

DayToBuy = Optimize("DTB",1,1,31,1);
Buy = DayToBuy == Day();
Sell = BarsSince(Buy) >=1;
```

FIGURE 11.1 SEASONALITY DAY OF MONTH - TESTING

The in-sample period is 1/1/1995 through 1/1/2005. Using 513 active stocks with data from 1995 to the present, the program summarized the profit for each day of the month. As the next chart shows, there are three strongly positive periods – the 1st through 5th, 10th through 16th, and 21st through 31st.

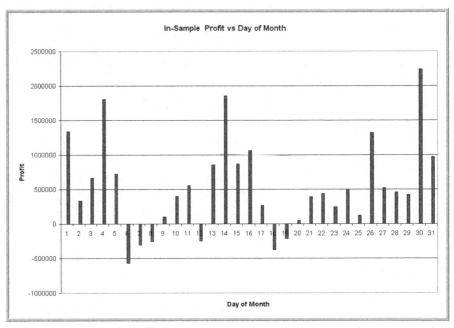

FIGURE 11.2 DAY OF MONTH, IN-SAMPLE

Based on the in-sample results, the results were used to create a trading system. The program was set to buy at the beginning of any of those strong periods and sell at the beginning of the intervening periods. Since there were no prolonged periods of losing days, we do not anticipate that taking short trades will be very profitable. Nevertheless, the code has been set up to enable testing of either long or short trades.

```
//   SeasonalityDayOfMonth_System.afl
//
//   Test for seasonality based on the day of the month.
//   This version is the trading system resulting
//   from analysis of the day-by-day testing.
//
SetTradeDelays(0,0,0,0);
BuyPrice = Close;
SellPrice = Close;
```

```
Cover = Buy = (Day() >= 1 AND Day() <=5) OR
              (Day() >=10 AND Day() <=16) OR
              (Day() >=21 AND Day() <= 31);
Short = Sell = (Day() >=6 AND Day() <=9) OR
              (Day() >= 17 AND Day() <=20);
```

FIGURE 11.3 SEASONALITY DAY OF MONTH - SYSTEM

Each of the 513 stocks was tested individually using the trading system version of the program over the in-sample period. 499 of 513 stocks
(97%) were profitable for long-only trades, with a median annual gain of
23%. 235 (46%) were profitable for short-only trades, with a median annual loss of 1%. 442 (86%) were profitable for long and short trades, with
a median annual gain of 21%.

The out-of-sample period is 1/1/2005 through 1/1/2007 – the two years
immediately following the in-sample period. The results of running the
version that tests for day-by-day profitability are a little less well defined,
as the next chart shows. But no changes will be made based on out-of-
sample results.

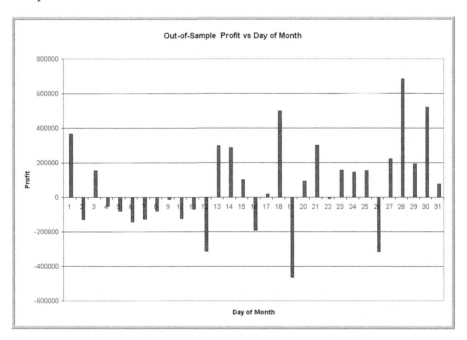

FIGURE 11.4 DAY OF MONTH, OUT-OF-SAMPLE

Testing individual stocks in the out-of-sample period, with no change
to the program, 428 of 513 (83%) stocks were profitable for long-only trades,
with a median annual profit of 18%. For short-only trades, 292 (57%) were

profitable with a median annual gain of 2%. 413 (80%) were profitable for long and short trades, with a median annual gain of 20%.

Day of the Month - Summary			
		Percent Profitable	Median Annual Gain
In-Sample	Long	97%	21%
	Short	46%	-1%
	Long & Short	86%	21%
Out-of-Sample	Long	83%	18%
	Short	57%	2%
	Long & Short	80%	20%

FIGURE 11.5 DAY OF THE MONTH - SUMMARY

The seasonality pattern based on the end of the month looks very promising.

TRADING DAY OF THE MONTH

It could be that trading day is more important than calendar day. That can be tested as well. The first trading day of the month is identified as the Day Of Interest (DOI). The program code will determine how many trading days the bar that is being evaluated is before or after the DOI. Long trades are entered on the close, and held one day. A trade entered on the DOI is defined to be a trade entered on Day 0 (zero), relative to the DOI.

```
//   SeasonalityTradingDay_Testing.afl
//
//   Test for seasonality based on trading day of the month.
//   This version does the day-by-day testing.
//
//   This program looks ahead to see whether there is
//   trading the next day.  That is OK.  We will not
//   be looking ahead when we trade, and the programming
//   is greatly simplified by looking ahead during
//   the testing.
//
SetTradeDelays(0,0,0,0);
BuyPrice = Close;
SellPrice = Close;

//   We will specify one day as the Day Of Interest -- DOI.
//   In this program, DOI is the first trading day of a month.
```

```
//  A trade made on DOI is a trade made on Day 0.
//  A trade made one day after DOI is a trade made on Day +1.
//  A trade made one day before DOI is a trade made on Day -1.
//
//  There are about 22 trading days in a month.
//  Centered at DOI, we will investigate from Day -8
//  to Day +8.
//

DOI = Month()!=Ref(Month(),-1);
Minus8 = Ref(DOI,8);
Daynumber = -8 + BarsSince(Minus8);

DayToBuy = Optimize("DayToBuy",0,-8,8,1);
Buy = Daynumber == DayToBuy;
Sell = BarsSince(Buy) >= 1;

Plot(Daynumber,"DN",colorBlue,styleDots);
```

FIGURE 11.6 SEASONALITY TRADING DAY - TESTING

The in-sample period is 1/1/1995 through 1/1/2005, and uses the same 513 stocks as the end-of-month example. Based on the in-sample results, there is a period of strong profitability beginning with Day -3 and extending through Day 2.

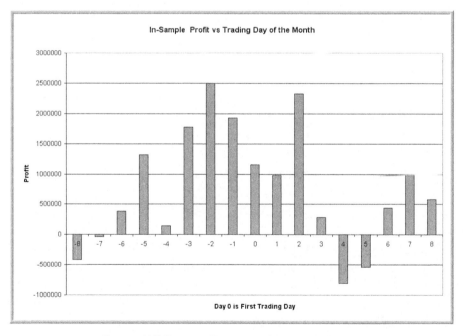

FIGURE 11.7 TRADING DAY OF THE MONTH, IN-SAMPLE

The trading system based on this pattern buys at the close of Day -3 and sells at the close of Day 3. It is long for six days. There is no period of losing days within a few days of the first trading day of the month, so no provision is made for short positions.

```
//   SeasonalityTradingDay_System.afl
//
//   Test for seasonality based on trading day of the month.
//   This version is the trading system resulting
//   from analysis of the day-by-day testing.
//
//   This program looks ahead to see whether there is
//   trading the next day.  That is OK.  We will not
//   be looking ahead when we trade, and the programming
//   is greatly simplified by looking ahead during
//   the testing.
//
SetTradeDelays(0,0,0,0);
BuyPrice = Close;
SellPrice = Close;

//   We will specify one day as the Day Of Interest -- DOI.
//   In this program, DOI is the first trading day of a month.
//   A trade made on DOI is a trade made on Day 0.
//   A trade made one day after DOI is a trade made on Day +1.
//   A trade made one day before DOI is a trade made on Day -1.
//
//   There are about 22 trading days in a month.
//   Centered at DOI, we will investigate from Day -8
//   to Day +8.
//

DOI = Month()!=Ref(Month(),-1);
Minus8 = Ref(DOI,8);
Daynumber = -8 + BarsSince(Minus8);

Buy = (Daynumber >= -3) AND (Daynumber <=2);
Sell = (Daynumber >=3) OR (Daynumber <=-4);

Plot(Daynumber,"DN",colorBlue,styleDots);
```

FIGURE 11.8 SEASONALITY TRADING DAY - SYSTEM

In-sample, 485 out of 513 (94%) stocks were profitable for long-only positions, with a median annual gain of 13.0%. Since there was not a strongly negative period within a few days of the first trading day of the month, short positions were not tested.

The out-of-sample period was 1/1/2005 through 1/1/2007. The day-by-day results show the seasonality continuing into the out-of-sample period.

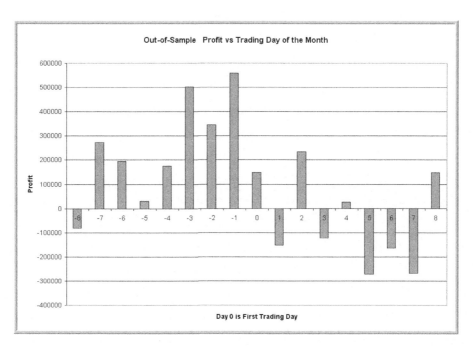

FIGURE 11.9 TRADING DAY OF THE MONTH, OUT-OF-SAMPLE

Testing the system on the out-of-sample period, and continuing to buy on the close of Day -3 and sell on the close of Day 3, 442 of 513 (86%) stocks showed a profit. The median annual gain was 14%.

Trading Day of the Month - Summary			
		Percent Profitable	Median Annual Gain
In-Sample	Long	94%	13%
Out-of-Sample	Long	86%	14%

FIGURE 11.10 TRADING DAY OF THE MONTH - SUMMARY

The seasonality appears to continue.

OPTIONS EXPIRATION DAY

Another possible Day Of Interest is options expiration day – the third Friday of the month in the United States. Trades are entered on the close. A trade entered on the Friday of options expiration is entered on Day 0 (zero).

```
//   SeasonalityOptionsExpiration.afl
//
//   Test for seasonality based on options expiration day,
//   the third Friday of the month in the US.
//
//   This program has the code for both the day-by-day
//   testing, and the resulting trading system.
//   Change from one to the other commenting-out
//   the code that is not needed.
//
//   This program looks ahead to set the Day Of Interest.
//   That is OK.  We will NOT
//   be looking ahead when we trade, and the programming
//   is greatly simplified by looking ahead during
//   the testing.
//
SetTradeDelays(0,0,0,0);
BuyPrice = Close;
SellPrice = Close;

//   We will specify one day as the Day Of Interest -- DOI.
//   In this program, DOI is the third Friday of a month.
//   A trade made on DOI is a trade made on Day 0.
//   A trade made one day after DOI is a trade made on Day +1.
//   A trade made one day before DOI is a trade made on Day -1.
//
//   There are about 22 trading days in a month.
//   Centered at DOI, we will investigate from Day -8
//   to Day +8.
//

//   DayOfWeek() returns 5 for Friday.

DOI = (DayOfWeek() == 5) AND ((Day() >= 15) AND (Day() <= 21));
Minus8 = Ref(DOI,8);
Daynumber = -8 + BarsSince(Minus8);

//   Do the day-by-day testing.
//DayToBuy = Optimize("DayToBuy",0,-8,8,1);
//Buy = Daynumber == DayToBuy;
//Sell = BarsSince(Buy) >= 1;

//   Use the day-by-day results in a trading system.
Buy = ((Daynumber >= -6) AND (Daynumber <=-2)) OR
        ((Daynumber >= 2) AND (Daynumber <= 4));
Sell = ((Daynumber >= -1) AND (Daynumber <= 1)) OR
        (Daynumber >= 5);
Short = ((Daynumber >= -1) AND (Daynumber <= 1));
Cover = (Daynumber >= 2);

Plot(Daynumber,"DN",colorBlue,styleDots);
```

FIGURE 11.11 SEASONALITY OPTIONS EXPIRATION

The in-sample period is 1/1/1995 through 1/1/2005, and uses the same 513 stocks. Based on the in-sample results, there is a five day period of strong profitability beginning with Day -6, followed by a three day period of weak or negative profitability beginning with Day -1, followed by a three day period of strong profitability beginning with Day 2. Day 6 and beyond are near the end of the month, have already been tested, and will not be included in this study.

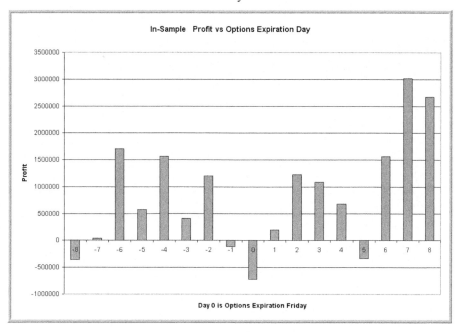

FIGURE 11.12 OPTIONS EXPIRATION IN-SAMPLE

The trading system starts flat, enters a long position on the close of Day -6, reverses to short on the close of Day -1, reverses back to long on the close of Day 2, goes flat on the close of Day 5.

In-sample, trading only long positions, 435 of the 513 (85%) are profitable, with a median annual gain of 10%. For short-only positions, 246 (48%) are profitable, with a median annual gain of 0%. Taking both long and short positions, 411 (80%) are profitable, with a median annual gain of 10%.

Out-of-sample, the day-by-day results show the same pattern, but with less strength.

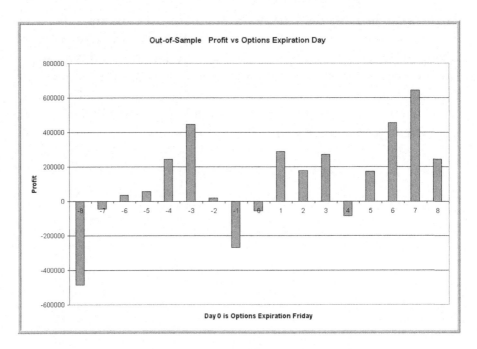

FIGURE 11.13 OPTIONS EXPIRATION OUT-OF-SAMPLE

Trading out-of-sample, taking only long positions, 408 of 513 (80%) are profitable, with a median annual gain of 9%. Short-only, 299 (58%) are profitable, with a median annual gain of 2%. Trading both long and short positions, 377 (73%) are profitable, with a median annual gain of 11%.

Options Expiration Day - Summary			
		Percent Profitable	Median Annual Gain
In-Sample	Long	85%	10%
	Short	48%	0%
	Long & Short	80%	10%
Out-of-Sample	Long	80%	9%
	Short	58%	2%
	Long & Short	73%	11%

FIGURE 11.14 OPTIONS EXPIRATION DAY - SUMMARY

The seasonality is profitable, with most of the profit coming from long positions.

PHASE OF THE MOON

The moon cycles from new moon through full moon and back to new moon approximately every 29.53 days, as seen from Earth. Starting with the occurrence of a new moon, we can compute the portion of the cycle that the moon has completed at any specific time – particularly the opening or closing of the market. The cycle runs from 0.00 to 0.99, then repeats. The program that follows is adjusted so that the cycle is measured at the close of the US equities markets – 4:00 PM EST. For the initial study, we will ignore Daylight Saving Time. If the results are promising, the code will be modified to account for DST.

Since the moon's cycle and the monthly calendar do not have matching divisions, the program divides the moon's cycle into 100 equal portions, and sets up a "slot" for each. Long positions are entered on the close of one day and exited on the close of the next. The profit for each trade is recorded according to the slot the moon was in when the trade was entered. 513 active stocks with data beginning in 1995 were selected. The in-sample period was 1/1/1995 through 1/1/2005, giving a sample set of 1,290,000 closed trades. Is that a large enough sample to give statistical validity?

For those interested in calibrating a lunar cycle model, several Internet sites give precise dates and times for new and full moon. The new moon used to calibrate this program was on December 20, 2006, at 14 hours 1 minute, Greenwich Mean Time, GMT. Subtract four hours from GMT to get Eastern Standard Time. When the market closes at 4:00 PM EST, it is 8:00 PM GMT, or 20 hours 0 minutes. On December 20, 2006, when the market closed the moon was 5 hours 59 minutes past new moon, which is 0.00844 of a cycle. The small adjustment is made in the program so that the market close on December 20, 2006, shows a phase of 0.00844.

```
//   SeasonalityMoon.afl
//
//   The moon has a cycle time of 29.53 days.
//   This program computes the profitability
//   relative to the new moon.
//
//   This program has the code for both the day-by-day
//   testing, and the resulting trading system.
//   Change from one to the other commenting-out
//   the code that is not needed.
//
//   The algorithm to calculate the age of the
//   moon in days is based on code contributed to
//   the AmiBroker Library by "Oz Falcon," which
```

```
//    is very similar to code posted by Paul Sadowski
//    on the Internet.

SetTradeDelays(0,0,0,0);
BuyPrice = Close;
SellPrice = Close;

// Constants
PI = 3.1415926535897932385;

// normalize values to range 0 to 1
function normalize( Val )
{
    Val = Val - floor( Val );
    Val = IIf(Val < 0, Val + 1, Val);
    return Val;
}

Y = Year();
M = Month();
D = Day();
Hr = Hour();
Mn = Minute();

// calculate the Julian Date at 12H UT
YY = Y - floor( ( 12 - M ) / 10 );
MM = M + 9;
MM = IIf(MM >= 12, MM - 12, MM);

K1 = floor( 365.25 * ( YY + 4712 ) );
K2 = floor( 30.6 * MM + 0.5 );
K3 = floor( floor( ( YY / 100 ) + 49 ) * 0.75 ) - 38;

//        for dates in Julian calendar
JD = K1 + K2 + D + 59;
//        for Gregorian calendar
JD = IIf(JD > 2299160, JD - K3, JD);

//   Calculate the moon's age as a percentage
//   of its cycle, with New Moon = 0.0
//   The small adjustment of 0.00407 is made
//   so that the new moon falls exactly at
//   December 20, 2006, 14 hours 1 minute GMT.
//   The US markets open (9:30 AM EST) 31 minutes
//   before that new moon.  The cycle age of the
//   market opening is -0.00073, which is 0.99927
//   of the 0 to 0.99999 cycle.
//   The US markets Close (4:00 PM EST)
//   5 hours 59 minutes after the new moon.  The
//   cycle age of the market closing is 0.00844.
//
IP = normalize( (( JD - 2451550.1 ) / 29.530588853)-0.00407 );

// Calculate the moon's age in days
AG = IP*29.53;
```

```
// Convert phase to radians
IP1 = IP;
IP = IP*2*PI;

//   For each of the 100 individual percentages
//   of the moon's age, compute the profitability of
//   buying at the close and selling at the next close.

Pct = int(100.0 * IP1);

//   Do the testing
//BuyTime = Optimize("Pct",10,0,99,1);
//Buy = Pct == BuyTime;
//Sell = BarsSince(Buy)>=1;

//   Use the results as a trading system.
Cover = Buy = (pct>=1 AND pct <=59) OR (pct >=79 AND pct <=99);
Short = Sell = (pct >=60 AND pct <=78);

_N(Title = " + Y + "/" + M + "/" +D +
" Hr:" + Hr + " Min:" + Mn +
      "    Age: " + AG +
      "    IP: " + IP1 + "    Pct: " + Pct);

Plot(Close, "C", colorBlack, styleCandle);

Plot(Pct,"Pct",colorBlue,styleDots|styleOwnScale);
```

FIGURE 11.15 SEASONALITY OF THE MOON

There seems to be strong seasonality, as the Figure 11.16, the in-sample chart, shows. Using common terminology, the system goes long about the time of the moon's third quarter, reverses to short at about the full moon, and reverses back to long at about the third quarter. In terms of the 100 slots, the system is long when the moon was anywhere in the 79 to 59 range, wrapping around the period of the new moon, and short when the moon is in the 60 to 78 range.

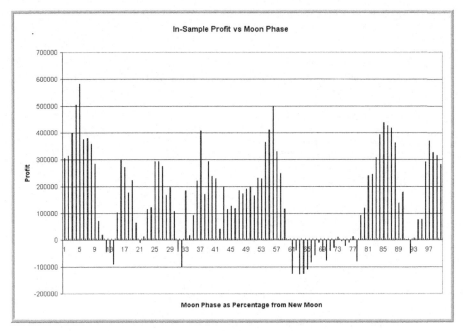

FIGURE 11.16 MOON IN-SAMPLE

For the in-sample period, it was profitable for 494 of 513 (96%) stocks, with a median annual gain of 20%. For short-only trades, it was profitable for 232 (45%), with a median annual loss of 1%. For both long and short trades, it was profitable for 458 (89%), with a median annual gain of 20%.

The out-of-sample period was 1/1/2005 through 1/1/2007 – the two years immediately following the in-sample period. Long-only, 285 of 513 (55%) were profitable, with a median annual profit of 2%. Short-only, 38 (7%) were profitable, with a median annual loss of 13%. Long and short, 140 (27%) were profitable, with a median annual loss of 11%.

The out-of-sample results are very different from the in-sample results. The slots from about 9 to 82 and 94 to 99 – about 80% of the slots – have inverted!

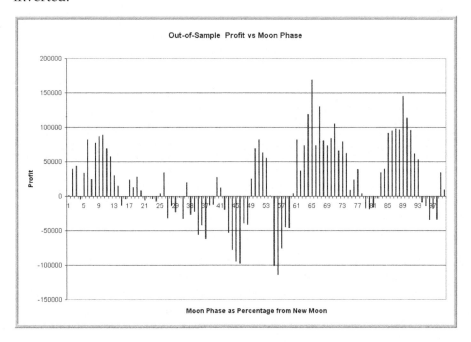

FIGURE 11.17 MOON OUT-OF-SAMPLE

Based on the model in the program listed here, there is no persistent pattern. It looks like there once was a pattern, but it has not been profitable lately. Even though the in-sample run produced 1,290,000 closed trades (significantly more than the 30 trades often suggested) to model 100 possible buy conditions, the model did not hold up out-of-sample. This illustrates again one of the central points of this book – the only statistics that count are those obtained from out-of-sample runs.

Moon Phase - Summary			
		Percent Profitable	Median Annual Gain
In-Sample	Long	96%	20%
	Short	45%	-1%
	Long & Short	89%	20%
Out-of-Sample	Long	55%	2%
	Short	7%	-13%
	Long & Short	27%	-11%

FIGURE 11.18 MOON PHASE SUMMARY

NOTE ABOUT THE END OF THE MONTH STUDY

The code for the day of the month study simply recorded the results for each date, without regard to the number of days in the month. Another study, perhaps a better one, could be done using the first of the month as a day of interest. Results for dates following the first would be unchanged, but results for dates preceding the first would change.

SECOND EDITION

End of the month seasonality. Using the code in figures 11.1 and 11.3, SPY was tested using CAR/MaxDD as the objective function, 1/1/1999 through 1/1/2006 as the in-sample period, and 1/1/2006 through 5/1/2011 as the out-of-sample period. In-sample, the best period to begin a four day long position was any day between the 25th and 31st. The best period to begin a four day short position was any day between the 14th and the 19th.

That system had a risk adjusted return, RAR, of 16.4% over the in-sample period, with CAR/MaxDD of 0.52. Figure 11.19 shows the equity and drawdown.

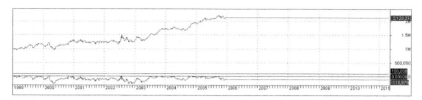

FIGURE 11.19 SPY END OF MONTH SEASONALITY -- IN-SAMPLE

Trading that same system using the out-of-sample data, it had a RAR of 1.99% and CAR/MaxDD of 0.06. Figure 11.20 shows the equity and drawdown for the entire period, with the vertical line at the start of the out-of-sample period.

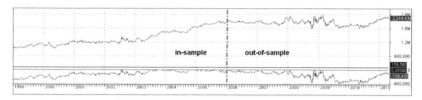

FIGURE 11.20 SPY END OF MONTH SEASONALITY -- ENTIRE PERIOD

Options expiration seasonality. Using the code in figure 11.11, SPY was tested for the in-sample period described earlier, 1/1/1995 through 1/1/2005, and then extended through 5/1/2011. Figure 11.21 shows the equity and drawdown for the entire period, with two vertical lines—one where the out-of-sample period begins in the original discussion, the second where the out-of-sample period ends in the original discussion.

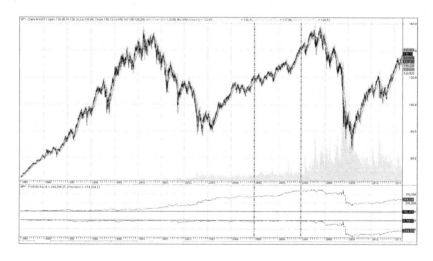

FIGURE 11.21 SPY OPTIONS EXPIRATION SEASONALITY

The entire equity is used to take each position. The system performed well through the market decline in 2001-2002 in the in-sample period, and in the two year out-of-sample period 2005-2006. It began flat performance in 2007, performed very poorly during the 2008-2009 decline, and has been profitable recently. The drawdown appears to be severe, and it is, due to the large positions taken. When a constant amount of $10,000 per trade is used, as is done to establish a baseline of performance and monitor current system health, the drop in performance is not as severe.

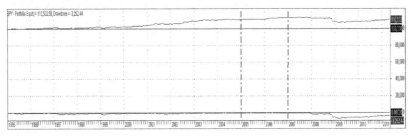

FIGURE 11.22 SPY OPTIONS EXPIRATION -- CONSTANT TRADE SIZE

This appears to be a case where the model (the logic) and the data (the price series) fell out of synchronization. *Modeling Trading System Performance* discusses ways to recognize that this is happening, and gives suggestions for dealing with it, including how to adjust position size.

12

Pattern Systems

PATTERN SYSTEMS CAN BE USED to identify potentially profitable opportunities in almost any type of market. "Buy after three down days," is anticipating a reversion to the mean. "Buy after three up days," is anticipating a trend. These might be meaningful patterns, and will be tested. The trading literature has many articles describing many other patterns, some of which have a reasonable basis and test well out-of-sample, others are simply the result of data mining and do not hold up to out-of-sample validation.

One way to test the "three days in a row" pattern is to compare the closing prices. A bar with a higher close than its predecessor puts that bar into the group of up days.

This example will use a different way. Each day will be evaluated strictly on the closing price, and will be classified as being an up day, flat day, or down day.

Measure the close to close percentage change for this day and for the past 60 trading days – about three months. Sort that list and determine what percentage change is required to be in the top third, middle third, or bottom third. Assign a value of 3, 2, or 1, to each day according to whether that day is in the top third, middle third, or bottom third, respectively. For each day, form a three number string with the most recent day as the final character. Three up days would be "333." Up, flat, down, with today being down, would be "321." There are 27 combinations. For each combination, test the profitability of being long one day.

The program that follows will do that. Rather than limit the groups

173

to thirds, a variable named *cutoff* allows the top and bottom groups to be more or less restrictive as the value of cutoff is lowered or raised. The *Percentile* function involves sorting data, so this program takes more time.

```
//   PatternDailyClose.afl
//
//   This program tests the profitability of a pattern
//   of daily closing prices.
//
//   Rank each daily percentage close to close change
//   according to where it fell in terms of the previous
//   three months.
//
//   If the change is in the top of the range, assign that day
//   a "3", in the middle a "2", in the bottom a "1".
//
SetTradeDelays(0,0,0,0);
BuyPrice = Close;
SellPrice = Close;

PctC = (C-Ref(C,-1))/C;
//   Set the Cutoff to select the exclusivity of the
//   top and bottom groups.
//   Cutoff = 33 will create three equal-sized groups.
//   Cutoff = 15 will make it more difficult to qualify
//   for the top and bottom groups.
Cutoff = 33;

TopGroup = PctC >= Percentile(PctC,60,100-Cutoff);
BottomGroup = PctC <= Percentile(PctC,60,Cutoff);
MiddleGroup = (NOT TopGroup) AND (NOT BottomGroup);

//   Set a single variable with the group
//   category of the bar.
Position = IIf(TopGroup,3,IIf(middleGroup,2,1));

//   Form a single identifier for each bar for its
//   three day sequence.
Sequence = 100 * Ref(Position,-2) + 10
           * Ref(Position,-1) + Position;

//   These AddColumn statements display the categories
//   each day is assigned to, and help verify that the
//   program works as it should.
//   Run as an Exploration with Current Symbol and
//   Last Days set to 100.
Filter = 1;
AddColumn(C,"C",1.9);
AddColumn(PctC,"PctC",1.9);
AddColumn(TopGroup,"Top",1.0);
AddColumn(MiddleGroup,"Middle",1.0);
AddColumn(BottomGroup,"Bottom",1.0);
AddColumn(Position,"Position",1.0);
AddColumn(Sequence,"Sequence",1.0);
```

```
//   ----Block of code in use when optimizing
//   When optimizing, uncomment this block
//   and comment-out all of the
//   code below the ==== dashed line.
//
//   Create a set of optimizations that
//   will cycle through all the possible sequences.
TwoDaysAgo = Optimize("TwoDaysAgo",1,1,3,1);
OneDayAgo = Optimize("OneDayAGo",1,1,3,1);
ThisDay = Optimize("ThisDay",1,1,3,1);

Selected = 100 * TwoDaysAgo + 10 * OneDayAgo + ThisDay;

Buy = Selected == Sequence;
Sell = BarsSince(Buy) >= 1;
//
//   ----End of code for optimizing


//================================================
//   ----Block of code in use when testing as a trading system
//   When testing, uncomment one set of sequences.
//   Buy the strong patterns,
//   short the weak patterns.
/*
//   33% Cutoff -- Strongest sequences
Buy = (Sequence == 111) OR
      (Sequence == 223) OR
      (Sequence == 323) OR
      (Sequence == 311) OR
      (Sequence == 313) OR
      (Sequence == 213) OR
      (Sequence == 131) OR
      (Sequence == 331) OR
      (Sequence == 113);
Sell = BarsSince(Buy) >= 1;
//   33% Cutoff -- Weakest sequences
Short = (Sequence == 132) OR
      (Sequence == 332) OR
      (Sequence == 232) OR
      (Sequence == 231) OR
      (Sequence == 221) OR
      (Sequence == 322) OR
      (Sequence == 333) OR
      (Sequence == 133) OR
      (Sequence == 122);
Cover = BarsSince(Short) >= 1;
*/
/*
//   15% Cutoff -- strongest sequences
Buy = (Sequence == 111) OR
      (Sequence == 211) OR
      (Sequence == 311) OR
      (Sequence == 121) OR
      (Sequence == 112) OR
      (Sequence == 223) OR
      (Sequence == 131) OR
```

```
                  (Sequence == 113) OR
                  (Sequence == 221);
Sell = BarsSince(Buy) >= 1;
//   15% Cutoff -- weakest sequences
Short = (Sequence == 333) OR
        (Sequence == 331) OR
        (Sequence == 332) OR
        (Sequence == 132) OR
        (Sequence == 232) OR
        (Sequence == 133) OR
        (Sequence == 233) OR
        (Sequence == 123) OR
        (Sequence == 313);
Cover = BarsSince(Short) >= 1;
*/
/*
//   Long only -- strongest single sequence
Buy = (Sequence == 111);
Sell = BarsSince(Buy) >= 1;
*/
//   These AddColumn statements display the Buy, Sell, Short,
//   and Cover signals, and the gain on the following day.
//GainAhead = (Ref(C,1)-C)/C;
//AddColumn(Buy,"Buy",1.0);
//AddColumn(Sell,"Sell",1.0);
//AddColumn(Short,"Short",1.0);
//AddColumn(Cover,"Cover",1.0);
//AddColumn(GainAhead,"GainAhead",1.9);
```

FIGURE 12.1 PATTERN DAILY CLOSE

USING A 33% CUTOFF

The first runs used a cutoff value of 33. The in-sample test results appear in the following chart, sorted left to right in order of their pattern sequence. The metric used is Risk Adjusted Return (RAR).

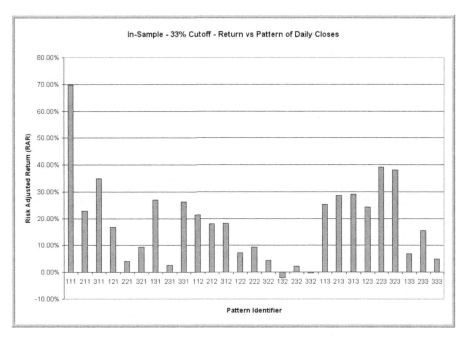

FIGURE 12.2 33% CUTOFF, IN-SAMPLE

There is definitely a pattern in the in-sample data. The best performance is bimodal – buy after weakness (patterns ending in 1) and buy after strength (patterns ending in 3).

Strongest	Weakest
111	132
223	332
323	232
311	231
313	221
213	322
131	333
331	133
113	122

FIGURE 12.3 33% CUTOFF, IN-SAMPLE

178   Quantitative Trading Systems

The program is extended to be a trading system which buys the nine
strongest patterns, and shorts the nine weakest patterns.

In-sample, 1/1/1995 through 1/1/2005, long-only, 464 of 513 (90%) were
profitable with a median annual gain of 12%. Short-only, 109 (21%) were
profitable with a median annual loss of 6%. Long and short, 327 (63%)
were profitable with a median annual gain of 6%.

Out-of-sample, 1/1/2005 through 1/1/2007, long-only, 378 of 513 (73%)
were profitable with a median annual gain of 8%. Short-only, 220 (42%)
were profitable with a median annual loss of 2%. Long and short, 303
(59%) were profitable with a median annual gain of 5%.

The chart of the out-of-sample results is very similar to the chart of
the in-sample results. The sequences that ranked high in-sample continue to rank high out-of-sample, and the sequences that ranked low
continue to rank low. It appears that the three-day pattern of closes is
persistent. But it may not be strong enough to be profitable as a trading
system of its own.

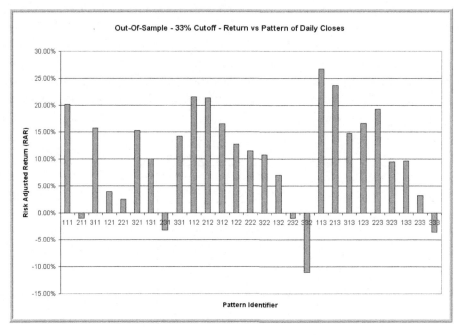

Figure 12.3 33% Cutoff, Out-of-Sample

33% Groups - Summary		Percent Profitable	Median Annual Gain
In-Sample	Long	90%	12%
	Short	21%	-6%
	Long & Short	63%	6%
Out-of-Sample	Long	73%	8%
	Short	42%	-2%
	Long & Short	59%	5%

FIGURE 12.4 33% CUTOFF, SUMMARY

USING A 15% CUTOFF

The criteria for being counted as an up day or down day might be too loose. The in-sample data was retested using a cutoff of 15%. One result we can anticipate is far fewer occurrences of multiple up or multiple down days. With the cutoff set at 33%, each sequence was expected to occur approximately equally – about 3.7%. With the cutoff set at 15%, a sequence of three up days or three down days is expected to occur only 0.3%.

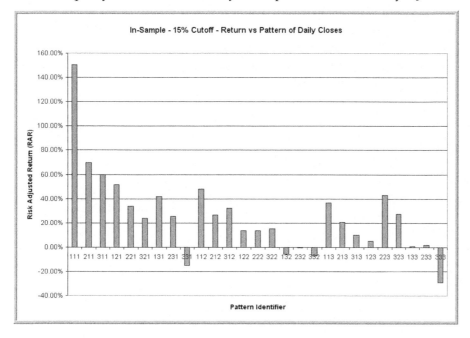

FIGURE 12.5 15% CUTOFF, IN-SAMPLE

The result is dramatic. Every sequence that has two or more days when the decline was in the deepest 15% of any three day period is among the strongest nine sequences. And every sequence that has two or more days when the rise was in the top 15% of any three day period is among the nine weakest sequences.

Strongest	Weakest
111	333
211	331
311	332
121	132
112	232
223	133
131	233
113	123
221	313

FIGURE 12.6 15% CUTOFF, IN-SAMPLE

In-sample, 1/1/1995 through 1/1/2005, long-only, 436 of 513 (85%) were profitable with a median annual gain of 8%. Short-only, 204 (40%) were profitable with a median annual loss of 2%. Long and short, 347 (68%) were profitable with a median annual gain of 6%.

Out-of-sample, 1/1/2005 through 1/1/2007, long-only, 305 of 513 (59%) were profitable with a median annual gain of 2%. Short-only, 261 (50%) were profitable with a median annual gain of 0%. Long and short, 286 (56%) were profitable with a median annual gain of 0%.

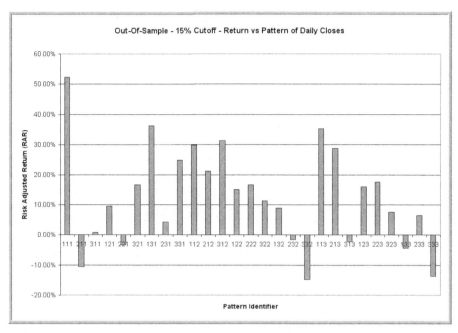

FIGURE 12.7 15% CUTOFF, OUT-OF-SAMPLE

15% Groups - Summary			
		Percent Profitable	Median Annual Gain
In-Sample	Long	85%	8%
	Short	40%	-2%
	Long & Short	68%	6%
Out-of-Sample	Long	59%	2%
	Short	50%	0%
	Long & Short	56%	2%

FIGURE 12.8 15% CUTOFF, SUMMARY

Even though the in-sample results have about 1,290,000 data points, none of these three-day patterns are strong enough or persistent enough when tested in the out-of-sample period to be used as trading systems. Perhaps they could be used in conjunction with other indicators or as filters.

13

Anticipating Signals

IF YOUR TRADING SYSTEMS are designed to trade at the closing price on the day the signal is generated, you must either:

*   be able to monitor the market near the close, estimate the closing price, and act very near the close
*   precalculate the price that will trigger a signal and place a limit-on-close order before the close

MAKE AN ESTIMATE

One technique is to create the next price bar during the trading day, get a real-time quotation near the close, enter those prices into the AmiBroker database using either the AmiBroker Quotation Editor or AmiQuote, and run the system.

In the example on the next chart, the system is a moving average crossover, it is in a long position, and it calculates its signal based on the closing price. The moving average lengths are 1 and 36, yesterday's Close was 41.12, the fast moving average is 41.12, and the slow moving average is 40.5875. If the price drops a little from yesterday, a Sell signal will be generated.

Figure 13.2 shows the code for the simple trading system to use to illustrate these techniques.

```
//    MACrossSystem.afl
//
//    The classic Moving Average crossover
//    using simple Moving Averages
//

//    Set up the lengths for the moving averages
Length1 = 1; //Optimize("Length1",6,1,81,2);
Length2 = 36; //Optimize("Length2",35,2,200,2);

//    The Moving Average calculations
MA1 = MA(C,Length1);
MA2 = MA(C,Length2);

//    The Buy and Sell logic
//    Buy when MA1 crosses from below MA2 to above MA2.
Buy = Cross(MA1,MA2);
Sell = Cross(MA2,MA1);

//    Compute the equity for the single ticker
e = Equity();
Maxe = LastValue(Highest(e));
Plot( Close, "Price", colorBlack, styleCandle );

//    Plot the MA lines.
Plot(MA1,"MA1",colorGreen,styleLine);
Plot(MA2,"MA2",colorBlue,styleLine);

//    Plot the Buy and Sell arrows.
shape = Buy * shapeUpArrow + Sell * shapeDownArrow;
PlotShapes(shape, IIf(Buy,colorGreen,colorRed), 0, IIf(Buy,Low,High));

//    Plot the equity curve
Plot(e,"Equity",colorBlue,styleLine|styleOwnScale,0,Maxe);
Plot(10000,"",colorBlue,styleLine|styleOwnScale,0,Maxe);
GraphXSpace = 5;
```

FIGURE 13.2 MOVING AVERAGE CROSSOVER SYSTEM

To enter estimated prices for the next bar:
- On the **Symbol** menu, select **Quote Editor.**
- In the Quote Editor window, left-click the top line in the quote list – the one that says "new."
- Set the date, and enter the latest price quotations.
- Click **OK** to save the quotes. The new data will immediately be displayed in the chart window, along with the Sell arrow if a signal is generated.

Quotations editor

Mode	Ticker	Date	Close	Open	High	Low	Volume	Open ...
⦿ Current symbol/all quotes	ADBE	(new)						
◯ All symbols/single quote (very slow)	ADBE	12/29/2006	41.12	41.36	41.8	41	2,687,200	0
	ADBE	12/28/2006	41.53	41.78	41.84	41.25	3,036,700	0
	ADBE	12/27/2006	41.79	41.76	41.89	41.35	2,921,000	0
Ticker: ADBE	ADBE	12/26/2006	41.44	40.75	41.55	40.75	2,332,300	0
	ADBE	12/22/2006	40.75	41.32	41.62	40.58	2,459,400	0
Date: 12/30/200(	ADBE	12/21/2006	41.38	42.01	42.04	40.99	3,064,000	0
	ADBE	12/20/2006	41.87	42.29	42.44	41.6	5,123,500	0
Time: 12:00:00 AI	ADBE	12/19/2006	41.45	40.77	41.55	40.45	5,763,400	0
Open: 41.20	ADBE	12/18/2006	41.29	42.45	42.55	41.05	7,575,000	0
	ADBE	12/15/2006	42.81	43.15	43.22	42.22	19,193,400	0
High: 41.25	ADBE	12/14/2006	40.81	40.46	41.59	40.05	12,668,000	0
Low: 40.65	ADBE	12/13/2006	40.3	40.6	40.75	39.53	4,541,800	0
	ADBE	12/12/2006	39.97	39.95	40.09	39.34	4,872,200	0
Close: 40.70	ADBE	12/11/2006	39.98	39.69	40.36	39.18	7,320,600	0
Volume: 0	ADBE	12/8/2006	38.88	38.15	39.39	37.99	5,687,500	0
	ADBE	12/7/2006	37.75	38.76	38.85	37.61	5,653,500	0
Open Int.: 0	ADBE	12/6/2006	38.54	39.15	39.43	38.33	4,298,000	0
	ADBE	12/5/2006	39.15	39.62	39.62	38.72	3,600,000	0
Delete	ADBE	12/4/2006	39.29	39.54	40	39.07	3,988,500	0

OK   Cancel

FIGURE 13.3 QUOTE EDITOR

If the market closes with the prices as you entered them, with a Close of $40.70, there is no sell signal.

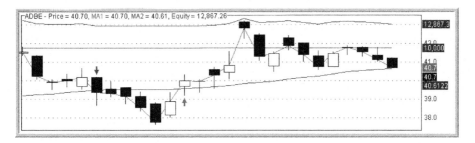

FIGURE 13.4 NO NEW SIGNAL

But, if the price drops further, and you estimate that the close will be $40.60, there is a sell signal.

FIGURE 13.5 NEW SIGNAL

When the actual closing prices are downloaded later, after the market closes, the actual prices will automatically replace those you entered as estimates.

PRECALCULATE KNOWING FORMULA

Another technique is to run a program that calculates the price at which the cross will take place. For Simple Moving Averages, this is pretty straight forward algebra. Figure 13.6 shows the code for a stand-alone routine (without error checking).

```
//    SimpleMovingAverageCrossover.afl
//
//    Given the lengths of two Simple Moving Averages,
//    each of which uses the value of the Close to compute
//    its average, compute the closing price that will
//    cause the two moving averages to intersect.
//
//    Moving average lengths.
FastLength = 1;
SlowLength = 36;
Price = C;
MAfast = MA(Price,FastLength);
MASlow = MA(Price,SlowLength);
MAFM1 = IIf(FastLength>1,MA(Price,FastLength-1),0);
MASM1 = IIf(SlowLength>1,MA(Price,SlowLength-1),0);
Filter = BarIndex() == LastValue(BarIndex());
PartA = FastLength*(SlowLength-1)*MASM1;
PartB = SlowLength*(FastLength-1)*MAFM1;
LenDiff = SlowLength-FastLength;
MACrossClose = ( PartA - PartB ) / (LenDiff);
AddColumn(FastLength,"FL",1.0);
AddColumn(SlowLength,"SL",1.0);
AddColumn(MAfast,"MAF",1.9);
AddColumn(MASlow,"MAS",1.9);
AddColumn(MACrossClose,"Crosses",1.9);
```

FIGURE 13.6 MOVING AVERAGE CROSSOVER PREDICT

Running the program as an Exploration (without any estimate for the next day's prices) shows that a closing price below $40.61 will generate a sell signal.

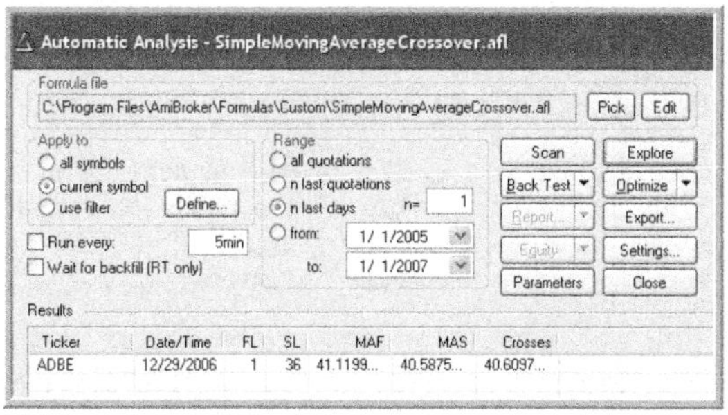

FIGURE 13.7 SMA CROSSOVER PREDICTION

It would be tedious to have to have a separate stand alone program to compute the cross over point for each system, but we can combine the two – the trading system and the cross over computation – into one AFL code module, as shown in Figure 13.8.

```
//   MACrossSystemWithPredict.afl
//
//   The classic Moving Average crossover
//   using simple Moving Averages
//

//   Set up the lengths for the moving averages
Length1 = Param("Length1",6,1,81,2);
Length2 = Param("Length2",35,2,200,2);

//   The Moving Average calculations
MA1 = MA(C,Length1);
MA2 = MA(C,Length2);

//   The Buy and Sell logic
//   Buy when MA1 crosses from below MA2 to above MA2.
Buy = Cross(MA1,MA2);
Sell = Cross(MA2,MA1);

//   Compute the equity for the single ticker
e = Equity();
Maxe = LastValue(Highest(e));
Plot( Close, "Price", colorBlack, styleCandle );

//   Plot the MA lines.
Plot(MA1,"MA1",colorGreen,styleLine);
Plot(MA2,"MA2",colorBlue,styleLine);

//   Plot the Buy and Sell arrows.
shape = Buy * shapeUpArrow + Sell * shapeDownArrow;
```

```
PlotShapes(shape, IIf(Buy,colorGreen,colorRed), 0, IIf(Buy,Low,High));

//   Plot the equity curve
Plot(e,"Equity",colorBlue,styleLine|styleOwnScale,0,Maxe);
Plot(10000,"",colorBlue,styleLine|styleOwnScale,0,Maxe);
GraphXSpace = 5;

//////////////////////////////////////////////////
//   SimpleMovingAverageCrossover.afl
//
//   Given the lengths of two Simple Moving Averages,
//   each of which uses the value of the Close to compute
//   its average, compute the closing price that will
//   cause the two moving averages to intersect.
//

//Retrieve the current values of the moving average lengths.
st = _PARAM_VALUES() ;
Cp = StrFind(st,",");
P1 = StrMid(st,1,Cp-2);
Ccp = StrFind(st,")");
P2 = StrMid(st,Cp,Ccp-Cp-1);

//   Moving average lengths.
//FastLength = Length1;
//SlowLength = Length2;
FastLength = StrToNum(p1);
SlowLength = StrToNum(p2);

Price = C;

MAfast = MA(Price,FastLength);
MASlow = MA(Price,SlowLength);
MAFM1 = IIf(FastLength>1,MA(Price,FastLength-1),0);
MASM1 = IIf(SlowLength>1,MA(Price,SlowLength-1),0);

Filter = BarIndex() == LastValue(BarIndex());

PartA = FastLength*(SlowLength-1)*MASM1;
PartB = SlowLength*(FastLength-1)*MAFM1;
LenDiff = SlowLength-FastLength;
MACrossClose = ( PartA - PartB ) / (LenDiff);

AddColumn(FastLength,"FL",1.0);
AddColumn(SlowLength,"SL",1.0);
AddColumn(MAFast,"MAF",1.9);
AddColumn(MASlow,"MAS",1.9);
AddColumn(MACrossClose,"Crosses",1.9);

//AddTextColumn(st,"Params",1.0);
//AddColumn(cp,"cp",1.0);
//AddTextColumn(P1,"P1",1.0);
//AddColumn(ccp,"ccp",1.0);
//AddTextColumn(P2,"P2",1.0);
```

FIGURE 13.8 MA CROSS WITH PREDICTION

To use the system requires two steps. First, Select and Insert the trading system.

FIGURE 13.9 SELECT TRADING SYSTEM

Right-click the window pane with the system.
Select **Parameters**.
Set the lengths of the moving averages, if necessary.
Click **OK**.

FIGURE 13.10 SET LENGTHS

Observe the indicators and note that a signal may be coming at today's close.
On the **Analysis** menu, select **Automatic Analysis**, pick the system.
When it is open, click **Parameters**, set them to match the parameters that were set in the trading system's window.
Click **OK**.

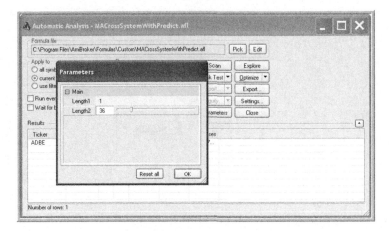

FIGURE 13.11 SET PARAMETERS

Click Explore, and read the predicted price at which the two moving averages cross.

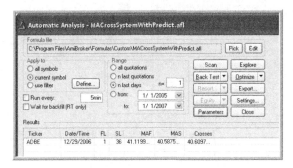

FIGURE 13.12 READ PREDICTION

Near closing time, check real-time quotations. If it appears that the Close will be $40.61 or below, place an order to Sell, MOC or LOC.

PREDICTION WITHOUT KNOWING FORMULA

The computational method above does give the closing price that corresponds to the two averages exactly meeting. But that example requires that we are able to first write the formulae and second solve for the prediction.

Binary search is a method used to find roots of equations that are well behaved, even if the formula is not known or the closed form solution is difficult or impossible. Make two guesses about the closing price – one that is too high and the other than is too low – and see that no signal was generated from the guess that was too high and a signal was generated from the guess that was too low. But guessing the closing price that just barely gives the signal will take a lot of trial and error. Provided that there is only one point between the too-high guess and the too-low guess where the curves cross, and providing that both moving averages are well defined (no divide by zero, or similar errors) for the entire range of data between the two initial guesses, then the binary search technique will work.

The technique is as follows:
- Guess a value for the close that is known to be too high.
- Evaluate the moving averages, or other more complex functions and indicators, using the high value.
- Guess a second value that is known to be too low.
- Evaluate the functions using the low value.
- Set some condition that will stop the loop about to be entered. An accuracy target is a good choice, with a limit on the number of iterations as a back up. Say the accuracy target is $0.0001 – one-one-hundredth of a cent.
- Compute the accuracy of the guesses so far. The accuracy is the difference between the high value and the low value.
- Stay in this loop until the accuracy is less than the accuracy target:
  - Compute the mid point between the high and low values.
  - Evaluate the functions at the mid point.
  - Decide whether the mid point is too high or too low, and replace either the existing high or low guess with the mid point guess.
  - Compute the accuracy.

When the program finishes the loop, the high value and low value will still be on opposite sides of the crossing value, but they will be very close together – close enough that either value, or the mid point, represents the predicted crossing price for our purposes.

Each pass through the loop cuts the difference between the high value and low value in half. For any reasonable choices of the initial high value, initial low value, and desired accuracy, the solution will be found within about 20 iterations.

Figure 13.13 following shows the AFL code to find the crossing point of two simple moving averages using the binary search method. This method does not require that we can solve the algebra for the prediction, or even that we know the formula.

```
//   GenericBinarySearch.afl
//
//   This routine uses a binary search to find the
//   value that sets the function defined in
//   "ZeroToFind" to 0.
//

//   Set any global values before the function definition.
//
Length1 = 1;
Length2 = 36;
AccuracyTarget = 0.0001;

function ZeroToFind(P)
//   Code whatever you want to find a zero for
//   into this function.
//   In this example, we are looking for the
//   value of a closing price that makes the
//   two moving averages, call them MA1 and MA2,
//   equal.
//   That is, we want MA1 - MA2 to equal 0.
{
    FTZ = MA(P,Length1) - MA(P,Length2);
    return FTZ;
}

//   BC is the index of the final bar in the existing
//   array.
BC = LastValue(BarIndex());

//   TF is the temporary array used for the
//   calculations.
//   Extend TF by one artificial value.
//   TF does not look into the future,
//   this is just a convenient way to put
//   the value being tested at the end
//   of a known array.
//   This code assumes that the variable being
//   searched is the Closing price.
//   If it is something else, use that
//   instead of "C" in the following line.
TF = Ref(C,1);

//   Set HGuess to 10 times the previous
//   final value.
TF[BC] = HGuess = TF[BC-1] * 10.0;

//   Find the sign associated with HGuess.
//   It could be either positive or negative,
//   depending on the function definition.
//   We do not care which, we just remember it.
HSign = IIf(LastValue(ZeroToFind(TF))>0,1,-1);
```

```
//   Set LGuess to 0.1 times the previous
//   final value.
TF[BC] = LGuess = TF[BC-1] * 0.1;

//   Find the sign associated with LGuess.
LSign = IIf(LastValue(ZeroToFind(TF))>0,1,-1);

//   If the signs are the same, there is no
//   zero in between them.
//   Set the return value to zero and return.
//   Otherwise loop through the binary search.
if (HSign==LSign)
{
    HGuess = 0.0;
}
else
{
    while(abs(HGuess - LGuess)>AccuracyTarget)
    {
        MGuess = (HGuess + LGuess)/2;
        TF[BC] = MGuess;

        MSign = IIf(LastValue(ZeroToFind(TF))>0,1,-1);
        HGuess = IIf(HSign == MSign, MGuess,HGuess);
        LGuess = IIf(LSign == MSign, MGuess,LGuess);
    }
}

//   When the loop finishes, HGuess and LGuess
//   will be very close together. Either one
//   is an acceptable value for our purposes.

Filter = BarIndex() == BC;

AddColumn(HGuess,"Zero if Close is:",1.9);
```

FIGURE 13.13 GENERIC BINARY SEARCH

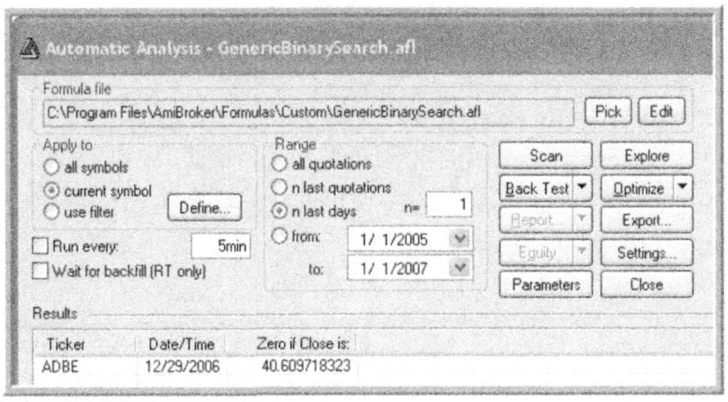

FIGURE 13.14 GENERIC BINARY SEARCH RESULT

This result agrees with the previous solutions.

14

Sector Analysis

THE CLOSEST MEETING between quantitative analysis and fundamental analysis is in the mutual funds and exchange traded funds that focus on one sector of the economy. Fidelity has about 40 sector-oriented mutual funds, most of which have been trading since about 1988. Standard & Poors has nine sector-oriented exchange traded funds that have been trading since December 1998. Both of these series give an opportunity to analyze the relationship between different sectors and between stocks and their sector.

To carry out these studies, it will be necessary to have data from two or more series in a single AmiBroker program. The next few figures illustrate some very basic tools for doing that.

Figure 14.1 gives the AFL code to export a data series from the Ami-Broker database to a Comma Separated Value (CSV) formatted file in a directory of your choice. One of the reasons for wanting to do this is to create test data series with dates that align with the other series in the database, and signal characteristics that are specially created to test AFL programs.

The outline is:
- Export a data series
- Use a spreadsheet to modify the OHLCV values
- Import the new test data series back into AmiBroker
- Run tests using AFL code

The specific steps are:
- Use Windows Explorer to create the directory to receive the data being exported from AmiBroker
- Enter the path name into the code of this program
- Note that any slash characters required to separate subdirectories in the path name must be entered as double slashes in the AFL code
- Make the data series you want to export the active series
- Open this file, ExportDataSeries.afl, in Automatic Analysis
- Click the verify syntax icon
- A file named Exported.csv will be written to the directory specified
- Use whatever spreadsheet or editor you wish to modify the data
- Save it back into CSV format with a new file name – say signals.csv
- If the date is formatted yyyy-mm-dd, the ASCII Import default format will read it correctly
- Within AmiBroker, from the File menu, select Import ASCII
- Navigate to signals.csv and import it.
- It will show up in the list of Symbols as Signals
- Use the signals data series as you would any other data series

```
//   ExportDataSeries.afl
//
//   This code taken from the "fputs" entry of the
//   AmiBroker help files.
//
fh = fopen( "C:\\Program Files\\AmiBroker\\
                CSVData\\exported.csv", "w");
if( fh )
{
    fputs( "Date,Open,High,Low,Close,Volume\n", fh );
    y = Year();
    m = Month();
    d = Day();
    for( i = 0; i < BarCount; i++ )
    {
        ds = StrFormat("%04.0f-%02.0f-%02.0f,",
        y[ i ], m[ i ], d[ i ] );
        fputs( ds, fh );

        qs = StrFormat("%.4f, %.4f, %.4f, %.4f, %.0f\n",
        O[ i ], H[ i ], L[ i ], C[ i ], V[ i ] );
        fputs( qs, fh );
    }
    fclose( fh );
}
```

FIGURE 14.1 EXPORT DATA SERIES

Figure 14.2 shows a plot of the Close of the signals series. All of the data for the Close component has been set to a value of 10.0, except for values of 15.0 for those days when a specific buy signal is desired and a value of 5.0 for those days when a specific sell signal is desired.

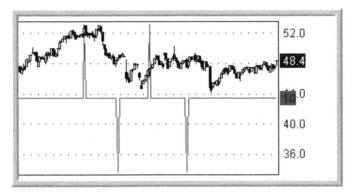

FIGURE 14.2 SIGNAL DATA

The AFL program to make use of that series is shown in figure 14.3. Since the signal series has only the signals, the code must read and remember that "base data", then go on to process other data series specified by the "current symbol" or defined group. The Foreign and SetForeign statements load the base data. Foreign loads a single component – one of OHLCVI – into a single variable. SetForeign loads all six components into the default variables Open, High, Low, Close, Volume, and OpenInt. Perform whatever calculations are desired, and assign whatever results to other AFL variables. Then use the RestorePriceArrays statement to inform AmiBroker that data from the current symbol is to be used from that point on.

```
//   ProcessSignals.afl
//
//   This program assumes that the file names "signals"
//   has been imported into the AmiBroker database.
//
//   Any close greater than or equal to 15.0 will be
//   taken as a "buy" signal, and any close less than
//   or equal to 5.0 will be taken as a "sell" signal.
//
//   Load the signals into variable sigs,
//   then return to normal processing of whatever
//   ticker is loaded.
//
sigs = Foreign("signals","C");
RestorePriceArrays();
```

```
Buy = sigs >= 14.0;
Sell = sigs <= 6.0;

Plot (C, "C", colorBlack, styleCandle);
Plot (sigs, "Signals", colorRed, styleLine|styleOwnScale);
```

FIGURE 14.3 PROCESS SIGNALS

A more interesting, and only slightly more complex, example uses data from one series to compute buy and sell signals, then applies those signals to all the issues in the defined group. Figure 14.4 contains the AFL code. Here the OEX, the index tracking fund that follows the S&P100, is used to calculate buy and sell signals. Since the SetForeign statement was used, the OEX data was loaded into OHLCV without the need for separate variables. Note that those values will be replaced by the OHLCV for whatever issue is loaded in the next part of the code. The equity computed is the equity from trades in the current symbol or defined group.

```
//   SignalsFromCommonSeries.afl
//
//   This code reads one data series that will be
//   used to compute the trading signals for
//   a group of issues.
//
//   Use the S&P 100 as the base series --
//   Yahoo ticker ^OEX
SetForeign("^OEX");

//   At this point, all calculations will be done with
//   the OHLCV of ^OEX.
Buy = Cross(MA(C,7),MA(C,3));
Sell = BarsSince(Buy) >=3;

//   From this point on, use the data in the
//   Selected data series.
RestorePriceArrays();

e = Equity();
Plot(e, "equity", colorRed, styleLine);

//   Use the Charts menu and Insert this program.
//   Place the cursor on a trade near the end of
//   the data series.
//   Cycle through, making several other data series
//   the current one, and note that trades always
//   take place at the same date.
```

FIGURE 14.4 SIGNALS FROM COMMON SERIES

Even though the sector funds have a narrow focus, and even though they represent trades made, use them as representatives of economic sectors with some caution. A notice posted on the Fidelity web site states that: "On October 1, 2006, the fund began comparing its performance to a different benchmark and adjusted its investments."

An advantage of performing quantitative analysis using sector funds is the smoothing that they provide. Since the components of the fund are chosen to have similar characteristics, the resulting fund has lower variance than the individual components. So the sector, hopefully, has less noise and a higher signal to noise ratio, making analysis easier. The disadvantage of using sector funds is that the profit from trading them is usually less than the profit from taking the same trades in the component issues.

One application of the use of a foreign data series is creation of a mini-portfolio of stocks that track a sector. As shown in figure 14.5, use the Foreign statement to load the data for a sector, compute perfect buy and sell signals that correspond to whatever trading frequency is desired, then use the Backtest system to determine the profitability of trading individual stocks. Form a mini-portfolio of the stocks that perform best and trade them based on signals that are derived from applying actual trading systems to sector data.

```
//   SectorCorrelation.afl
//
//   Use Foreign to load the data from a sector
//   mutual fund or ETF.
//   Use the ZigZag function to determine perfect
//   buy and sell signals based on the sector.
//   Test a large number of individual issues to
//   determine which trade best using those signals,
//   and form a mini-portfolio to be traded.
SetTradeDelays(0,0,0,0);
BuyPrice = C;
SellPrice = C;

SetForeign("FSELX");  //Fidelity Select Electronics
zz = Zig(C,10);
Buy = (zz<Ref(zz,-1)) AND (zz<Ref(zz,1));
Sell = (zz>Ref(zz,-1)) AND (zz>Ref(zz,1));

RestorePriceArrays();

e = Equity();
Plot(e,"equity",colorRed,styleLine);
```

FIGURE 14.5 SECTOR CORRELATION

Of course it is impossible to buy at the perfect bottom and sell at the perfect top, but Figure 14.6 shows what trading Fidelity Select Electronics Fund, FSELX, based on perfect FSELX signals produced.

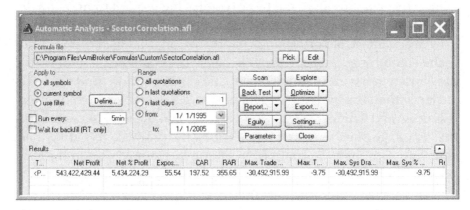

FIGURE 14.6 PERFECT TRADING FSELX

Changing the symbol to be traded from FSELX to a group defining the 500 stocks in the S&P 500 index, the issues that ranked highest using RAR as the metric are shown in Figure 14.7.

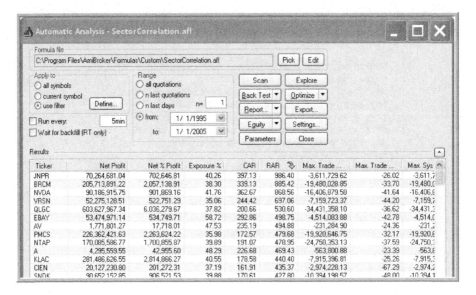

FIGURE 14.7 RANKED BY RAR

The issues that ranked highest using K-ratio as the metric are shown in Figure 14.8.

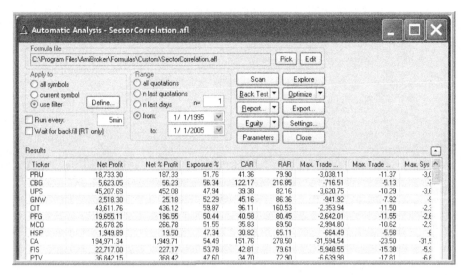

FIGURE 14.8 RANKED BY K-RATIO

Changing to the Fidelity Select Utility Fund, FSUTX, produces the results shown in figure 14.9 when trading the fund itself.

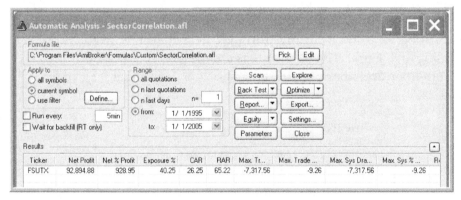

FIGURE 14.9 PERFECT TRADING FSUTX

And, when tested against the 500 stocks in the S&P 500, figure 14.10 shows those results, ranked by RAR.

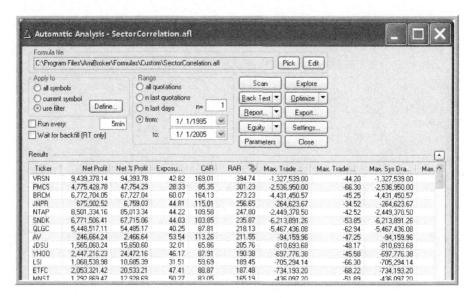

FIGURE 14.10 RESULTS TRADING FSUTX

Wait a minute. The highest ranking stocks are not utilities. What are Verisign, PMC Sierra, Broadcom, Juniper Networks, and Network Appliance doing tracking the utilities? It looks like those stocks were is such a strong up trend from 1995 through 2005, that they would score well using any signal. The AFL code is changed so that positions are taken both Long and Short. Figure 14.11 shows the modified AFL code.

```
//    SectorCorrelation.afl
//
//    Use Foreign to load the data from a sector
//    mutual fund or ETF.
//    Use the ZigZag function to determine perfect
//    buy and sell signals based on the sector.
//    Test a large number of individual issues to
//    determine which trade best using those signals,
//    and form a mini-portfolio to be traded.
SetTradeDelays(0,0,0,0);
BuyPrice = C;
SellPrice = C;

SetForeign("FSUTX"); //Fidelity Select Utilities
zz = Zig(C,10);
Cover = Buy = (zz<Ref(zz,-1)) AND (zz<Ref(zz,1));
Short = Sell = (zz>Ref(zz,-1)) AND (zz>Ref(zz,1));
```

```
RestorePriceArrays();

e = Equity();
Plot(e,"equity",colorRed,styleLine);
```

FIGURE 14.11 TRADING LONG AND SHORT

And figure 14.12 shows the results of trading the S&P 500 stocks, both long and short.

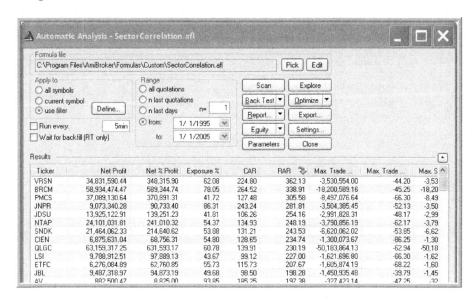

FIGURE 14.12 LONG AND SHORT RANKED BY RAR

Those technology stocks are still at the top of the list. Should the technology stocks be traded based on utility sector signals? An out-of-sample test will help answer. FSUTX has not had a 10% retracements since 2005, so there are no signals based on the code shown above. To get signals, the 10% retracements in the Zig function is changed to a 1%. The in-sample period was retested and those same technology stocks were among the very top. A watchlist was formed from the 12 stocks that tested best in-sample, and it was tested out-of-sample, with results shown in figure 14.13.

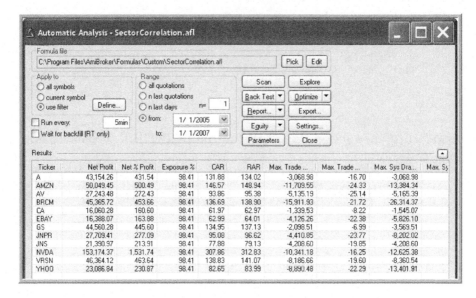

FIGURE 14.13 OUT-OF-SAMPLE

Figure 14.14 shows trading the FSUTX on its own signals for that period.

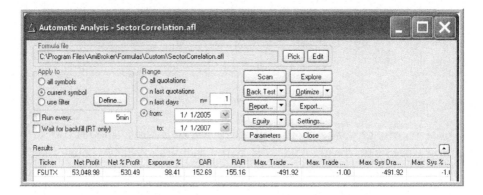

FIGURE 14.14 FSUTX TRADING ITS OWN SIGNALS, OUT-OF-SAMPLE

These results are OK, but the leverage expected from trading individual stocks rather than the sector fund has disappeared. A watchlist was made up of the 31 companies that are the current components of the S&P Utility ETF, ticker XLU, and that list traded out-of-sample on the FSTUX signals. Figure 14.15 shows clearly that there is an advantage in choosing stocks that have some reason to be correlated, rather than just those that appear at the top of the profitability list.

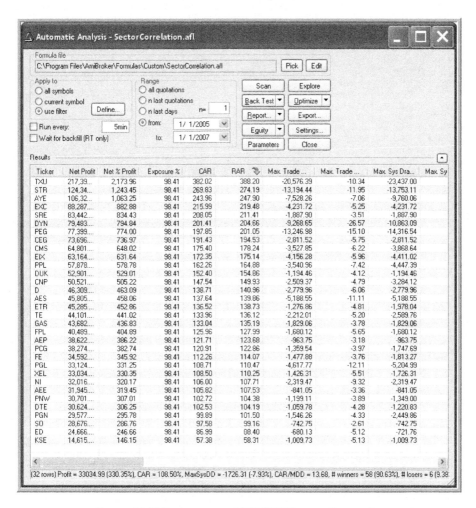

FIGURE 14.15 STOCKS OF THE XLU ETF TRADED OUT-OF-SAMPLE

15

Rotation

ROTATIONAL TRADING SYSTEMS deal with a small group of issues – usually about five to twenty. A fixed number of positions are held at all times. At the end of each period – usually a day or a week – some metric is computed for each of the group members and the issues are ranked from high to low. Long positions are taken in the issues with the highest positive rank. As time passes and conditions change, issues drop down in rank. If any issue has dropped below an established lower limit of rank, exit that position and replace it with the issue with the highest rank that is not already held.

Success depends on choosing a metric that correlates with the percentage change coming over the next few bars. High rank correlates with the strongest gains in the near future, while low rank correlates with the steepest losses in the near future.

Optionally, short positions are taken in the issues with the most negative rank. In some systems, particularly those that hold long-only positions, a risk-free choice, such as a money market fund, that will always have a positive rank is included.

For example, a group might consist of ten issues, each from a different sector of the market, perhaps represented by sector-oriented mutual funds. The system will always be long two issues and short two issues. A long position will be held as long as it is among the four highest ranked issues, and a short position will be held as long as it is among the four weakest issues.

Rotational systems are good candidates to beat a broad market average. They select the best from among a limited population, and rotate among the choices.

The economy progresses through regular cycles, with sectors of the economy rising and falling in sequence with some predictability. While the economy may be difficult to predict, and the specific sequence of progression may change from time to time, an accurate metric will identify which sector is currently strong or gaining strength.

In the 1980's and 90's, the strong upward bias to the equity markets made comparative relative strength the metric of choice. (That is, true relative strength, not the RSI indicator.) This was particularly true when the group was comprised of sector mutual funds. Since 2000, rotational systems that hold only long positions, have relatively long holding periods, and use relative strength as the metric, have not done well.

Rotational trading, as implemented in AmiBroker, does not use buy signals, sell signals, stops, profit targets, or intra-bar transactions. All exchanges are made at the price and delay specified on the settings menu.

For rotational systems, consider using a population of mutual funds, exchange traded funds, or market sector indices as the population from which to choose. You do not necessarily invest in these directly, but rather use them to indicate which sector of the economy is coming into strength. When the system signals that positions should be taken in a new issue, the actual trades may be taken from a mini-portfolio of issues that are correlated with the issue used in the rotational system, but have higher beta.

The group of issues among which the example in this chapter rotates consists of the nine Standard and Poor's sector exchange traded funds.

    XLB Materials
    XLE Energy
    XLF Financial
    XLI Industrial
    XLK Technology
    XLP Consumer Staples
    XLU Utilities
    XLV Health Care
    XLY Consumer Discretionary

Figure 15.1 shows the AFL code for the rotational trading system used in this chapter.

```
//    SectorRotation.afl
//
//    Compute a score based on the recent Rate Of Change
//    of the closing price.
//
//    Rotate among the nine S&P sector ETFs
//
//    Program options include allowing short positions or not
//    and interpreting the ROC as a mean reverting indicator
//    by turning it "upside down".

EnableRotationalTrading();

//    The number of issues to hold at a time
NumberHeld = 2; //Optimize("NumberHeld",1,1,4,1);

//    Allocate funds equally among all issues
PositionSize = -100/NumberHeld;

//    Set WorstRankHeld to be some number greater
//    than the number of positions held.
NumberExtras = 3; //Optimize("NumberExtras",0,0,4,1);
WorstRank = NumberHeld + NumberExtras;
SetOption("WorstRankHeld", WorstRank);

//    The LookBack period for the Rate of Change indicator
LookBack = 5; //Optimize("LookBack",7,2,20,1);

//    UpDown allows the ROC to be inverted
//    to treat a rising ROC as a "sell" signal
UpDown = 2; //Optimize("UpDown",2,1,2,1);

//    Value of 1 allows short positions
//    Value of 2 blocks short positions
AllowShort = 2; //Optimize("AllowShort",1,1,2,1);

Multiplier = IIf(UpDown==1,1,-1);
Score = Multiplier*ROC(C,LookBack);
Score = IIf(AllowShort==1,Score,Max(Score,0));
PositionScore = Score;
```

FIGURE 15.1 SECTOR ROTATION

The system was optimized over the in-sample period from the beginning of the funds existence in 1998 through 1/1/2005. The results were sorted by three metrics. One was risk adjusted return (RAR), another RAR/MDD, and the third K-ratio. RAR gives the highest total profit for the period a position is held, but it often has high drawdown and sometimes does not trade well in the out-of-sample period. RAR/MDD divides RAR by the maximum drawdown, and K-ratio is a metric based on the angle and smoothness of the equity curve. Both of the last two typically have a lower percentage return, but both usually trade well in the out-of-sample period.

For each of the three metrics, the variables were set to values associated with the highest ranking result and were retested for the period 1998 through 1/1/2007. This includes a test of the out-of-sample data. The figures below show the equity curves for the entire period, with a vertical line at 1/1/2005 where out-of-sample results begin. Although the optimization allowed short positions to be taken, many traders will not take short positions. Each result is shown in two versions – one allowing short positions and one prohibiting them.

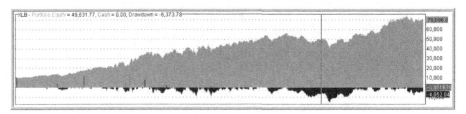

FIGURE 15.2 RANKED BY RAR, ALLOW SHORTS

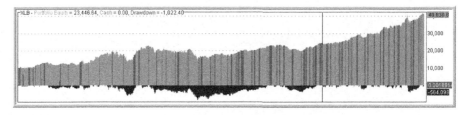

FIGURE 15.3 RANKED BY RAR, PROHIBIT SHORTS

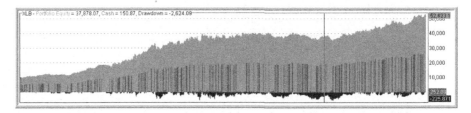

FIGURE 15.4 RANKED BY RAR/MDD, ALLOW SHORTS

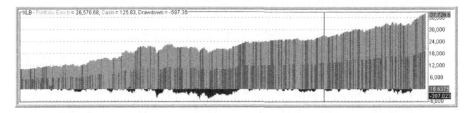

FIGURE 15.5 RANKED BY RAR/MDD, PROHIBIT SHORTS

FIGURE 15.6 RANKED BY K-RATIO, ALLOW SHORTS

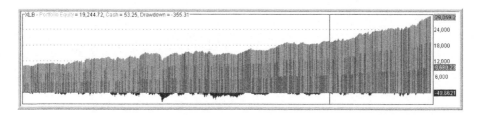

FIGURE 15.7 RANKED BY K-RATIO, PROHIBIT SHORTS

SECOND EDITION

Results presented in the first edition covered the period through 1/1/2007. How does this technique perform during the market volatility of 2008 through 2010?

The code shown in Figure 15.1 was modified slightly so that each position would be the same number of dollars. An additional line of code insures that the number of issues held is limited. Figure 15.8 shows the code as it was run.

```
//   The number of issues to hold at a time
NumberHeld = 1; //Optimize("NumberHeld",1,1,4,1);

//   Allocate funds equally among all issues
//PositionSize = -100/NumberHeld;
SetPositionSize(10000,spsValue);

//   Set WorstRankHeld to be some number greater
//   than the number of positions held.
NumberExtras = Optimize("NumberExtras",0,0,2,1);
WorstRank = NumberHeld + NumberExtras;
SetOption("WorstRankHeld", WorstRank);
SetOption("MaxOpenPositions",NumberHeld);
```

FIGURE 15.8 MODIFIED SECTION OF FIGURE 15.1 CODE

The watchlist used contained four major ETFs: SPY, IWM, EEM, and

QQQ. Short positions were allowed and the system was allowed to be mean reverting. The date range used was 1/1/2006 through 5/6/2011. The objective function was K-ratio.

Setting NumberHeld to 1 selects the issue with the highest Position-Score, taking a long position if positive, a short position if negative. Figure 15.9 shows the equity chart.

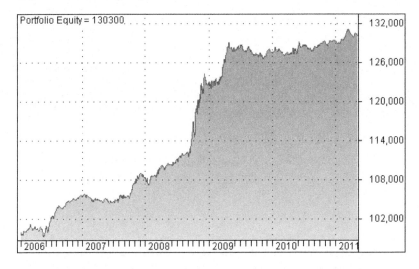

FIGURE 15.9 FOUR MAJOR ETFS - BEST ONE

Setting NumberHeld to 2 selects the two issues with the two highest PositionScores. Figure 15.10 shows the equity chart.

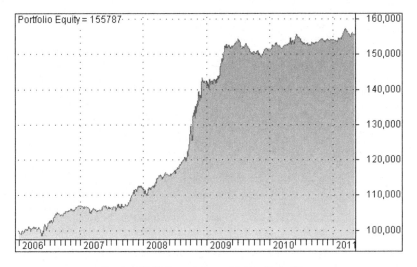

FIGURE 15.10 FOUR MAJOR ETFS - BEST TWO

16

Portfolios

ONE OF THE STRONGEST FEATURES of AmiBroker is its capability to manage a portfolio. The portfolio could be a single trading system with a single set of parameter values being applied to all the issues in a group, or it could be a single trading system with specific parameter values associated with individual issues, or it could be several trading systems.

Unlike the portfolios traded using the rotational methods described in the previous chapter, there are essentially no restrictions when dealing with general portfolios – almost anything that can be done with an individual issue can be done with a portfolio, plus the many features related to portfolio management. Buy and Sell signals are used to enter and exit positions; buyprice, sellprice, and trade delays control the timing and price of the entries and exits; any number of simultaneous positions can be held; trades can be scaled into and scaled out of; restrictions can be placed on the holding period and trading frequency to comply with mutual fund family rules; and so forth.

The simplest portfolio expands a simple trading system – from working with a single issue to working with a group of issues. That change is made by selecting Use Filter rather than Current Symbol on the Automatic Analysis menu, as shown in Figure 16.1. Clicking the Define button opens up the menus that allow any meaningful group to be selected – a market, group, sector, industry, or watchlist. The scan, explore, back test, and optimize functions will then work on all of the issues that are members of that group. If the command is Back Test or Optimize, the group is treated either as a portfolio of issues, or as a list of single issues, depending on the options chosen on the submenus.

213

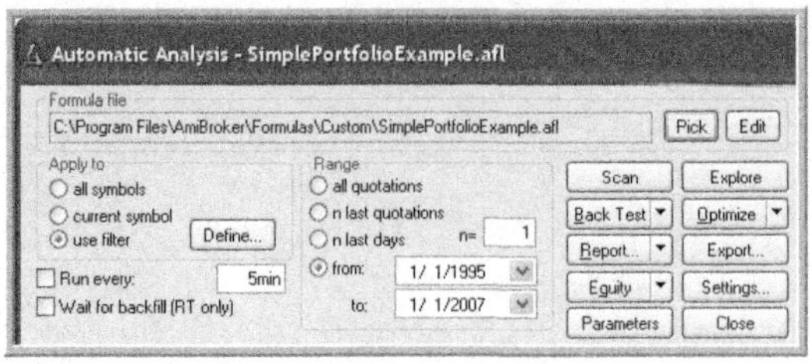

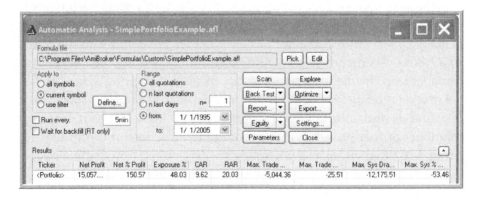

FIGURE 16.1 AUTOMATIC ANALYSIS MENU

Figure 16.2 shows the AFL code for a simple trading system that can be applied to a single issue or to a portfolio.

```
//   SimplePortfolioExample.afl
//
//   The basic system is a simple moving average crossover
//
SetTradeDelays(0,0,0,0);
BuyPrice = C;
SellPrice = C;

MA1Length = 8;
MA2Length = 7;

MA1 = MA(C,MA1Length);
MA2 = MA(C,MA2Length);

Buy = Cross(MA1, MA2);
Sell = Cross(MA2, MA1);

Plot(C,"C",colorBlack,styleCandle);
```

FIGURE 16.2 SIMPLE PORTFOLIO EXAMPLE

Make Alcoa (ticker AA) the current symbol and click the BackTest button. The Results show the profit and other metrics, and show "<Portfolio>" as the Ticker.

FIGURE 16.3 DEFAULT BACKTEST

When the Back Test menu is pulled down, Portfolio Backtest is shown to be the default operation, as in Figure 16.4. That means that the backtest calculations are applied to all of the issues in the group, the rules provided by the AFL code and the AmiBroker backtest engine for creating a portfolio are applied, and the result for the portfolio is reported.

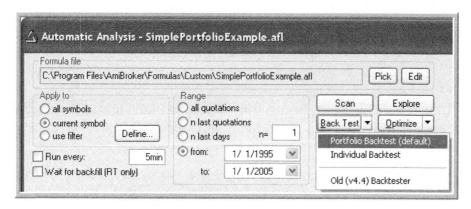

FIGURE 16.4 SHOWING PORTFOLIO BACKTEST

If the Individual Backtest option is chosen, then the trading system is applied to each issue in the group individually, and the results are reported individually. Figure 16.5 illustrates this. Since current symbol is still selected, and Alcoa is the current symbol, the Results pane, Figure 16.5, now shows the Ticker to be AA.

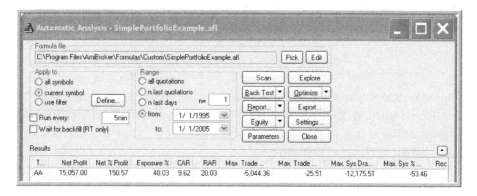

FIGURE 16.5 INDIVIDUAL BACKTEST

By selecting use filter, then clicking the Define button, a watchlist containing six issues is selected. See Figure 16.6.

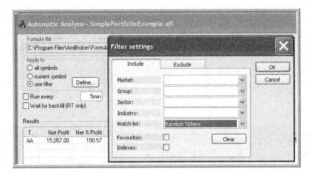

FIGURE 16.6 SELECTING A WATCHLIST

Pulling down the Back Test menu and selecting Individual Backtest runs the system on each ticker individually and reports the results separately, as Figure 16.7 shows.

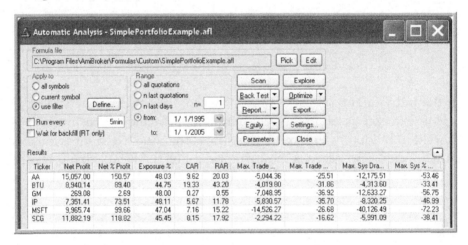

FIGURE 16.7 INDIVIDUAL BACKTESTS OF GROUP

Just clicking the Back Test button instructs AmiBroker to compute the results assuming that the six issues are a single portfolio. Figure 16.8 shows a single line in the results pane. Note that the results that do not match any of the six components.

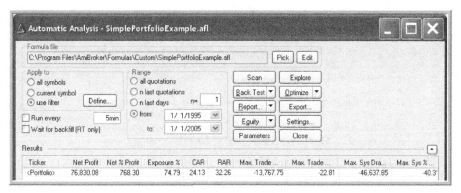

FIGURE 16.8 PORTFOLIO BACKTEST OF GROUP

Click the Report button, then the trades tab, to see the individual trades taken as a portfolio, as shown in Figure 16.9. The Results summary, in Figure 16.8, shows an exposure of 74.79%, which is higher than any of the individual exposures as seen in Figure 16.7. Because the moving averages cross over for different issues at different times, there are more signals and a higher exposure. Figure 16.9 shows that there is only one trade active at any time.

SimplePortfolioExample - Backtest Report - HtmlView

File   View   Help

Statistics | Charts | **Trades** | Formula | Settings | Symbols

Trades

Trade list

Ticker	Trade	Entry	Exit	% change	Profit	Shares	Pos. value	Cum. profit	# bars	Profit/bar	MAE/MFE	Scale In/Out
IP	Long	1/3/1995 25.1	1/9/1995 25.97	3.47%	346.61 3.47%	398.406	10000.00	346.61	5	69.32	-1.00% 3.47%	0/0
GM	Long	1/13/1995 21.03	2/6/1995 19.55	-7.04%	-728.15 -7.04%	491.993	10346.61	-381.54	17	-42.83	-12.10% 1.18%	0/0
GM	Long	2/10/1995 19.9	2/13/1995 20.08	0.90%	87.00 0.90%	483.34	9618.46	-294.53	2	43.50	-1.88% 0.93%	0/0
AA	Long	2/13/1995 8.15	2/15/1995 8.27	1.47%	142.90 1.47%	1190.85	9705.46	-151.63	3	47.63	-0.78% 1.58%	0/0
MSFT	Long	2/17/1995 3.26	2/27/1995 3.33	2.15%	211.47 2.15%	3020.97	9848.37	59.84	6	35.24	-1.64% 2.98%	0/0
AA	Long	2/27/1995 8	3/10/1995 7.74	-3.25%	-326.94 -3.25%	1257.48	10059.84	-267.11	10	-32.69	-6.38% 3.49%	0/0
AA	Long	3/13/1995 7.72	3/16/1995 7.74	0.26%	25.21 0.26%	1260.74	9732.89	-241.89	4	6.30	-3.28% 1.31%	0/0
AA	Long	3/17/1995 7.62	3/20/1995 7.79	2.23%	217.70 2.23%	1280.59	9758.11	-24.19	2	108.85	-0.35% 2.33%	0/0

FIGURE 16.9 PORTFOLIO RESULT TRADES

To allow for more than one simultaneous position, a change must be made to the AFL code. See Figure 16.10. Note the lines that set Number-Positions and PositionSize. No other changes were made.

```
//    SimplePortfolioExampleMultipleTrades.afl
//
//    The basic system is a simple moving average crossover
//
//    This version allows multiple simultaneous positions,
//    and allocates available funds equally among them.
//
SetTradeDelays(0,0,0,0);
BuyPrice = C;
SellPrice = C;

//    Set the number of positions.
NumberPositions = 2;
SetOption("MaxOpenPositions", NumberPositions);

//    Allocate available funds equally among them.
PositionSize = -100 / NumberPositions;

MA1Length = 8;
MA2Length = 7;

MA1 = MA(C,MA1Length);
MA2 = MA(C,MA2Length);

Buy = Cross(MA1, MA2);
Sell = Cross(MA2, MA1);

Plot(C,"C",colorBlack,styleCandle);
```

FIGURE 16.10 SIMPLE PORTFOLIO EXAMPLE - MULTIPLE TRADES

Allowing two simultaneous positions, results change considerably, as shown in Figure 16.11. Some systems benefit from holding multiple positions, others do not.

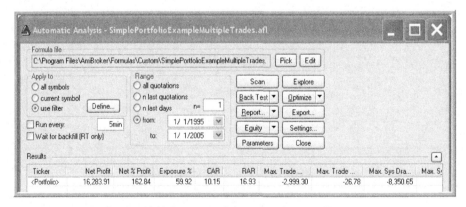

FIGURE 16.11 PORTFOLIO BACKTEST MULTIPLE TRADES

The Trades tab shows that there are overlapping positions, as can be seen in Figure 16.12.

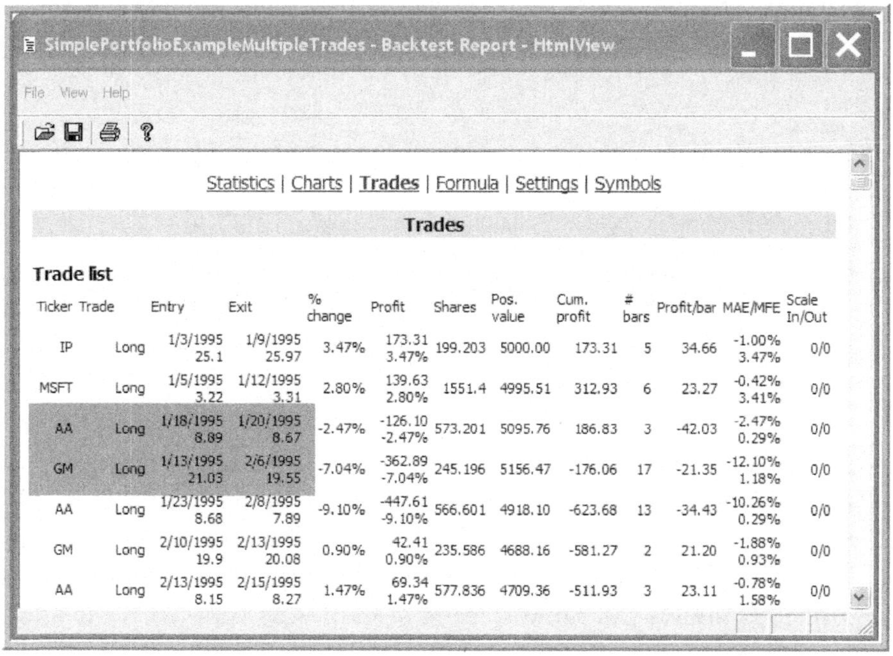

Ticker	Trade	Entry	Exit	% change	Profit	Shares	Pos. value	Cum. profit	# bars	Profit/bar	MAE/MFE	Scale In/Out
IP	Long	1/3/1995 25.1	1/9/1995 25.97	3.47%	173.31 3.47%	199.203	5000.00	173.31	5	34.66	-1.00% 3.47%	0/0
MSFT	Long	1/5/1995 3.22	1/12/1995 3.31	2.80%	139.63 2.80%	1551.4	4995.51	312.93	6	23.27	-0.42% 3.41%	0/0
AA	Long	1/18/1995 8.89	1/20/1995 8.67	-2.47%	-126.10 -2.47%	573.201	5095.76	186.83	3	-42.03	-2.47% 0.29%	0/0
GM	Long	1/13/1995 21.03	2/6/1995 19.55	-7.04%	-362.89 -7.04%	245.196	5156.47	-176.06	17	-21.35	-12.10% 1.18%	0/0
AA	Long	1/23/1995 8.68	2/8/1995 7.89	-9.10%	-447.61 -9.10%	566.601	4918.10	-623.68	13	-34.43	-10.26% 0.29%	0/0
GM	Long	2/10/1995 19.9	2/13/1995 20.08	0.90%	42.41 0.90%	235.586	4688.16	-581.27	2	21.20	-1.88% 0.93%	0/0
AA	Long	2/13/1995 8.15	2/15/1995 8.27	1.47%	69.34 1.47%	577.836	4709.36	-511.93	3	23.11	-0.78% 1.58%	0/0

FIGURE 16.12 PORTFOLIO RESULT TRADES MULTIPLE TRADES

If the population of the group is expanded, there will be more signals, including multiple signals on days when there are not enough open positions or funds to take them all. Change the group to be the 100 stocks that comprise the NASDAQ 100 and set the program to allow two simultaneous positions. On the setting menu, report tab, select detailed log. Click Backtest (requesting the default portfolio backtest), and rerun the program. The detailed log will appear in the results pane, as shown in Figure 16.13. The first line of the entry for each day shows the tickers that have signals that day. There are several each day, and each has a score of 1 listed next to it.

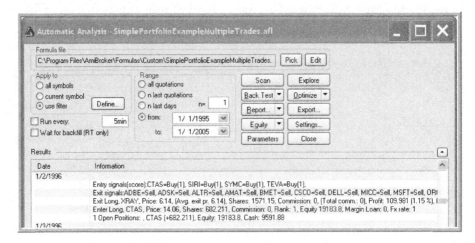

FIGURE 16.13 PORTFOLIO BACKTEST DETAILED LOG

A metric, computed using ordinary AFL code and stored in the variable named PositionScore, is used to differentiate among multiple signals. This metric is similar to the one used in the rotational trading, but its only use is to break ties when there are more signals than entry places. Figure 16.14 shows the same trading system, this time with the additional AFL necessary to compute PositionScore.

```
//    SimplePortfolioExampleMultipleTrades.afl
//
//    The basic system is a simple moving average crossover
//
//    This version allows multiple simultaneous positions,
//    and allocates available funds equally among them.
//
SetTradeDelays(0,0,0,0);
BuyPrice = C;
SellPrice = C;

//    Set the number of positions.
NumberPositions = 2; //Optimize("NumPos",1,1,6,1);
SetOption("MaxOpenPositions", NumberPositions);

//    Allocate available funds equally among them.
PositionSize = -100 / NumberPositions;

MA1Length = 8;
MA2Length = 7;

MA1 = MA(C,MA1Length);
MA2 = MA(C,MA2Length);

Buy = Cross(MA1, MA2);
Sell = Cross(MA2, MA1);
```

```
Plot(C,"C",colorBlack,styleCandle);

// ----------------------------- //
//  Compute the PositionScore metric to break
//  ties when there are more signals than
//  can be funded.
//
Lookback = 5;
PositionScore = -ROC(C,Lookback);
```

FIGURE 16.14 SIMPLE TRADING SYSTEM WITH POSITIONSCORE

The detailed summary shown in Figure 16.15 illustrates the PositionScore values that result. All possible entering trades are listed in order of their PositionScore, and as many as can be accommodated will be executed.

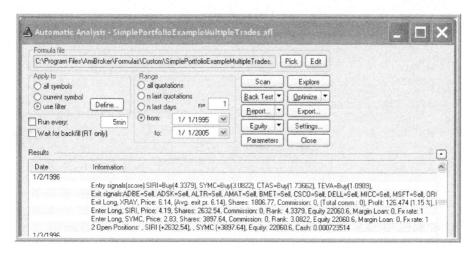

FIGURE 16.15 PORTFOLIO BACKTEST POSITION SCORE DETAILED LOG

That PositionScore algorithm seems to work pretty well. Compare Figure 16.16, which shows the result for the group of 100 Nasdaq stocks without PositionScore, with Figure 16.17, which shows the result when the PositionScore is used to break ties.

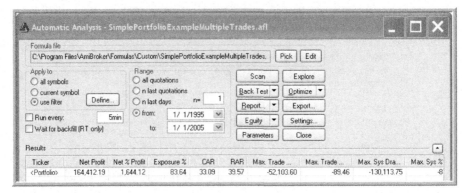

FIGURE 16.16 NASDAQ 100 - NO POSITION SCORE

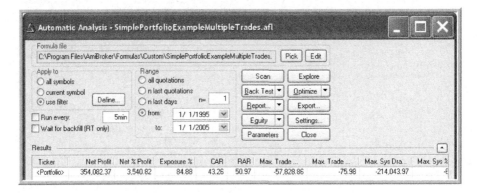

FIGURE 16.17 NASDAQ 100 - POSITION SCORE COMPUTED

After a backtest is completed, a click of the equity button (see Figure 16.1) will display the portfolio equity. Funds that are in trades are colored blue on your monitor; those in cash are in green.

Figures 16.18 and 16.19 display the portfolio equity corresponding to Figures 16.16 and 16.17. The two backtests were rerun, this time with the date range up through 1/1/2007. The area of the curve to the right of the vertical line is out-of-sample performance.

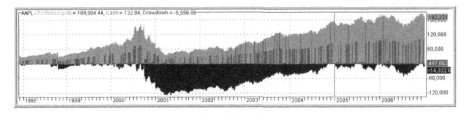

FIGURE 16.18 NASDAQ 100 EQUITY - NO POSITION SCORE

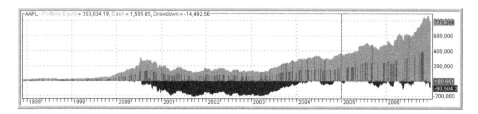

FIGURE 16.19 NASDAQ 100 EQUITY - POSITION SCORE COMPUTED

Of course, calculation of PositionScore is limited only by your own imagination.

Please refer to the AmiBroker user's guide or help system for more information about backtesting and portfolios. The articles *backtesting your trading ideas* and *portfolio-level backtesting,* in particular.

17

Filters and Timing

FILTERS ARE INDICATORS created specifically to permit or prohibit trades. They often use information outside an individual trading system to indicate whether conditions are favorable to trade or not. (Note, filters discussed in this chapter are different than the filters selected on the Automatic Analysis menu that define groups of issues to be analyzed.)

The filter might be based on:
- Analysis of data other than that being traded.
- Confirmation using a different time frame.
- Overall market timing.
- Performance of the system itself through equity curve feedback.
- Advisory services or newsletters.

Filters can be industry specific, based on a fundamental relationship between the issue being traded and the characteristics of the data used in the filter. For example, a filter based on interest rates may work for stocks in the financial service industry, but not for stocks in the mining industry. But it is not necessary that the two data series be directly related with changes in one causing changes in the other, just that they be correlated and remain correlated.

You are limited only by your imagination, and sound validation techniques, in creating filters. It is acceptable to use stocks, stock indices, bonds, mutual funds, commodities, seasonality, or anything else; always with the caveat that the data is reported with acceptable lag, is reported on the same or nearly the same granularity as the tradable, and is not subjective or subject to revision.

Using a filter as a component of a trading system turns the trading system into a two step process. First, define the filter so that it identifies some characteristic of the market you plan to trade. For instance, the filter could identify the direction of the trend. Second, use the filter as a permission switch to allow or prohibit positions in assets that are well correlated with the filter. For example, take only long positions when the filter indicates the direction is up and only short positions when the filter indicates the direction is down.

When developing filters, be careful to observe good modeling technique. That is, use one set of data to develop the filter, and a second set to verify that it works out-of-sample. Do not contaminate the out-of-sample data when determining which stocks to trade. Alternatively, code both the filter and the trading system into the same logic so they share the in-sample period. Out-of-sample testing is then out-of-sample for both components. But due to the increased complexity, beware of curve-fitting.

ANALYSIS OF OTHER DATA

Analysis of data other than that being traded falls into two categories.
- In the first, which is intermarket analysis, the frequency of signals based on the external data is the same as the trading frequency.
- In the second, which is a true filter, signals based on the external data are much less frequent – the filter signals hold their state for much longer than the trading position is held.

To begin, we will take a brief look at intermarket analysis – analyzing two series of data and taking positions in one based on the other or on the relationship between the two.

Many of the well publicized intermarket trading systems focus on commodities and futures; and using a continuous futures contract as one or both of the components works well. Traders who do not have commodities data, or who are not interested in trading commodities or futures, will still be able to experiment with intermarket systems by using either indices or exchange traded funds.

Chapter 14, Sector Analysis, introduced the use of the Foreign and SetForeign statements to load data other than that of the current symbol. Many of the examples in this chapter will use foreign data.

Interest Rates as Intermarket Model

The first example uses analysis of interest rates to trade equities.

Yahoo maintains several interest rate-related data series. ^IRX is the 90 day interest rate, ^FVX is the yield on the Five Year Note, and ^TXN is the yield on the Ten Year Note.

Figure 17.1 shows the basic version of an intermarket trading system. The external data is ^FVX. The issue being traded is the current symbol.

```
//   IntermarketFiveYearNoteBasic.afl
//
//   The BuyPrice and SellPrice come from the
//   issue being traded.
SetTradeDelays(0,0,0,0);
BuyPrice = C;
SellPrice = C;

//   The indicators and signals are computed from the
//   Five Year Note, Yahoo Ticker ^FVX
ForeignC = Foreign("^FVX","C");

//   Compute the RSI
ForeignRSI = RSIa(ForeignC,15);

//   Compute the Stochastic of the ForeignRSI
ForeignStochRSI = 100 * (ForeignRSI - LLV(ForeignRSI,24))
        / (HHV(ForeignRSI,24) - LLV(ForeignRSI,24));
ForeignStochRSI = EMA(ForeignStochRSI,3);

//   The Buy and Sell signals will be taken from the
//   crossing of the StochRSI indicator with itself, smoothed
Sm = Param("Sm",3,1,100,1);
FStRSISm = DEMA(ForeignStochRSI,Sm);

Buy = Cross(ForeignStochRSI,FStRSISm);
Sell = Cross(FStRSISm,ForeignStochRSI);

e = Equity();

//   Plotting the "current symbol"
Plot(C,"C",colorBlack,styleCandle);
PlotShapes(Buy*shapeUpArrow + Sell*shapeDownArrow,
    IIf(Buy,colorGreen,colorRed));

//   Plotting the indicator created from the Five Year Note
Plot(ForeignStochRSI,"FStRSI",colorRed,
        styleLine|styleLeftAxisScale);
Plot(FStRSISm,"FStRSISm",colorGreen,
        styleLine|styleLeftAxisScale);

//   Plotting the equity of trading the
//   current symbol based on the Five Year Note
Plot(e,"Equity",colorRed,styleLine|styleOwnScale);
GraphXSpace = 10;
```

Figure 17.1 Basic Intermarket Analysis

In the program above, all of the computation is done based on values that came from the Five Year Note data, except the prices at trade entry and trade exit – they came from the current symbol. The results of applying this system to one of the stocks in the S&P Financial sector is shown in Figure 17.2. No search was done for the best values of the arguments or the stocks that trade most profitably, so even though this is nicely profitable there is probably a lot of room for improvement.

FIGURE 17.2 BASIC INTERMARKET EQUITY

This is a very high frequency trading system. Trading VNO long-only for the period 1/1/1995 through 1/1/2005, there are 394 trades in the ten year in-sample period, each trade held an average of about 4 days, each trade showing a profit of about 0.4%, slightly over 50% of the trades are winners.

INTEREST RATES AS A FILTER SYSTEM

In order to turn the intermarket system into a filter system, the frequency of the signal changes coming from the filter series must be slowed down. Perhaps that can be accomplished by taking additional moving averages before the signals are calculated.

Instead the program in Figure 17.3 uses a different trading system to create the filter. The first part of the code uses the ^FVX data to create a permission variable. The second part of the code uses data from the current symbol to generate signals. The third part of the code combines the two. Read the comments in the code for step by step explanation.

```
//    IntermarketFiveYearNoteIntermediate.afl
//
//    The Yield on the Five Year Note will be used
//    as a filter to permit or block trades
//
//    First step -- find a profitable trading
//    for ^FVX that has longer holding periods
//    than the one in Figure 17.1.
```

```
SetTradeDelays(0,0,0,0);
BuyPrice = C;
SellPrice = C;

//   The indicator and signals are computed from the
//        Five Year Note, Yahoo ticker ^FVX
//   Load the data from ^FVX into OHLC;
SetForeign("^FVX");

//   Compute the stochastic (Position In Range)
//   indicator based on the MACD.
StochMACD = 100 * (MACD()-LLV(MACD(),30))
         / (HHV(MACD(),30)-LLV(MACD(),30));

//   Using a BuySellLevel, compute the
//   permission.
BuySellLevel = 95;

//   The Buy and Sell signals that are commented out
//   in the next lines are profitable for trading
//   the yield on the five year note.
//Buy = Cross(StochMACD, BuySellLevel);
//Sell = Cross(BuySellLevel,StochMACD);

//   But the price of the five year note and its
//   yield are inversely related.
//   So the signals need to be reversed so they
//   are profitable for the equities.
BuyS = Cross(StochMACD, BuySellLevel);
SellS = Cross(BuySellLevel,StochMACD);

//   The Buy and Sell signals that are commented out
//   in the next lines are profitable for trading
//   individual stocks based on the yield of the
//   five year note.
//Buy = SellS;
//Sell = BuyS;
//Short = Sell;
//Cover = Buy;
//   Use those signals from the five year note
//   to filter permission for a trading system that
//   trades more frequently.
Permit = SellS;
Block = BuyS;

//   At this point, Permit and Block are only set
//   on the bar when the signal changes.
//   Use the "flip" command to set all the bars
Permit = Flip(Permit,Block);
Block = Flip(Block,Permit);
//   Uncomment the next line to see the Permit variable
Plot(Permit,"Permit",colorBlue,styleDots);

//   Stop using data from ^FVX
RestorePriceArrays();
//   This is the end of the filter portion.

//
// ----------------------------------------
//
```

```
//    The second step -- have a trading system that
//    profitable in its own right.
//
//    Start an ordinary trading system using the
//    data from current symbol to generate
//    its signals.

//    Compute the RSI
RSIValue = RSIa(C,15);

//    Compute the Stochastic of the RSI of the current symbol
StochRSI = 100 * (RSIValue - LLV(RSIValue,24))
         / (HHV(RSIValue,24) - LLV(RSIValue,24));
StochRSI = EMA(StochRSI,3);

//    The Buy and Sell signals will be taken from the
//    crossing of the StochRSI indicator with itself, smoothed
Sm = Param("Sm",3,1,100,1);
StochRSISm = DEMA(StochRSI,Sm);

SRSIBuy = Cross(StochRSI,StochRSISm);
SRSISell = Cross(StochRSISm,StochRSI);

//    -------------------------------------------------------
//
//    The third step -- combine the trading signal with the
//    permission variable.
//
//    The final Buy and Sell signals come from a
//    combination -- the signals from the high
//    frequency trading system with permission
//    from the lower frequency filter.
Buy = Permit AND SRSIBuy;
Sell = Block OR SRSISell;

//    Remove the extra signal arrows.
Buy = ExRem(Buy,Sell);
Sell = ExRem(Sell,Buy);

e = Equity();

Plot(C,"C",colorBlack,styleCandle);
PlotShapes(Buy*shapeUpArrow+Sell*shapeDownArrow,
           IIf(Buy,colorGreen,colorRed));

Plot(StochMACD,"StochMACD",colorBlue,styleLine|styleOwnScale);
Plot(StochRSI,"StochRSI",colorBlue,styleLine|styleOwnScale);

Plot(e,"Equity",colorRed,styleLine|styleOwnScale);

GraphXSpace = 10;
```

FIGURE 17.3 INTERMARKET FILTER

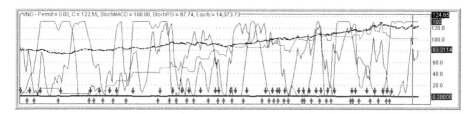

FIGURE 17.4 INTERMARKET FILTER EQUITY

HEINE INTEREST RATE FILTER

Credit for this filter goes to work done by Richard Heine and reported by Nelson Freeburg in his excellent journal, *Formula Research*. Contact information for Mr. Freeburg is in the Appendix - Resources.

As described by Heine and Freeburg, the filter is based on weekly data of five indices: Dow Jones 20 Bond Index, Long Term Bond Yields, 13 Week T Bill Yield, Dow Jones Utility Index, and CRB Index. Score +1 when the DJ20 is above its 24 week Simple Moving Average (SMA). Score +1 when Long Term Bond Yield is below its 6 week SMA. Score +1 when 13 Week Yield is below its 6 week SMA. Score +1 when the DJ Utility Index is above its 10 week SMA. Score +1 when the CRB Index is below its 20 week SMA. Score 0 when those conditions are not met. Add up the five scores. Allow Long positions when the total score is +3 or higher, allow Short positions when the total score is +2 or lower. The Heine Filter was designed to time the Dow Jones 20 Bond Index.

With AmiBroker's ability to use multiple time frames, the Heine filter could be implemented as designed using weekly data. Heine's work can also be adapted to use daily data. Almost any combination of the five data series using average periods between 5 and 250 days works well when used to time the Dow Jones 20 Bond Index. It also works well for many common stocks, particularly those with a strong relationship to interest rates.

The Dow Jones 20 Bond Index has always been quirky. Data for a more stable index (the Dow Jones Corporate Bond Index) begins about January 2002. To bring the Heine filter up to date on daily data, replace the DJ 20 Bond Index with the Dow Jones Corporate Bond Index. For back testing, you may need to splice together the earlier data from the DJ 20 Bond Index. Then use Exponential Moving Averages with lengths 20, 150, 100, 100, and 200 respectively.

The resulting filter is not very good for the general stock indices, but it is a good filter for long term interest rates and related securities. The model is very stable relative to the values of its parameters. The technique used to create the filter is the important point of this section.

OTHER RELATIONSHIPS

Other relationships worth investigating include:
- Volatility as measured by VXO or VXN and broad indices
- Dollar and equities
- Dollar and gold
- Dollar and oil
- Oil and transportation
- Cattle feed and cattle
- Crops and weather

MULTIPLE TIME FRAMES

MANY TRADING SYSTEMS are built on the principle that action at one time interval must be confirmed by action at a longer time interval – confirm a daily signal with a weekly signal; or use a weekly setup and a daily signal.

The time frame manipulation features of AmiBroker make it possible to perform all the calculations within one program. Figure 17.5 shows an example.

```
//   TimeFrameWeekly.afl
//
//   This is not a good trading system.
//   Its purpose is to illustrate the use
//   of TimeFrameSet, TimeFrameExpand, and
//   TimeFrameRestore.
//
//   The time frame modification features of AmiBroker
//   are very powerful, but it is easy to overlook
//   a necessary conversion and get incorrect results.
//
SetTradeDelays(0,0,0,0);
BuyPrice = C;
SellPrice = C;

//   Start out working with daily data, as is normal
//
//   Compute the Position In Range indicator on daily data.
//   If the term stochastic had not been coined first,
//   what is now called the stochastic oscillator might
//   be called the PositionInRange indicator.
//   PIR is an unsmoothed stochastic.
//
```

```
//   In pseudo-code, PIR = (C-LLV)/(HHV-LLV);
//
//   Set the lookback length for the daily indicator
//   As usual, this could be a Param or Optimize statement
DailyLB = 20;

//   Compute the PIR using Daily data
PIRDaily = (C - LLV(C,DailyLB))
        / (HHV(C,DailyLB) - LLV(C,DailyLB));
//   Plot the Daily PIR
Plot(PIRDaily, "PIRDaily", colorRed,styleLine);

//   Switch to weekly data
TimeFrameSet(inWeekly);

//   C is now the Weekly Close
//   As are O, H, L, V, OI
//   There are only one-fifth as many data points
//   for the weekly data, and they are stored in
//   the data arrays near the "current date" end.
//
//   Set the lookback length for the weekly indicator
//   This can also be an Optimize statement
WeeklyLB = 5;

//   Compute the PIR using Weekly data
PIRWeekly = (C - LLV(C,WeeklyLB)) / (HHV(C, WeeklyLB) - LLV(C,WeeklyLB));

//   Plot the Weekly PIR
//   If the "TimeFrameExpand" is omitted from the plot command,
//   there will be a blue line at the current end of the chart,
//   but it will not extend all the way to the left.
Plot(TimeFrameExpand(PIRWeekly,inWeekly),
            "PIRWeekly", colorBlue, styleLine);

//   Switch back to daily data
TimeFrameRestore();

//   Set the levels at which signals are triggered.
WeeklyLevel = 0.10;
DailyLevel = 0.15;

//   Check for signals
//   If the "TimeFrameExpand" is omitted from this line,
//   the PIRWeekly data will be concentrated at the current end
//   of the chart, and the dates will be misaligned.
//   Signals will be generated, but since they are using
//   misaligned data, they are wrong.
Buy = (TimeFrameExpand(PIRWeekly,inWeekly) <= WeeklyLevel)
            AND (Ref(PIRDaily,-1) <= DailyLevel)
            AND (PIRDaily>Ref(PIRDaily,-1));
Sell = BarsSince(Buy) >=3;

//   To see what is happening, remove one or more of
//   the "TimeFrameExpand" from the lines above,
//   and look at the data produced by the
//   Exploration that follows.
Filter = 1;
```

```
AddColumn(C,"C",1.4);
AddColumn(PIRDaily,"PIRDaily",1.4);
AddColumn(TimeFrameExpand(PIRWeekly, inWeekly),"PIRWeekly",1.4);
```

FIGURE 17.5 TIME FRAME WEEKLY

There are explanatory and cautionary comments in the program, but they bear repeating. It is easy to overlook one of the commands that compress or expand the data. When that happens, the data series will not align properly and the results will be inaccurate. It is instructive to modify the program by removing one or more of the TimeFrameExpand commands and note the effect that has, so that you will be able to recognize the problem and know its solution in other programs.

Here is another example, this time using the slope of the MACD Difference line to permit or block trades. Two versions are programmed – one using daily data for the MACD, the other using weekly data. Figure 17.6 shows the version that uses daily data.

```
//    WeeklyMACDFilterDailyData.afl
//
//    Use a MACD to allow or block trades signaled
//    by some other system.
//
//    -----------------------------------
//    Set up the Permission filter
//
//    The traditional MACD is the smoothed difference of
//    two moving averages.

//    Using daily data for the permission filter

p = 5; //Optimize("P",17,3,36,2);
q = 37; //Optimize("Q",29,3,52,2);
r = 7; //Optimize("R",9,3,15,1);

EMA1= EMA(C, p);
EMA2= EMA(C, q);
Diff = EMA1 - EMA2;
SmDiff = EMA(Diff, r);

Plot(SmDiff, "SmDiff", colorRed,styleLine);

//   Permit trades when the line is rising
Permit = SmDiff > Ref(SmDiff,-1);

//   Test using the permission filter
PermitSwitch = 1; //Optimize("PermFilter",1,1,2,1);
Permit = IIf(PermitSwitch==1,Permit,0);

//    -----------------------------------
//
//    Put the trading system here
```

```
//
MA1 = MA(C, 8);
MA2 = MA(C, 7);
BuySignal = Cross(MA1,MA2);
SellSignal = Cross(MA2,MA1);
Buy = Buysignal AND Permit;
Sell = SellSignal OR (NOT permit);
```

FIGURE 17.6 WEEKLY MACD FILTER USING DAILY DATA

Testing the 100 stocks in the current NASDAQ 100 from 1/1/1995 to 1/1/2005, the system is profitable for most stocks with median RAR about 20%.

Figure 17.7 shows the AFL code when the time frame modifications are made.

```
//   WeeklyMACDFilterWeeklyData.afl
//
//   Use a weekly MACD to allow or block trades signaled
//   by some other system.
//
//   ------------------------------------
//   Set up the Permission filter
//
//   The traditional MACD is the smoothed difference of
//   two moving averages.

//   Using weekly data for the permission filter

TimeFrameSet(inWeekly);

p = 19; //Optimize("P",17,3,36,2);
q = 23; //Optimize("Q",29,3,52,2);
r = 14; //Optimize("R",9,3,15,1);

EMA1= EMA(C, p);
EMA2= EMA(C, q);
Diff = EMA1 - EMA2;
SmDiff = EMA(Diff, r);

Plot(SmDiff, "SmDiff", colorRed,styleLine);

//   Permit trades when the line is rising
Permit = SmDiff > Ref(SmDiff,-1);

//   Test using the permission filter
PermitSwitch = 1; //Optimize("PermFilter",1,1,2,1);
Permit = IIf(PermitSwitch==1,Permit,0);

//   Expanded Permit to have daily periodicity
Permit = TimeFrameExpand(Permit,inWeekly);

//   Return to daily
TimeFrameRestore();
```

```
// -----------------------------------
//
//   Put the trading system here
//
MA1 = MA(C, 8);
MA2 = MA(C, 7);

BuySignal = Cross(MA1,MA2);
SellSignal = Cross(MA2,MA1);

Buy = Buysignal AND Permit;
Sell = SellSignal OR (NOT Permit);

Plot(Permit,"Permit",colorBlue,styleDots);
```

FIGURE 17.7 WEEKLY MACD FILTER USING WEEKLY DATA

Using the same values for the MACD calculation, profitability improves. And making a few optimization runs reveals other profitable and stable sets of arguments.

Another scheme that has supporters is a dual time frame Bollinger Band system. A version of it is shown in Figure 17.8. There are several possibilities for trading Bollinger Bands – buy the breakouts, fade the breakouts, etcetera. The code has several of the options in place, but commented out. None of them seemed to work well on the issues and time periods tested.

```
//   DualTimeFrameBollingerBand.afl
//
//   This program uses daily data to take trades, providing
//   the weekly data permits the trade.
//
//   Both daily and weekly look at the position of the most
//   recent close within the Bollinger Bands.
SetTradeDelays(0,0,0,0);
BuyPrice = C;
SellPrice = C;

//   Set up the weekly filter
TimeFrameSet(inWeekly);

WeeklyLookBack = Optimize("WkLB",8,2,10,2);
WeeklyBandWidth = Optimize("WkBW",1.1,1,2.5,.1);

BBPctWeekly = (C - BBandBot(C,WeeklyLookBack,WeeklyBandWidth))
         / (BBandTop(C,WeeklyLookBack,WeeklyBandWidth)
          - BBandBot(C,WeeklyLookBack,WeeklyBandWidth));
BBPctWeekly = TimeFrameExpand(BBPctWeekly,inWeekly);

//   Return to daily data
TimeFrameRestore();
```

```
// --------------------------------------------
//   Set up daily trading system
DailyLookBack = Optimize("DyLB",5,5,30,5);;
DailyBandWidth = Optimize("DyBW",1.1,1,2.5,.1);

BBPctDaily = (C - BBandBot(C,DailyLookBack,DailyBandWidth))
        / (BBandTop(C,DailyLookBack,DailyBandWidth)
        - BBandBot(C,DailyLookBack,DailyBandWidth));

//   There are a lot of conditions that might work --
//   Buy breakouts
//   Fade breakouts
//   Buy returns into bands


//   Buy breakouts
Buy = (BBPctWeekly >= 0.90) AND (BBPctDaily >= 0.90);
Sell = BBpctDaily <= 0.10;
//Sell = BarsSince(Buy) >=3;
Short = (BBPctWeekly <= 0.10) AND (BBPctDaily < 0.10);
Cover = BBPctDaily >= 0.90;
//Cover = BarsSince(Short) >=3;


//   Fade breakouts without waiting for prices to move
//   back into the band.
//   This does not work very well, at least
//   on the issues I tested.
//Buy = (BBPctWeekly <= 0.10) AND (BBPctDaily <=0.10);
//Sell = (BBPctDaily >= 0.90);
//Short = (BBPctWeekly >= 0.90) AND (BBPctDaily >= 0.90);
//Cover = (BBPctDaily <= 0.10);


//   Buy returns to the bands after excursions outside.
//   This does not work very well, at least
//   on the issues I tested.
//Buy = ((BBpctWeekly <= 0.10) OR (Ref(BBPctWeekly,-1) <= 0.10))
//        AND (Ref(BBPctDaily,-1) <= 0.10)
//        AND (BBPctDaily > Ref(BBPctDaily,-1));
//Sell = (BBPctDaily >= 0.90);
//Short = ((BBPctWeekly >= 0.90) OR (Ref(BBPctWeekly,-1) >= 0.90))
//        AND (Ref(BBPctDaily,-1) >= 0.90)
//        AND (BBpctDaily < Ref(BBPctDaily,-1));
//Cover = (BBPctDaily <= 0.10);


Buy = ExRem(Buy,Sell);
Sell = ExRem(Sell,Buy);
Short = ExRem(Short,Cover);
Cover = ExRem(Cover,Short);

Plot(C, "C", colorBlack, styleCandle);
PlotShapes(Buy*shapeUpArrow + Sell*shapeDownArrow,
        IIf(Buy,colorGreen,colorRed));
PlotShapes(Short*shapeHollowDownArrow
        + Cover*shapeHollowUpArrow,
                IIf(Short,colorRed,colorGreen));
```

```
Plot(BBPctWeekly,"BBPctWk",colorBlue,
        styleLine|styleLeftAxisScale);
Plot(BBPctDaily,"BBPctDy", colorGreen,
        styleLine|styleLeftAxisScale);
```

FIGURE 17.8 DUAL TIME FRAME BOLLINGER BANDS

BROAD MARKET TIMING

BROAD MARKET TIMING is based on characteristics of the market itself, using artifacts such as the number of new highs, advancing volume, or declining issues to create indicators which provide some insight into the market.

It is often easier to develop profitable trading systems for broad market timing than for individual equities. This may be because the broad market consists of many individual equities and the averaging effect of combining them contributes a natural smoothing.

It is still easier to develop models for market sectors. The combination of individual equities in the sectors provides some smoothing, and the components are correlated, so the sector indexes trend well.

USING AMIBROKER'S ADD TO COMPOSITE FUNCTIONALITY

A very powerful feature of AmiBroker is the AddToComposite (ATC) function. The AmiBroker web site has an excellent tutorial in the use of ATC written by Herman van den Bergen. A typical use of ATC is to process all the issues in a watch list and accumulate sums, averages, and counts of selected information. For example, count the number of stocks that are at new 90 day highs. Indicators formed in this manner are described as diffusion indicators.

The form of the AddToComposite function is:
    AddToComposite(array, "ticker", "fields", flags);
- Array is the array being added into the composite.
- "ticker" is the ticker of the composite being formed.
- "fields" are the data fields within "ticker" that are being updated.
- flags govern the actions of ATC.

As its name suggests, ATC adds information into a composite data series. Typical operation is:
- Decide what array will be accumulated, and compute it.
- Use the AddToComposite function to accumulate the data in one or more fields of a composite data series.
- Refer to the newly created data series as you would any other data series.

There are some guidelines for working with ATC:
- The ticker symbol for a composite should start with the tilde "~" character.
- The ticker symbol should be at most 15 characters long.
- All the composite data series will be created in Group 253.
- ATC can be used while in Scan, Explorer, Backtest, or Optimize mode.
- The composite series can be stored in the O, H, L, C, V, or I fields.
- If you plan to use one of OHLC, use the "X" code instead – it puts identical values in all of OHLC so data inconsistencies do not arise.

SIMPLE EXAMPLE OF ATC

Following is an AmiBroker program that computes and displays an Advance Decline Oscillator for the 500 stocks currently in the S&P 500 index.

```
//   ATCSimpleTest.afl
//
//   Demonstration of the AddToComposite (ATC) function
//
//   In Automatic Analysis:
//       In Apply to, with the Use Filter and Define menus,
//           Select a group to process
//               For example, select a Watchlist containing the
//               500 stocks that make up the S&P 500 index.
//       In Range, use any settings, they make no difference
//       Click the Scan button
//
//   This program creates four composite tickers.
//       ~Counter -- contains the number of issues processed
//       ~AdvIss  -- contains the number of issues Up each day
//       ~DecIss  -- contains the number of issues Down each day
//       ~UncIss  -- contains the number of issues Unchanged
//   The Volume field of each series is used to store the counts
//
```

```
//   Since no explicit Flag parameter is specified,
//   the default flags are in effect.
//       ATC should Reset the composite series
//           before adding data to them,
//       the series should be stored in Group 253.
//
//   Click the Apply Indicator icon and the ADO will be
//   plotted in its own window pane
AddToComposite(1,"~Counter","V");

AdvIss = C > Ref(C,-1);
AddToComposite(AdvIss,"~AdvIss","V");

DecIss = C < Ref(C,-1);
AddToComposite(DecIss,"~DecIss","V");

UncIss = C == Ref(C,-1);
AddToComposite(UncIss,"~UncIss","V");
//   Scan mode requires that the afl program have
//   Buy and Sell signals.
//   Just set them to zero -- no buy and no sell.
Buy = 0;
Sell = 0;

//   The four new data series are immediately available.
//   Create and plot an Advance Decline Oscillator using them
AdvIss = Foreign("~AdvIss","V");
DecIss = Foreign("~DecIss","V");
UncIss = Foreign("~UncIss","V");
Count = Foreign("~Counter","V");

ADO = (AdvIss - DecIss)/IIf(Count<=0,1,Count);

Plot(ADO,"AdvDecLine",colorRed,styleLine);
```

FIGURE 17.9 ATC SIMPLE TEST

Figure 17.10 shows the results. Note that the oscillator has peaks on days the S&P 500 closed higher and valleys on days it closed lower.

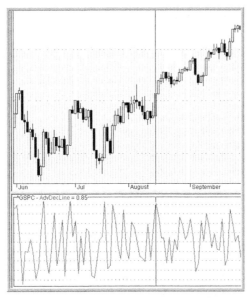

FIGURE 17.10 ATC SIMPLE TEST RESULT

DIFFUSION INDEX

An excellent use of ATC is creation of diffusion indexes of various kinds. A diffusion index is an index that represents the summation of an indicator over many issues in a group. The resulting diffusion index is usually an oscillator. The index can either be a sum of an oscillator already associated with each member of the group, such as summing up the RSI of each member; or it can be formed by first accumulating data from each member, then creating the oscillator. With just a little more code, the simple test in Figure 17.9 could become a useful oscillator. Those additions are incorporated into the code in Figure 17.11.

```
//   SimpleDiffusionIndex.afl
//
//   Create a simple diffusion index using ~AdvIss, ~DecIss,
//   and ~Counter that were created in an earlier run.
//   Since those data series will not change until
//   another day of data is added to the database,
//   there is no need to recalculate them for every run.
//   There is no AddToComposite statement in this program.
//
SetTradeDelays(0,0,0,0);
BuyPrice = C;
SellPrice = C;
```

```
//   Read the data series containing the number of
//   advancing issues, declining issues, and
//   total issues.
AdvIss = Foreign("~AdvIss","V");
DecIss = Foreign("~DecIss","V");
Count = Foreign("~Counter","V");

ADO = (AdvIss - DecIss)/IIf(Count<=0,1,Count);

//   This optimization does not involve the ATC function.
LookBack = Optimize("LookBack",24,2,100,2);

SmoothedADO = DEMA(ADO,LookBack);
Trigger = DEMA(SmoothedADO,3);

Plot(SmoothedADO,"AdvDecLine",colorRed,styleLine);

Buy = Cross(SmoothedADO,Trigger);
Sell = Cross(Trigger,SmoothedADO);

PlotShapes(Buy*shapeUpArrow+Sell*shapeDownArrow,
     IIf(Buy,colorGreen,colorRed));

Filter = 1;
AddColumn(C,"C",1.4);
AddColumn(AdvIss,"AdvIss",1.4);
AddColumn(ADO,"ADO",1.4);
```

FIGURE 17.11 SIMPLE DIFFUSION INDEX

The median Risk Adjusted Return (RAR) for the 500 individual stocks that make up the S&P 500 for the in-sample period was about 35%. Figure 17.12 shows the stocks with the highest RAR.

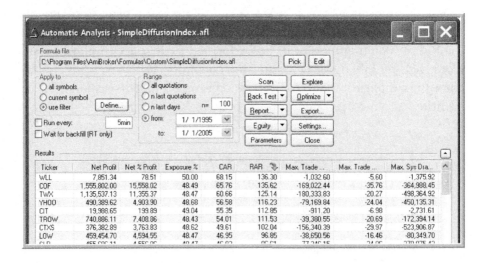

FIGURE 17.12 SIMPLE DIFFUSION INDEX RESULT

A watchlist containing the 100 stocks that performed best in-sample based on RAR was formed, and those stocks were tested out-of-sample, 1/1/2005 to 1/1/2007. The median RAR was about 16%.

Since the signals are coming from a single indicator, all the stocks get a Buy signal on the same day, so a good PositionScore method should be added to the code in Figure 17.11 to differentiate which stocks to buy.

ANOTHER SIMPLE DIFFUSION INDEX

In the program shown in Figure 17.13, the diffusion index is formed by averaging indicators associated with each individual issue. In this example, the oscillator part is computed before the ATC part. Within the program, the ZScore will be added into the composite. ZScore values are both positive and negative, and they are small in absolute value – seldom over 3.0. AmiBroker handles the negative values without any problem, but the small numbers lose all the significance beyond the decimal point. To overcome that, multiply the ZScore by 100 or 1000 before adding it in. There is no need to reverse the transformation before computing the indicator – just think of a ZScore of 0.80 as a ZScore of 80 percent of one standard deviation and work with the 80 instead of the 0.80.

As each member of the group is processed, compute the ZScore of every closing price. The ZScore measures the amount, measured in standard deviations, that the data point is above or below the mean. For this example, the group chosen is XLE, the S&P Energy Exchange Traded Fund. If the diffusion index is successful, the plan is to trade the most profitable of the issues that make up XLE, the XLE itself, or options on XLE.

Figure 17.13 shows the code for creating this diffusion index, again using ATC. The ZScore is calculated using the function ExampleZScore. ExampleZScore computes the ZScore in the ordinary way, but it has been compiled into a custom DLL. The creation of custom DLLs is described in the Appendix – Extending AmiBroker.

```
//   ATCExampleZScore.afl
//
//   Note the flags in the ATC statement.
//   Flag 1: Reset
//   Flag 2: Save results in Group 253
//   Flag 8: Enable ATC in Backtest mode
//
LB = 5;
ZlookbackLength = LB;
```

```
zs = 1000* ExampleZScore(C,Zlookbacklength);
//Plot(zs,"zs",colorRed,styleLine);

AddToComposite(zs,"~XLEZScore","V",1+2+8 );
AddToComposite(1,"~Counter","V",1+2+8 );

xlez = Foreign("~XLEZScore","V");
xlezcount = Foreign("~Counter","V");

xlez = xlez / IIf(xlezcount<=0,1,xlezcount);

xlezsm = DEMA(xlez,20);
trigger = DEMA(xlezsm,3);
Filter = 1;

Plot(xlezsm,"xlezsm",colorRed,styleLine|styleLeftAxisScale);
Plot(trigger,"trigger",colorBlue,styleLine|styleLeftAxisScale);

Buy = Cross(xlezsm,trigger);
Sell = Cross(trigger,xlezsm);

PlotShapes(Buy*shapeUpArrow+Sell*shapeDownArrow,
    IIf(Buy,colorGreen,colorRed));
```

FIGURE 17.13 DIFFUSION INDEX FROM ZSCORE

If you want to find out how the group does as a portfolio, click the Backtest button and accept the default of Portfolio Backtest. Similarly to the previous example, the code in Figure 17.13 will give all the issues in the group Buy and Sell signals on the same day, so it is important to have a PositionScore method.

If you want to find out how each individual in the group does, pull down the small menu on the Backtest button and select Individual Backtest. That is how the results in Figure 17.14 were produced. Be sure to check individual performance – very often the performance of the group is influenced by one or two strong performers, or by a data error that appears to be a very profitable trade. In this example, XTO produces about three times the profit of the next most profitable issue.

XLE, the ETF itself, was included as one of the tickers along with the components that make up XLE. Note that the profitability of trading XLE ranks near the bottom of the list. Trading the individual components will be a better choice.

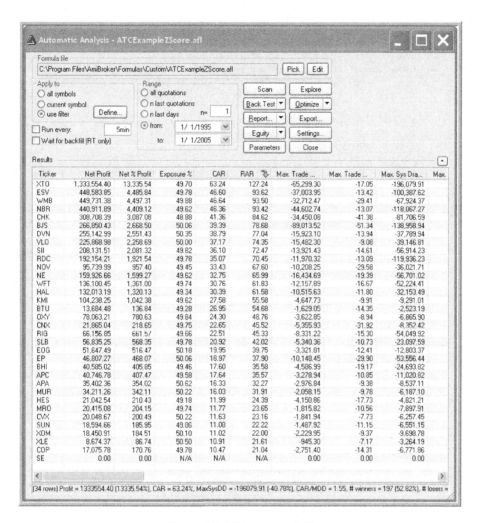

FIGURE 17.14 ZSCORE ON XLE

OPTIMIZING WITHIN ATC

The previous examples computed one composite, then used optimization to search for the best use for it. Another approach, as is shown in Figure 17.15, is to search for the best composite by optimizing, creating several alternatives, and choosing among them.

```
//   ATCExampleZScoreOptimize.afl
//
LB = Optimize("LB",20,5,50,5);
ZlookbackLength = LB;
```

```
zs = 1000* ExampleZScore(C,Zlookbacklength);
//Plot(zs,"zs",colorRed,styleLine);

AddToComposite(zs,"~XLEZScore"+WriteVal(LB,1.0),"V",1+2+8 );
AddToComposite(1,"~Counter"+WriteVal(LB,1.0),"V",1+2+8 );
xlez = Foreign("~XLEZScore"+WriteVal(LB,1.0),"V");
xlezcount = Foreign("~Counter"+WriteVal(LB,1.0),"V");

xlez = xlez / IIf(xlezcount<=0,1,xlezcount);

xlezsm = DEMA(xlez,20);
trigger = DEMA(xlezsm,3);
Filter = 1;
Plot(xlezsm,"xlezsm",colorRed,styleLine|styleLeftAxisScale);
Plot(trigger,"trigger",colorBlue,styleLine|styleLeftAxisScale);

Buy = Cross(xlezsm,trigger);
Sell = Cross(trigger,xlezsm);

PlotShapes(Buy*shapeUpArrow+Sell*shapeDownArrow,
    IIf(Buy,colorGreen,colorRed));
```

FIGURE 17.15 OPTIMIZING WITH ATC

Caution – using this program, there will be two files created in Group 253 for every combination of values for the optimization variables.

If you want to find out how the group performs as a portfolio, click the Optimize button and accept the default of Portfolio Optimization.

If you want to find out how the individuals within the group perform, drop down the small menu on the optimize button and select Old (V4.4) Optimizer. That is what was done, using XLF, the S&P Financial ETF, and its components, to produce Figure 17.16. Run 2, the best as measured by Net Profit, used a Lookback length of 10. We would see the 10 in the rightmost column if we scrolled across.

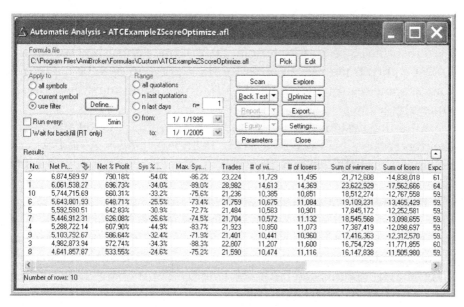

FIGURE 17.16 ZSCORE OPTIMIZED ON XLF

The AddToComposite function in AmiBroker is extremely powerful and the diffusion indices that can be created using it are very profitable.

EQUITY CURVE FEEDBACK

Two traders are discussing their experiences. One says that periods of drawdown are buying opportunities; the other says that they are indications that the trading system has stopped working. The last 12 trades show the following gains, all in dollars:

Gain	+400	-200	+300	+100	+200	+450	+150	+200	+600	-200	-100	-300
Label										A	B	C

TABLE 17.1 TRADE RECORD

Who is right? (We will come back to A, B, and C)

Isn't this the same as asking whether a particular market is trending or in a trading range? In a trending market, rising prices are usually followed by rising prices, falling prices are usually followed by falling prices, and several declines following a period of rising prices indicates a change in trend. In a trading range market, rising prices are usually followed by falling prices, falling prices are usually followed by rising prices, and several declines following a period of rising prices does indicate a buying opportunity.

Substitute closed trades for daily bars – trade entry, highest equity, lowest equity, trade exit. In order for the equity curve to be a filter for trades, some technique similar to a trading system must be accurate when applied to trade bars.

A trading system that is profitable in a trending market stays with the trend and exits or reverses when the trend changes. A trading system that is profitable in a trading range market takes positions opposite the trend.

There are statistical tests that identify trend versus trading range. One is the *runs* test. Given a time series, assign each data point a "+" if it is higher than its predecessor and a "-" if it is lower or unchanged. A run is a sequence of any number of data points that have the same sign. The data points can be of any length – hourly bars, daily bars, or closed trades.

Take this series of 15 data points and 14 changes:

Data	40	36	38	41	40	38	34	33	36	34	40	40	47	53	57
Change		-4	+2	+3	-1	-2	-4	-1	+3	-2	+6	0	+7	+6	+4
Sign		-	+	+	-	-	-	-	+	-	+	-	+	+	+

TABLE 17.2 ANALYZING RUNS

The number of points, N, is 14.
The number of wins (+ sign), W, is 7.
The number of losses (- sign), L, is 7.
The number of runs, R, is 8.

The formula for the Z statistic is:

$$Z = \frac{N*(R-0.5)-X}{\sqrt{\dfrac{(X*(X-N))}{(N-1)}}}$$

where $X = 2*W*L = 2*7*7 = 98$

$$Z = \frac{14*7.5-98}{\sqrt{\dfrac{98*(98-14)}{13}}} = \frac{7}{25.16} = 0.278$$

The Z being discussed in this section is the Z-statistic — different than the ZScore used in earlier sections.

If Z is negative, there is a positive serial dependency, which implies trending, and fewer but longer streaks – wins follow wins and losses follow losses.

If Z is positive, there is a negative serial dependency, which implies trading range, and more, but shorter streaks – wins follow losses and losses follow wins.

The magnitude of Z indicates how far from the expected random value this data series is.

Since we accept the sign of Z as correct and want to know whether it is significant, we use a one-tailed test. Z must be greater than 1.65 in absolute value to be significant at the 0.05 level, and greater than 2.33 to be significant at the 0.01 level.

For a very rough estimate – for wins and losses approximately equal in number, if 10 data points have 3 or fewer runs or 8 or more runs, the Z statistic is significant at the 0.05 level, and the mode is trending or trading, respectively. If 20 data points have 6 or fewer runs (trending) or 14 or more runs (trading), the Z statistic is significant at the 0.05 level.

Our two traders could compute the Z value for the series of closed trades listed in Table 17.1. If Z is -1.65 or more negative, the series is of trades is trending, and since the last three trades are losers, the system is broken. If Z is +1.65 or greater, the series is a trading range and buying the dips is a good strategy.

Long ago, they decided to use a 10 trade sequence on which to base their equity curve analysis. After Trade A, Z = 0.32 – not significant. After Trade B, Z = -1.33 – not significant. After Trade C, Z = -2.11 – significant at the 0.05 level, and indicating that the series is trending and the system is broken. They should stop trading it until the system and the market it trades return to synchronization.

A short program will compute and plot the Z value for daily bars.

```
//   PlotRunTest.afl
//
//   Compute the Runs Test
//   and plot the result.

function ComputeRunZ (P, N)
{
    w1 = IIf(P>Ref(P,-1),1,0);

    for (i=0; i<N; i++)
    {
        Z[i] = 0.0;
```

```
      }
      for (i=N; i<BarCount; i++)
      {
          Runs[i] = 1;
          Win[i] = 0;
          Lose[i] = 0;
          for (j=0; j<N; j++)
          {
              if (wl[i-j] == 1)
              {
                  Win[i]++;
              }
              else
              {
                  Lose[i]++;
              }
          }
          for (j = 0; j<n-1; j++)
          {
              if (wl[i-j] != wl[i-j-1])
              {
                  Runs[i]++;
              }
          }
          if ( Win[i] >= N )
              Z[i] = -5.0;
          else
              if ( Lose[i] >= N )
                  Z[i] = 5.0;
              else
              {
                  x = 2 * Win[i] * Lose[i];
                  Num = N * ( Runs[i] - 0.5 ) - x;
                  Denom = sqrt( ( X * ( X - N ) ) / ( N - 1 ) );
                  Z[i] = Num / Denom;
              }
      }

      return Z;
}

n = Param("n",10,2,50,1);

Z = ComputeRunZ(C,n);

Plot(C,"C", colorBlack,styleCandle|styleOwnScale);

Plot(Z,"Z",colorBlue,styleLine,-2,2);
Plot(-1.65,"",colorBlue,styleDots);
Plot(1.65,"",colorBlue,styleDots);
```

FIGURE 17.17 PLOT RUN TEST

Changing the time frame can change the mode of the market. Five days up followed by five days down looks like trends on a daily or shorter time frame, but looks like a trading range on a weekly time frame.

Another approach to equity curve analysis is to see whether a trend following system, such as moving average crossover, or a trading range system, such as stochastic oscillator, is more accurate when applied to trade "bars."

Advisory services

There are many, many advisory services willing to take our subscription fees and offer us advice. Some act as filters – permitting trades or blocking trades – which is why the discussion of advisors is in this chapter.

Before subscribing to an advisory service or newsletter, check to see if it is tracked by The Mark Hulbert Financial Digest. Contact information for Hulbert is in the Appendix – Resources. Note that very few of the services he follows have annual rates of return above 10 percent for two years or more.

Newsletter writers cover the range from very professional and very ethical down to very unethical. One of the difficulties with advice from any advisor – newsletter writer, stock broker, television commentator, economist, etcetera – is for any one customer to detect unethical behavior or even to differentiate between skill and luck.

The scenario described here does not reflect any real person, living or dead, and there is no indication that this ever happened. But imagine an unethical person wanted to convince people to subscribe to his expensive newsletter. He compiles a list of ten thousand people who are known to be interested in investing.

He begins a ten week program. At the beginning of week one, he write two versions of his newsletter – one forecasting that the coming week the broad market average he trades will be up, the other than it will be down. He e-mails the up letter to 5,000 randomly chosen people and the down letter to the other 5,000, along with a message saying that they have been chosen to receive a free ten week trial subscription. At the beginning of week two, he again writes two versions of his newsletter – one forecasting that the next week will be up, the other that it will be down. He mails the up letter to 2,500 who got the up letter last week and to 2,500 who got the down letter last week. The down letter goes to the others. He continues this process for ten weeks in all, splitting the recipients in half each time.

At the end of ten weeks, one person of every 1024 – 9 out of the 10,000 – will have gotten newsletters with perfect predictions – ten out of ten correct. Another 97 received nine out of ten correct, and 439 received eight correct. He informs them that his regular subscription rate of $100 per month will be going up, and they can subscribe for a non-refundable $1000 per year if they hurry. Even those who received zero correct will sign up, planning to do the opposite of his advice. A sizable percentage sign up and pay the fee, and the newsletter writer goes out of business due to serious health problems.

EXPECTATIONS OF PROFITABILITY

If the advisors, newsletters, money managers, or fund managers are good (better than random), at least some of them should be profitable. And their level of profitability should provide some indication of the returns individual traders can expect. Given the large number of advisors making predictions and recommendations every day, week, and month, some of them will have excellent annual returns strictly due to luck.

There are several sources of information that report returns by category of investment. Futures magazine, and other monthly periodicals, regularly publish the results for the most recent month and year to date. The source quoted is often the Barclay Trading Group. It is rare to see annual returns in excess of 10% per year for two or more years. The five most profitable Commodity Trading Advisors for the entire year of 2006, as reported in December 2006 issue of Futures, averaged about 19% for the year. The worst five lost 19% for the year.

Firms that trade options do little better. And firms that trade currencies not only do no better, but also have month to month swings of profit and loss greater than their annual net profit.

According to the Hulbert Financial Digest, as reported in the December 2006 issue, only six newsletter services outperformed the Wilshire 5000 index in both up and down markets since 1990. Although there were both rising and falling periods, overall it was a very strong bull market with an annualized gain of 11.0% for the Wilshire. The best of the newsletters had an annualized gain of 15.4%.

Screens that select stocks based on a variety of fundamental metrics, such as AAII and Value Line, suffer from common faults:
- All of their results come from in-sample testing.
- The data used has been reported and is not the result of trades made.
- The data is subject to revision.

The very strong upward bias to the equities markets since 1982 makes nearly any portfolio look profitable and nearly any portfolio manager look skillful.

To quote a friend of mine who is both observant and cynical, do not confuse brains with a bull market.

18

In-Sample – Out-of-Sample

DIVISION OF DATA into in-sample and out-of-sample periods gives us a method of evaluating the ability of a trading system to identify and synchronize with the characteristics of the market. In order to trade profitably, the trading system must recognize patterns that occur in the in-sample period, hoping that they persist through the out-of-sample period.

The market data always consists of two components—the signal component that is characteristic of the data and remains relatively stable over time, and the noise component that is random and unpredictable over time.

The distinction between signal and noise is, in part, an artificial distinction caused by our inability to detect patterns in the noise. If we could find persistent patterns in the noise, that portion of noise would become signal. Anything that is not specifically recognized as signal is noise—even if it contains profitable information that could be recognized by some other model.

Through optimization, the trading system will learn the patterns in the in-sample period – both signal and noise – as well as it can, given its rules and parameters. If the market is sufficiently stationary and the trading system sufficiently clever, the patterns that it learned by examining the in-sample period will continue to be identified in the out-of-sample period.

The trading system will be successful if the profits are coming from the signal component of the in-sample data rather than the noise component. The only way to test this is to look at the results from applying

253

the trading system to data that was not used during its learning process – the out-of-sample data.

How optimization works

There is nothing special about optimization. An optimization is simply an organized search of a number of alternatives. Each of the parameters that will be searched has a list or range of values established for it. One parameter might be the lookback period of a simple moving average. The length of the moving average will be varied from 2 to 30 in steps of 2. The maximum number of days that a position may be held will be varied from 1 to 20 in steps of 1. The total number of runs necessary to test all combinations is the product of the number of steps for the individual variables. In this case, it is 300 (15 times 20). For each test, the in-sample data period specified is loaded into memory, the model is set with a specific length for the moving average lookback and a specific time for the holding period, buy and sell signals are issued, and the values of the metrics including the objective function are computed. At the end of all 300 runs, there is a list of the 300 individual runs and the performance statistics for each.

The important step is ranking the alternatives. The entry at the top of the list is the best. Best because its objective function has the highest value. If you prefer any alternative other than the top one, modify your objective function until the alternatives are in the order of your preference.

Optimization is not limited to numerical arguments. It can include logical operators (equal, less than, greater than, and, or) and ticker symbols (that is, searching the symbol space) – all in hopes of discovering combinations of models, arguments, and tickers that scored high for the in-sample period and will continue to score high in the out-of-sample period.

Reasons for using long in-sample periods:

- *The trading system will be exposed to many different market conditions and, hopefully, will learn to recognize and make profitable signals for all of them.*

   The problem is that the model cannot adapt to many different conditions without having many variables, which risks overly-fit solutions. For example, a moving average crossover model with specific moving average lengths might work well over one period of time, but would need different lengths for other time periods, and rules to identify which lengths to use.

- *With many data points, the model has less risk of being curve-fit.*

   True, but unless the underlying market is stationary, the model will only fit (and be profitable for) a portion of the period.

- *A long data period will produce a large number of trades, which helps provide statistical validity.*

   If this were the out-of-sample period, that statement would be true. But the optimization was done using the in-sample period. All in-sample trade results are meaningless. Only the results from the following out-of-sample period are useful in estimating future performance. So it does not matter how many trades were produced.

REASONS FOR USING SHORT IN-SAMPLE PERIODS:

- *The series being modeled changes less in a short period of time than in a long period. There are fewer conditions for the model to learn and a greater chance that it can learn them accurately.*

   The problem is the risk of curve-fitting a model to a short in-sample period. Examination of the out-of-sample results for the following time period will indicate whether the model is valid or not.

HOW CAN THE PROPER OR BEST LENGTH OF THE IN-SAMPLE PERIOD BE DETERMINED?

There is no general relationship or rule of thumb to suggest the answer. The best or proper length of the in-sample period is that length that maximizes the model's ability to recognize the signal portion of the data while at the same time minimizing the influence of the specific noise in the data. That length can only be determined by experimentation for each model and each data series.

IS IT NECESSARY TO HAVE AN OUT-OF-SAMPLE DATA PERIOD?

Yes. Models that have been created by an extensive search will have used up all the available degrees of freedom and will be curve-fit solutions. Equity curve and trade statistics for in-sample trades are meaningless. The out-of-sample period is the only way to determine whether the model has prediction capability.

WHAT IS THE BEST OR PROPER LENGTH OF THE OUT-OF-SAMPLE PERIOD?

There is no rule of thumb or general relationship suggesting the best or proper length of the out-of-sample period. It is not related to the length of the in-sample period.

The best answer is that the length of the out-of-sample period is "as long as the model and the data remain in synchronization."

CAN OUT-OF-SAMPLE PERIODS PRECEDE IN-SAMPLE PERIODS?

No. A model that is fit to an in-sample period of 1985 to 1995 will probably show good results over the 1975 to 1985 period. But, the data we will eventually trade is always more recent than the in-sample period, never earlier. So the results over the earlier period have no predictive value. Testing the model over a later time period, such as from 1995 to the present, is meaningful. If the results over 1975 to 1985 are profitable but the results from 1995 to the present are not, that is an indication that the market has changed in such a way that the model being tested is no longer profitable. If the results over 1975 to 1985 are profitable and the results from 1995 to the present are also profitable, that is an indication that the model may continue to trade profitably. The positive results from 1975 to 1985 indicate that the underlying market is very stationary with regard to that model.

For the same reasons, it is inappropriate to use the *bootstrap*, *fold*, or *jackknife* technique for dividing data into in-sample and out-of-sample periods. These methods divide all the data into several periods – say ten. The modeling process makes ten passes; each pass treats nine of the periods as in-sample and reserves the other for out-of-sample. After the ten passes, the results from the ten out-of-sample periods are gathered together and analyzed as one out-of-sample period that includes all of the original data. Only one of the ten periods is truly out-of-sample. Results from the out-of-sample periods will overestimate the future performance of the system.

IS IT LEGITIMATE TO USE ARTIFICIAL DATA TO TRAIN A MODEL?

No. We are hoping to find some pattern within the data that will lead to profitable trades on actual market data that the model has never been exposed to. Certainly, we can create an artificial data file that has *some* of the same characteristics of the real data. But if we knew how to create an artificial data file that had the important characteristics of the actual data, then we would already know how to identify the patterns we are looking for. In any event, the model must perform profitably in true out-of-sample testing, which requires actual market data.

DOES A SYSTEM NEED TO DO WELL IN ALL MARKET CONDITIONS?

No. But the system should be able to recognize the type of market it does do well in, and remain out of the market when conditions are unfavorable. This can be accomplished in several ways.

- The system can take entries according to its rules, but stop out with small losses when the market conditions are unfavorable.
- The system can track its own performance and scale back during drawdowns.
- A filter can be included either within the trading system or as a separate program to identify favorable and unfavorable markets.

WILL THE BEST IN-SAMPLE RESULTS GIVE THE BEST OUT-OF-SAMPLE RESULTS?

When the question is asked a little differently it is apparent that the best hope for strong out-of-sample results comes from the best in-sample models.

"Are there any techniques that could be applied that have not already been applied that will help select any model other than the one that scored highest?"

If the answer is yes, then incorporate those techniques into the model and rerun the optimization. If the answer is no, then accept the model that ranks highest in-sample.

CAN OUT-OF-SAMPLE RESULTS BE AS GOOD AS OR BETTER THAN IN-SAMPLE RESULTS?

Perhaps for one or two out-of-sample periods, but long periods of out performance are unlikely.

The more complex a model is, the less likely out-of-sample results will be as good as in-sample results because of the model being somewhat fit to the noise. The less complex a model is, the less likely out-of-sample results will be as good as in-sample results because of the lack of stationarity of the data and the inability of the simple model to adapt.

If the out-of-sample performance was regularly better than the in-sample performance, that would create an inconsistent situation. Assume that the in-sample period is six months and the out-of-sample period is also six months. Each out-of-sample period becomes the in-sample period for the next walk forward step, and the optimization process insures that the profit will be at least as great when that six month period is in-sample as when it was out-of-sample. For the out-of-sample to be consistently more profitable than the in-sample, the trading system would become more profitable over time. However, experience shows that equity curves always flatten over time – they never show steeper rises for extended periods.

A wide search will have created and tested thousands of models, each slightly different. Just as the scam newsletter writer got lucky and sent some people perfect predictions by writing sequences of advisory letters that covered all the possibilities, some of these models got lucky and produced great results based solely on fitting the noise component of the data. To the extent that the model fits the signal component, good performance will continue as long as the characteristics of the signal remain stationary. To the extent the model fits the noise component, performance will drop considerably.

We cannot remove the noise from the historical data. If we could, we would simply do that and the performance due to fitting the noise would be removed and no longer an issue. But we can minimize fit to one specific series of noise found in the in-sample data by substituting our own noise. Take high scoring models and rerun them, each time adding a random noise component to the data. Alternatively, the optimization could be set up to run all models several times, adding random noise to each run, and reporting a composite score.

Chapter 22, Monte Carlo Analysis, has an example of adding noise to the price series to test the sensitivity of the model.

WHAT IS THE RELATIONSHIP BETWEEN THE IN-SAMPLE AND OUT-OF-SAMPLE RESULTS?

There is no general rule. The important measurement is whether the out-of-sample results are satisfactory. If the out-of-sample results are nearly as good as the in-sample results, that does indicate that the system is identifying nearly all of the profitable opportunities. If the out-of-sample results are much poorer, it might be possible to modify the system and improve it. But do not let perfect be the enemy of adequate. As discussed in detail in MTSP, the distribution of the results are as important, or perhaps more so, than the average. A less profitable, but smoother, system can be traded at a higher level of leverage, which may more than make up the difference between the two final equity values.

Beware of contaminating the out-of-sample data

Model development is rarely done in a completely unbiased manner. Every use of the out-of-sample data to adjust the model causes the model to lose generality and predictive ability.

Outliers

Outliers are valid data points that differ significantly, say more than two standard deviations, from data points near them. The sharp drop in the equity markets on October 19, 1987, is an example.

How should outliers such as these be handled, particularly in the in-sample data? We certainly hope the model will be holding the correct position when a similar outlier occurs again. Those systems that depend on catching a small number of big trades live or die by outliers. If the outlier is included in an in-sample period, no model that is wrong on that date will score well.

The answer depends in part on how the model will be used.
- If it will be used to buy or sell the data series that has the outlier, then that data is very important and should not be modified.
- If the model will be used to buy or sell options on the data series, the effect of being in the wrong position may be minimized – the maximum loss from a debit options position is the amount of the debit.
- If the model will be used as a broad market indicator or filter, then recognizing the sign of the move is more important than being credited for the amount of the move.

One technique to limit the effect of outliers is to limit the gain or loss on any single day. This process is called Winsorizing. All data points above, say, the 95th percentile are given the value of the 95th percentile.

Similarly, those below the 5th percentile are given the value of the 5th percentile. Performing the limit within the trading system before the objective function is computed insures that the outlier will not adversely affect that trading system's rank. In AmiBroker, this can be accomplished by recognizing the large price change and setting the BuyPrice or SellPrice variable to limit the effect of that trade.

Avoid the temptation to add a rule to the trading system to deal with unlikely events.

SECOND EDITION

Prior to the release of AmiBroker version 5.20, November 2008, all optimizations performed an exhaustive search; which meant that every combination of optimization variables was tested. With the release of version 5.20, it is now possible to use "non-exhaustive" search procedures.

OPTIMIZATION

Optimization is the process of finding the maximum or minimum of a given function. Any trading system can be considered to be a function of a number of parameters. The inputs to that function are the parameters to the AFL statements and the price data; the output is your optimization target (say CAR/MDD). You are looking for the arguments that maximize the value of the target. Since all possible combinations are tested when an exhaustive optimization is run, the global optimum of the space being searched will be found.

NON-EXHAUSTIVE OPTIMIZATION

Non-exhaustive (or "smart") methods will find either the global optimum or one of the local optima. The goal is of course to find the global one, but if there is a single sharp peak out of the many parameter combinations, non-exhaustive methods may fail to find this single peak. But, from a trader's perspective, finding the single sharp peak is not the best solution for trading—the resulting trading system would be too unstable and too sensitive to small changes in the data to be useful in real trading. In the optimization process we are rather looking for plateau regions with stable parameters, and this is the area where intelligent methods shine.

Some of smart optimization algorithms, such as the Particle Swarm Optimization and Tribes algorithms, are based on animal behavior;

some, such as Genetic algorithms, on biological processes; some, such as CMA-ES, on mathematical concepts derived by humans.

AmiBroker has several (three, as of this writing) non-exhaustive methods:
1. Covariance Matrix Adaptation Evolutionary Strategy (CMA-ES).
2. Standard Particle Swarm Optimizer (SPSO).
3. Adaptive parameterless particle swarm optimizer (Tribes).

Non-exhaustive search algorithms work as follows:
1. The optimizer generates some (usually random) starting population of parameter sets.
2. A backtest is performed by AmiBroker for each parameter set from that population.
3. The results of backtests are evaluated according to the objective function.
4. A new population of parameter sets is generated based on the results. If a new best is found, save it.
5. Return to step 2 and continue until stopping criteria are met.

Examples of stopping criteria include:
a. Reaching specified maximum number of iterations.
b. Stop if the range of best objective values of last X generations is zero.
c. Stop if adding 0.1 standard deviation vector in any principal axis direction does not change the value of objective value.
d. Others.

QUICK START

The simplest way to use the new non-exhaustive optimizer is to add a single line at the beginning of your AFL. Choose one of the lines shown below. Then start the optimization run as usual (using the Analysis menu, select Automatic Analysis, set up the dates and other parameters as you want them, click Optimize).

```
OptimizerSetEngine ("cmae"); // Use the CMA-ES method
OptimizerSetEngine ("trib"); // Use the Tribes method
OptimizerSetEngine ("spso"); // Use the Particle Swarm Optimization
method
```

There is a pair of additional and optional AFL statements that can also be used to specify the number of runs and the number of evaluations per single run. The behavior of each is engine-dependent. If these statements are omitted, the default values will be used and will probably be satisfactory.

WHICH METHOD TO USE

For relatively easy problems, all three methods will find the same optimal solution in about the same amount of time. As the complexity of the problem increases, CMA-ES may be the best method to use. According to scientific benchmarks, CMA-ES outperforms nine other popular evolutionary strategies (like PSO, Genetic and Differential evolution). Start by using CMA-ES, and by allowing AmiBroker to use the default number of runs and number of evaluations – that is, do not try to set them yourself.

COMPLETE EXAMPLE

The following example code uses CMA-ES method. Note that the parameter space being searched contains 10,000 combinations. If an exhaustive optimization is used, there will be 10,000 entries in the results table. When CMA-ES is used, there will be about 1000 entries in the table and the time required will also be about 10% of that required for the exhaustive optimization.

```
OptimizerSetEngine("cmae");
sl = Optimize("s", 26, 1, 100, 1 );
fa = Optimize("f", 12, 1, 100, 1 );
Buy = Cross( MACD( fa, sl ), 0 );
Sell = Cross( 0, MACD( fa, sl ) );
```

CAVEAT

It is important to understand that all smart optimization methods work best in continuous parameter spaces and with relatively smooth objective functions. If the parameter space is discrete, evolutionary algorithms may have trouble finding the optimal value. This is especially true for binary (on/off) parameters - they are not suited for any search method that uses gradient of objective function change (as most smart methods do). If your trading system contains binary parameters, you should not use smart optimizer directly on them. Instead, switch the binary parameters manually; then make runs to optimize only continuous parameters using smart optimizer.

OBSERVATIONS

It is normal that the procedure will skip some evaluation steps as it detects that the solution has been found. Therefore the optimization progress bar may move very fast at some points. The procedure also has ability to increase the number of steps over what was initially estimated if they are needed to find the solution. Due to the adaptive nature of the procedure, the "estimated time left" and/or "number of steps" displayed by the progress dialog is only a best guess at any time and may vary during the course of the optimization.

Note that decreasing the "step" parameter in Optimize() function calls does not significantly affect optimization times. The only thing that matters is the problem "dimension", that is, the number of different parameters (the number of Optimize function calls). The number of "steps" per parameter can be set without affecting the optimization time, so use the finest resolution you want. In theory the algorithm should be able to find the solution in at most 900*(N+3)*(N+3) backtests where "N" is the dimension. In practice it converges a lot faster. For example the solution in 3 (N=3) dimensional parameter space (say 100*100*100 = 1 million exhaustive steps) can be found in as few as 500-900 CMA-ES steps.

In a forum posting, Tomasz Janeczko states:

"CMAE via its internal convergence logic tends to find plateaus. However, if the size of the problem (of the parameter space) is large and the number of tests is several orders of magnitude smaller, it may find local optima instead of the global one. To determine the stability of the solution you should perform small exhaustive searches near the solution point (these could be as small as +/- one step in each dimension). Without doing that, it is just guessing. Using the source codes provided, it is possible to add extra sensitivity tests into the search, but that does not add as much good as one may think in case of CMAE."

And a forum member wrote:

"You know TJ, now that you put it that way, I think you are right. I am not sure if I should call them "plateaus", but I am referring to groups of similar parameter values that return consistent results. Actually, it does seem to find *some* plateau or another almost always, but often it is not the higher (i.e., most profitable) ones that I

know are there and want it to find. So I think the shorter/
less profitable plateaus are probably broader and more
numerous and easier to find.

Thank you for reminding me about the source code, it looks
like you put a lot of work into commenting and making
it easy for us (thank you!) so I think I can understand
enough of it to make some tweaks if I want to try that
later..."

I will add a caution to beware of having the search for the global best
parameters become the goal – rather than the search for an acceptably
profitable trading system.

All the non-exhaustive procedures are implemented through use of
a plug-in. The full source code for each is included in the ADK.

Please refer to the release notes for version 5.20 and the AmiBroker
User's Guide for more complete description.

19

Statistical Tests

COMPARISON OF TWO MEANS

One of the tests we will want to make is the comparison of two averages – two means. In developing trading systems, we will want to know whether one system has an advantage over another, and the certainty of our conclusion. To illustrate, we will first use an example that might be easier to understand, then go on to examining the validity of trading systems.

Assume that a petroleum chemist has developed a new additive, labeled Treatment B, for gasoline and wants to determine whether it improves gasoline mileage over the formulation currently in use, Treatment A. He performs some tests, gathers some data, computes some statistics, and tests a hypothesis.

STATEMENT OF HYPOTHESIS

The process of comparing two means begins with two statements that, together, include all possibilities. These statements describe the relative gasoline mileage when using Treatment A versus when using Treatment B. The statistical test will be used to reject one of the statements and, therefore, to accept the other. The statements are worded so that the statement the chemist hopes to reject is that his new additive does not improve gasoline mileage. The statement that is set up to be tested is called the Null Hypothesis. The chemist's null hypothesis, named H_0, is:

Treatment B does not improve the gasoline mileage when compared to Treatment A. The alternative statement, named H_1, is: Treatment B does improve the gasoline mileage when compared to Treatment A. Clearly, only one of these two statements can be correct. If the chemist is able to reject H_0, then he accepts H_1, and goes on to file a patent application.

The statistical level at which H_0 will be rejected is usually decided before the data is gathered. The 0.05 level is a good choice, and will be discussed later in this chapter.

COLLECTION OF DATA

He sets up an experiment in which he makes 45 runs on a test track, each 25 miles long, using the existing gasoline formula. He carefully records the gasoline mileage and labels it Treatment A. He makes 45 more runs

Gasoline Treatment Study					
Treatment A			Treatment B		
25.23	25.43	25.22	25.92	26.41	25.91
25.90	24.14	24.21	25.34	25.10	25.54
25.71	24.22	24.04	26.90	26.28	26.05
25.80	25.38	24.71	26.00	26.59	25.22
25.83	24.35	24.09	25.05	26.04	26.22
24.35	25.34	24.97	26.20	25.84	25.20
24.90	25.12	25.94	25.95	25.33	26.80
25.77	24.22	25.20	25.97	25.41	25.90
24.48	24.49	25.31	25.71	26.76	26.42
24.47	24.75	24.56	25.44	26.84	26.14
25.55	25.76	24.29	25.90	26.02	26.50
25.65	25.82	25.43	25.63	26.83	26.46
25.31	24.96	24.56	25.22	25.73	26.28
24.15	25.45	24.69	25.83	26.10	25.05
25.73	25.02	25.10	26.89	25.27	26.01
Mean 25.01			Mean 25.96		
StdDev 0.60			StdDev 0.54		
ZScore 7.90					
FIGURE 19.1 GASOLINE TREATMENT DATA					

using gasoline with his new additive, records the mileage, and labels it Treatment B. The miles per gallon figures are listed in Figure 19.1, along with the mean and standard deviation for both treatments.

The mean value of the 45 test runs using Treatment B is 25.96 miles per gallon, while the mean value for the 45 test runs using Treatment A is 25.01 miles per gallon. Treatment B's mean is greater than Treatment A's. If Treatment B's mileage was lower, the chemist would not have to go any further – he would know that his additive does not help. The question he must answer is: Could the results from his 45 test runs using Treatment B have come from Treatment A's population? That is, are the results because of an improvement, or because of luck? He will never know for certain, but he can assign a probability to the likelihood that the results came from luck. If that probability is small enough, usually 5% or less, then he will be satisfied that the results came from his additive.

When the chemist is making his test track runs using gasoline with the new additive, each run gave him one observation – one sample point actually observed drawn from the infinite population of all points. It is the population that he wants to know about, and each sample he takes – each run he makes – increases his knowledge. But, no matter how many runs he makes, he will not know with certainty the mileage of the population. He will only increase the probability that his estimate is correct. Our inability to know for sure is the reason the analysis is stated as a probability. When two alternatives are compared in laboratory studies, it is common for the result to be stated as, for example, "significant at the 95% level." This means that the null hypothesis can be rejected with 95% confidence – there is less than a 5% probability that the data from the two alternatives came from the same population, which would mean the results from his additive were higher by chance.

The experiment will have its null hypothesis stated in such a way that rejecting the null hypothesis confirms something – usually confirms the point the researcher wants to make. He states the null hypothesis, H_0: Treatment B is not better than Treatment A. That is, the mean of Treatment B is not higher than the mean of Treatment A. He states the alternative hypothesis, H_1: Treatment B is better than Treatment A.

One method of testing whether the two treatments are different is performed by computing the z-score associated with the two experiments. After first computing the mean and standard deviation of each set of results, the z-score is computed:

$$z = \frac{\left(\bar{X}_1 - \bar{X}_2\right)}{\sigma\left(\bar{x}_1 - \bar{x}_2\right)}$$

where, $\sigma_{(\bar{x}_1 - \bar{x}_2)} = \sqrt{\dfrac{var_1}{N_1} + \dfrac{var_2}{N_2}}$

In our example, $z = \dfrac{(25.96 - 25.01)}{\sqrt{\dfrac{0.60 * 0.60}{45} + \dfrac{0.54 * 0.54}{45}}} = 7.90$

STATISTICAL SIGNIFICANCE

Since the mean mileage for Treatment B is greater than the mean mileage for treatment A, and our chemist is only interested in further research for his new additive if it improves gasoline mileage, he decides to use a single-tailed test. The value of 7.90 represents the number of standard errors of the mean that the mean for Treatment B is greater than the mean for Treatment A. Is that a large enough number to justify a decision? There are statistical tables and formulas that tell us what the probability is that two sets of data could have come from the same distribution for any given z-score. The 95% level of confidence corresponds to a probability of 0.05. The z-score associated with 0.05 is 1.65; the z-score associated with 0.01 is 2.33. The probability associated with a z-score of 7.90 is much less than 0.000001 – one part in a million. Based on that probability, he rejects H_0, the null hypothesis, and accepts H_1, the alternative hypothesis. Note that he is never absolutely certain that his additive helped, only that the chance that it did not help is very, very small.

The graph that follows in Figure 19.2 shows the distribution of observed data from the two sets of test runs.

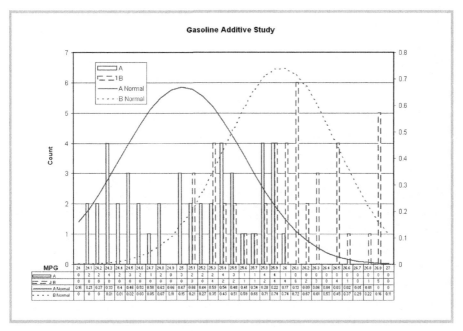

FIGURE 19.2 GASOLINE ADDITIVE STUDY

TYPE I AND TYPE II ERRORS

If there is no certainty, then there must be a possibility of making the wrong decision – rejecting H_0 when it should not have been rejected, or accepting H_0 when it should have been rejected. A diagram will help.

		Observed	
		H_0 True, H_1 False	H_0 False, H_1 True
Actual	H_0 True, H_1 False	Observations correctly confirm, or at least do not reject, H_0	**Type I Error.** Observations incorrectly reject H_0, implying H_1 is true when it is not.
	H_0 False, H_1 True	**Type II Error.** Observations incorrectly confirm H_0 as True, when H_1 is True.	Observations correctly reject H_0, implying H_1 is true.

FIGURE 19.3 TYPE I AND TYPE II ERRORS

APPLICATION TO TRADING SYSTEMS

Moving on to data that results from a trading system, we want to ask whether the new system is superior to a baseline system, which is perhaps a system that takes positions at random.

H_0, the null hypothesis, states: The New System is indistinguishable from a Random System. H_1, the alternative hypothesis, states: The New System is better than a Random System.

We want H_1 to be true, so we want to reject H_0. To do this, we collect observations about both the Random System and the New System, then describe the mean of the New System's observations in terms of the Random System's.

The level of confidence that you, as the person responsible for making your own trades, require is up to you. It need not be 95%, but the higher it is, the more likely your trading system will be profitable when traded.

Assume end-of-day data is being used, trades are held some number of days, and the day by day percentage gain over a fixed period of time for both systems can be recorded. If this is the test that will be used to decide whether or not to trade the New System, be certain that the data collected for this test is coming from out-of-sample periods. If either the baseline system or the New System has been optimized over this period, the resulting data will not be representative.

The New System has a total of 340 days in trades, mean gain of 0.0025 (0.25%) per day, standard deviation of 0.006; the Random System has a total of 225 days in trades, mean gain of 0.0020 (0.20%) per day, standard deviation 0.005.

We can apply the same calculations as the chemist.

$$\text{In our example, } z = \frac{(0.0025 - 0.0020)}{\sqrt{\dfrac{0.006 * 0.006}{340} + \dfrac{0.005 * 0.005}{225}}} = 1.07$$

The critical value for z for a one-tailed test at the 0.05 level is 1.65. (It always will be.) This implies that we cannot reject the null hypothesis at the 95% level, or even at the 90% level, where the critical value is 1.28. We can reject the null hypothesis at about the 85% level. That is, the results from the New System appear to be better than those of the Random System, but they could have resulted by chance – about once in every six times we perform the tests we could get results this good by chance.

The risk of rejecting H_0 and accepting H_1 is the risk of a Type I Error – the risk of trading an invalid system.

A MAJOR DIFFICULTY arises when designing statistical tests to be applied to trading results. The data points being analyzed are either the profit or loss from closed trades or day-to-day equity changes. Measuring as a percentage normalizes the data. The standard deviation of a series of trading outcomes typically exceeds the mean of that same series. Take any out-of-sample trading result and compute percent profit per trade for all closed trades. Then compute the mean and standard deviation of profit per trade in a 20 trade moving window. Invariably, the standard deviation is large in relation to the mean, and often exceeds it. Consequently, the lower limit of a plus-or-minus two standard deviation confidence interval is a negative number — so the statistical test of whether the mean could be zero says that indeed the mean could be zero. That is, these results could have come from a profitless system and results are profitable strictly from luck. Increasing the number of trades or days being analyzed reduces the width of the confidence bands, but increases the lag time between the time the system breaks and the time the statistical test verify that.

CHI-SQUARE TEST

Often we wish to know whether observed frequencies differ significantly from expected frequencies. For example, we ask whether one set of observed daily change data could have come from a normally distributed population with the same mean and standard deviation.

The chi-square test is a measure of the discrepancy between observed and expected frequencies.

Data to be analyzed using a one-way classification fits into a table such as the following:

Event	E_1	E_2	E_3	...	E_k
Observed Frequency	o1	o2	o3	...	ok
Expected Frequency	e1	e2	e3	...	ek

FIGURE 19.3 CHI-SQUARED CLASSIFICATION

Degrees of freedom = v = number of categories minus 1, that is, k - 1.

The chi-squared statistic is computed as:

$$\chi^2 = \frac{(o_1 - e_1)^2}{e_1} + \frac{(o_2 - e_2)^2}{e_2} + \cdots + \frac{(o_k - e_k)^2}{e_k}$$

$$\chi^2 = \sum_{i=1}^{k} \frac{(o_i - e_i)^2}{e_i}$$

If the total frequency is N,

$$\sum o_i = \sum e_i = N,$$

Then an equivalent expression is

$$\chi^2 = \sum \frac{o_i^2}{e_i} - N.$$

If $\chi^2 = 0$, observed and expected frequencies agree exactly.

The larger the value of χ^2, the greater the discrepancy.

If necessary, lump events together so that every event has at least a count of five for the expected frequency.

EXAMPLE (NOT FROM TRADING)

A coin is tossed 200 times and comes up heads 115 of those. The null hypothesis is that the coin is fair. Can we reject that hypothesis? If so, at what level of confidence?

Event	Heads	Tails
Observed Frequency	115	85
Expected Frequency	100	100

$$\chi^2 = \frac{(115 - 100)^2}{100} + \frac{(85 - 100)^2}{100} = 4.50$$
$$\nu = 2 - 1 = 1$$

Look up the percentile in a table.

For $\nu = 1, \chi^2_{.95} = 3.84, \chi^2_{.99} = 5.02$.

Since 4.50 > 3.84, the hypothesis can be rejected at the .05 level. But 4.50 < 5.02, so it cannot be rejected at the .01 level. The coin is probably not a fair coin.

WHY 30?

So many articles talk about the number of items being analyzed statistically and want a minimum of 30. There are a couple reasons.

For one reason, several important probability distributions have a behavior that is unique when the number of items being analyzed is small, but behave like the normal distribution when the number is large. The transition between small and large happens at about 30. The binomial distribution is one such example. "Student's t" distribution is another.

For another, when samples are drawn from a population and analyzed, corrections based on the sample size are necessary when the sample is small. For example, sample statistics, such as the standard deviation, are adjusted by multiplying them by $\sqrt{\dfrac{N}{N-1}}$ to estimate population parameters. When N is greater than about 30, the adjustment is less important and usually omitted.

When analyzing out-of-sample results, it is useful to test whether the the system is better than random—whether the results obtained could have come from a population with a mean of zero. When performing the statistical test, assume that the standard deviation of the random results have the same standard deviation as the out-of-sample results. The confidence factors are higher with more trades, but the calculations can be done with any number.

Reiterating a very important point, it is essential that tests, whether by eye-balling the equity curve or by formal tests of statistical significance, be used to compare only results from out-of-sample data. When in-sample results are analyzed, there is no number of closed trades, or of anything else, that is large enough to assure profitable out-of-sample performance. In-sample results are essentially meaningless. They are always good. We do not stop optimizing until they are good.

When development of a trading is complete, there is a high level of confidence that the system is working. After it has been traded for a period of time, performance will vary and eventually deteriorate. One of the most important questions is whether the trading system is working or is broken. Should it be traded with high position size, traded at reduced position size, or taken offline. *Modeling Trading System Performance* addresses that question, discussing several easily applied statistical tests.

20

Walk Forward Testing

WALK FORWARD TESTING is a process for mechanizing and automating the search for profitable, stable trading systems that adapt to changing market conditions.

It is easy to verify that markets change characteristics. Program any trading system and optimize it so that it is acceptable over some period of time. Acceptable in the sense that the objective function you prefer scores well – high profit, low drawdown, etcetera. Extend the time period and test again. Most likely there are periods of acceptable performance scattered among unacceptable periods. Look at the equity curve – it rises and falls. Without exception, the longer the time period tested, the worse the average performance will be. A trading system is a combination of a trading model and a market. The model did not change. So the market must have changed.

When using the walk forward technique, the time period is shortened in the hope that the market and the trading system remain in synchronization throughout – remain stationary, in statistical terms. If they do not eventually synchronize, then either the time period is too long, the market data is too low in information content, or the system is inadequate. If they do remain in synchronization for a period of time, we want that period to include all of the in-sample time plus enough out-of-sample time so that the market can be traded profitably. Stationarity is measured with respect to a specific model. Over the same period of data, a model might be stationary with respect to a moving average system, but not with respect to a breakout system.

As illustrated in figure 20.1, two lengths of time are chosen. One is

275

the length of the in-sample period, the other the length of the out-of-sample period. The out-of-sample period always immediately follows the in-sample period.

The model is optimized over the in-sample data, the best values for the optimization variables are selected and coded into the program, and the system is tested over the out-of-sample period. The out-of-sample results are saved, the start of the in-sample period is moved forward in time the length of the out-of-sample period, and the process is repeated. After all of the data has been processed, including yesterday, the out-of-sample results are concatenated together and examined – they provide an unbiased estimate of the performance we might expect when this procedure is continued and traded. If the equity curve and other trade statistics from the out-of-sample periods are acceptable, then the model can be traded. At the end of what would be the out-of-sample time period, the in-sample period is moved forward, the model reoptimized, and trading continues using the newly optimized parameter values.

The two lengths, the in-sample length and the out-of-sample length, are parameters of the model and are available for optimization themselves. Like other parameters of the model, they should be tested for stability. The specific amount of time between reoptimizations should be unimportant. Test this by reoptimizing after various lengths of time, much as you would test varying the length of a moving average. If the system is stable, the amount of time between reoptimizations will be forgiving. If results vary widely with small changes in the time between reoptimizations, then the system is unstable and probably unreliable.

The objective function must be predetermined and is not available for optimization. The highest ranking values must be accepted at every walk forward step.

Dakota carries this to an extreme, and does it very effectively. The validation period is one bar long.

No matter how validation is performed, including walk forward testing, it cannot guarantee that actual trades will be profitable. But strict adherence to rigorous validation increases the confidence in the model and the probability of profitable trades.

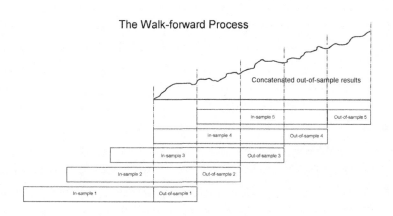

The Walk-forward Process

Concatenated out-of-sample results

In-sample 5	Out-of-sample 5
In-sample 4	Out-of-sample 4
In-sample 3	Out-of-sample 3
In-sample 2	Out-of-sample 2
In-sample 1	Out-of-sample 1

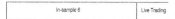

| In-sample 6 | Live Trading |

FIGURE 20.1 WALK FORWARD PROCESS

A WALK FORWARD EXAMPLE

Figure 20.2 shows the AFL code for a trading system called CCT CMO.

```
// CCT CMO Oscillator.afl
//
//   A CMO Oscillator
//
//

//   Two variables are set up for optimizing
CMOPeriods=Optimize("pds",21,1,101,10);
AMAAvg=Optimize("AMAAvg",96,1,101,5);

//   The change in the closing price is summed
//   into two variables -- up days and down days
SumUp = Sum(IIf(C>Ref(C,-1),(C-Ref(C,-1)),0),CMOPeriods);
SumDown = Sum(IIf(C<Ref(C,-1),(Ref(C,-1)-C),0),CMOPeriods);

//   The CMO Oscillator calculation
CMO = 100 * (SumUp - SumDown) / (SumUp + SumDown);

//Plot(CMO,"CMO",colorGreen,styleLine);

//   Smooth the CMO Oscillator
CMOAvg = DEMA(CMO,AMAAvg);
//   And smooth it again to form a trigger line
Trigger = DEMA(CMOAvg,3);
//   Buy when the smoothed oscillator crosses
```

```
//    up through the trigger line
Buy = Cross(CMOAvg,Trigger);
//    Sell on a downward cross, or 6 days,
//    whichever comes first
Sell = Cross(Trigger,CMOAvg) OR BarsSince(Buy)>=6;

Buy = ExRem(Buy,Sell);
Sell = ExRem(Sell,Buy);

Plot(C,"C",colorBlack,styleCandle);

PlotShapes(Buy*shapeUpArrow+Sell*shapeDownArrow,
    IIf(Buy,colorGreen,colorRed));
Plot (CMOAvg,"CMOAvg",colorGreen,
    style=styleLine|styleOwnScale|styleThick,-100,100);
```

FIGURE 20.2 CMO OSCILLATOR

The walk forward testing for this system was done using a single tradable, XLB, the S&P Materials ETF. The in-sample optimization period was two years, beginning January 1. The out-of-sample validation period was one year, beginning January 1 immediately following the in-sample period. The optimization was done five times.

I.   The first in-sample period was 1/1/2001 to 1/1/2003, followed by out-of-sample 1/1/2003 to 1/1/2004.
II. The second in-sample period was 1/1/2002 to 1/1/2004, followed by out-of-sample 1/1/2004 to 1/1/2005.
III. The third in-sample period was 1/1/2003 to 1/1/2005, followed by out-of-sample 1/1/2005 to 1/1/2006.
IV. The fourth in-sample period was 1/1/2004 to 1/1/2006, followed by out-of-sample 1/1/2006 to 1/1/2007.
V.   The final in-sample period was 1/1/2005 to 1/1/2007, followed by live trading if the results are acceptable.

A series of Figures, 20.3 through 20.17, illustrates the process of manually performing a walk forward analysis. The steps are numbered in roman numerals to indicate which walk forward period is being analyzed.

Before starting the walk forward, test the code and select the issue that will be used for the optimization.
• From the Automatic Analysis menu, pick the formula file.
• Apply to should be set to current symbol.
• Make certain the options under the Settings menus are as you want them.
• On the Report Tab, be sure Trade List is selected.

- Decide which metric will be used to rank the optimization results
  – I have picked K-ratio, just as it is provided by AmiBroker.

I. Set the date range to 1/1/2001 to 1/1/2003.
    - Click Optimize.
    - Sort the results by K-ratio.
    - Record the parameter values that rank highest.
    - Modify the AFL code so those values will be used on the next
      Backtest run.
    - Change the To date to 1/1/2004.
    - Click Test.
    - Note the profit on 1/1/2003, the last in-sample date, and the
      profit on 1/1/2004, the last out-of-sample date.
    - Click the Export button and save the trade list to a file in
      comma separated value (CSV) format. Give the file a name
      associated with the ticker, the system, and the beginning out-
      of-sample date.

Figure 20.3 shows Automatic Analysis ready to click Optimize for the
first walk forward step.

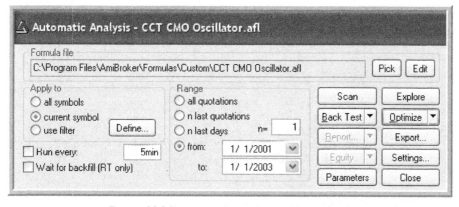

FIGURE 20.3 READY TO CLICK OPTIMIZE FOR WF 1

After optimizing, sort the results by K-ratio. Figure 20.4 shows the highest ranking results.

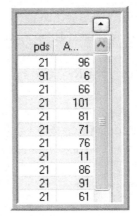

FIGURE 20.4 WF 1 BEST VALUES

Figure 20.5 shows the test results for both the two year in-sample and one year out-of-sample. The values of the optimizable variables have been set to those that were highest ranking.

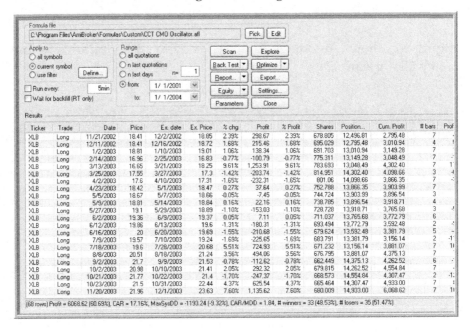

FIGURE 20.5 WF 1 OUT-OF-SAMPLE RESULTS

II. Change the From date to be 1/1/2002. The date range is now 1/1/2002 to 1/1/2004.
- Click optimize.
- Sort.
- Record.
- Modify the code.
- Change the To date to 1/1/2005.

- Click Test.
- Export.

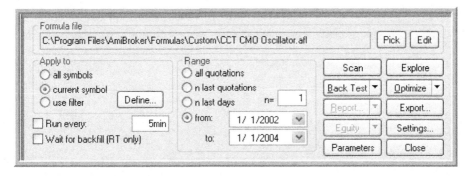

FIGURE 20.6 READY TO CLICK OPTIMIZE FOR WF 2

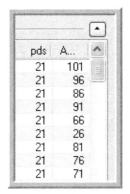

FIGURE 20.7 WF 2 BEST VALUES

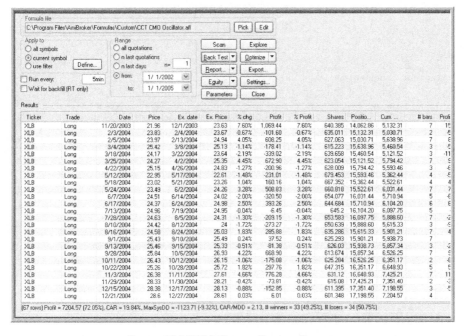

FIGURE 20.8 WF 2 OUT-OF-SAMPLE RESULTS

III. Change the From date to 1/1/2003.
- The date range is now 1/1/2003 to 1/1/2005.
- Perform the same steps.

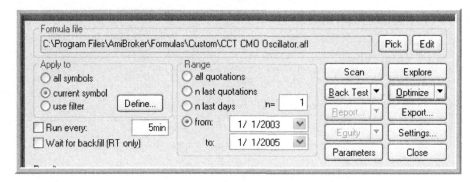

FIGURE 20.9 READY TO CLICK OPTIMIZE FOR WF 3

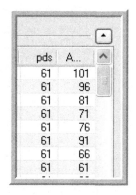

FIGURE 20.10 WF 3 BEST VALUES

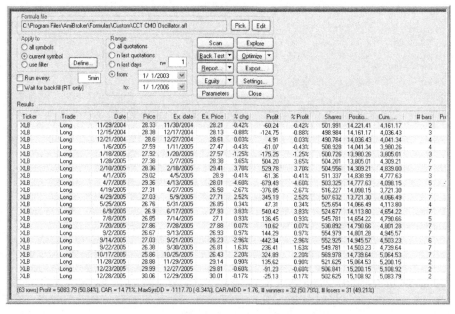

FIGURE 20.11 WF 3 OUT-OF-SAMPLE RESULTS

IV. The date range is now 1/1/2004 to 1/1/2006. Perform the same steps.

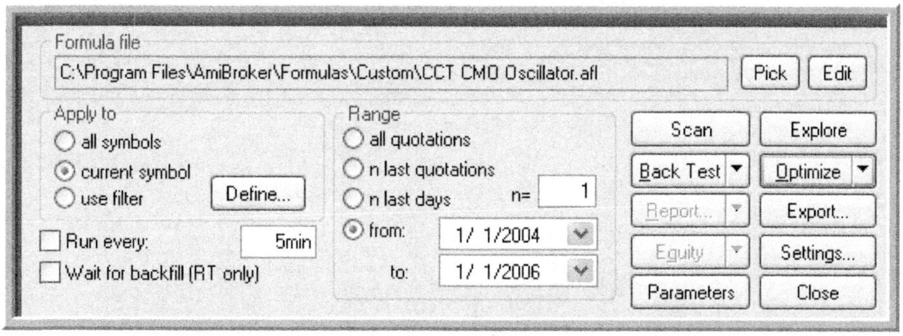

FIGURE 20.12 READY TO CLICK OPTIMIZE FOR WF 4

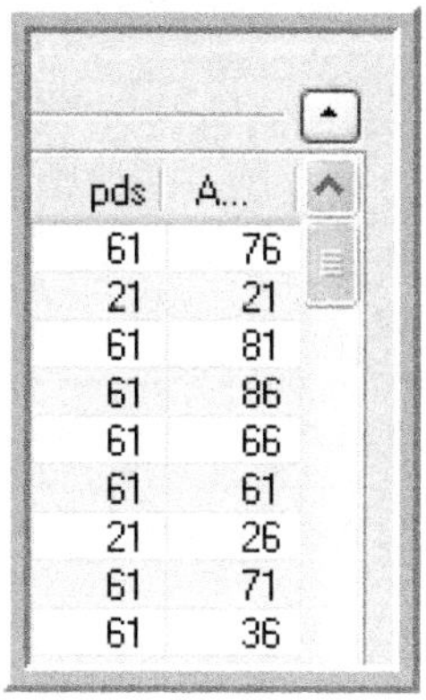

FIGURE 20.13 WF 4 BEST VALUES

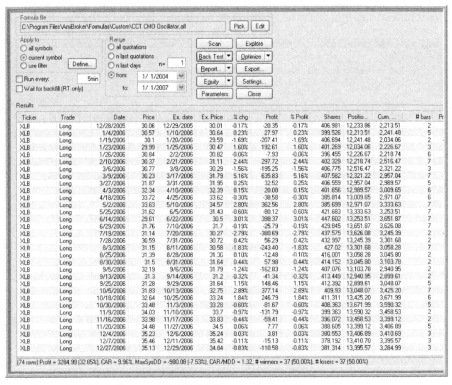

FIGURE 20.14 WF 4 OUT-OF-SAMPLE RESULTS

V. The date range is now 1/1/2005 to 1/1/2007. This is the last full optimization period, so it will be the last optimization.

- Sort by K-ratio.
- Record the parameter values that rank highest.
- Modify the code so those values will be used for the next tests, and to generate the buy and sell signals. Since this chapter is being written early 2007, there is only a short out-of-sample period.
- Export the out-of-sample results.

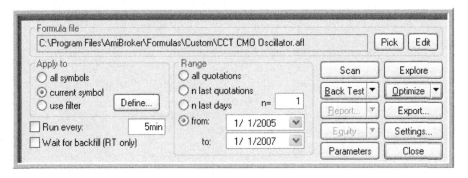

FIGURE 20.15 READY TO CLICK OPTIMIZE FOR WF 5

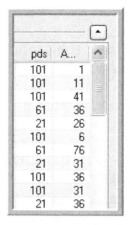

FIGURE 20.16 WF 5 BEST VALUES

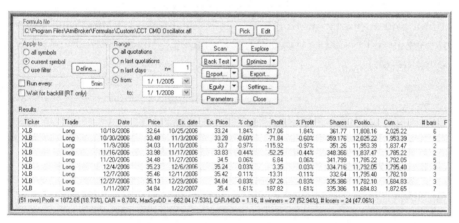

FIGURE 20.17 WF 5 OUT-OF-SAMPLE RESULTS

Figure 20.18 shows the in-sample and out-of-sample results for walk forward step V. Out-of-sample begins at the vertical bar.

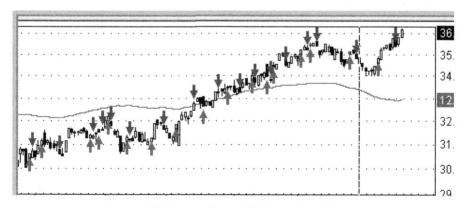

FIGURE 20.18 EQUITY CURVE WF 5 PLUS LIVE TRADES

Go to the directory where the CSV files were saved, and open all five files with a spreadsheet. Each file holds the in-sample and out-of-sample for one of the walk forward steps. Using the cut and paste capabilities of the spreadsheet, put all of the out-of-sample trades into a single time-ordered column. Because each of the walk forward steps has taken a different computational path, and the number of shares and equity will have discontinuities, you will have to work with the changes in price from trade entry to trade exit. Perform whatever analysis you wish on these results, then decide whether to trade this model – that is the combination of this code and this ticker.

Figure 20.19 shows the equity curve resulting from concatenating together the out-of-sample data from the four full years 2003, 2004, 2005, 2006 and the portion of 2007. The straightness of the out-of-sample equity curve is 96.5%. $10,000 as of 1/1/2003 becomes $16,670 1/22/2007 – a compound annual growth rate of 13.5%. It is unusual to find out-of-sample results with such a straight equity curve. This appears to be a very robust model.

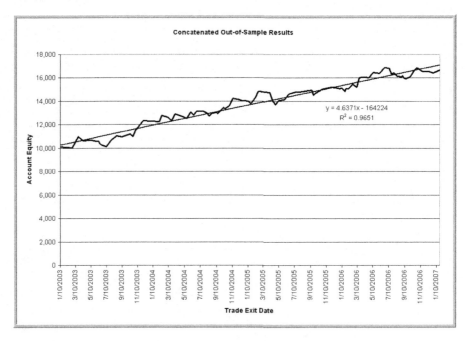

Figure 20.19 Combined Out-of-Sample Equity Curve

The in-sample results are interesting for comparison. Figure 20.20 shows the equity curve resulting from 1/1/2001 to 1/1/2003 from step I, then the second in-sample year from each of the other steps. The straightness of the equity curve is 98.6%. $10,000 on 1/1/2003 becomes $21,350 on 1/1/2007 – a compound annual growth rate of 13.5%.

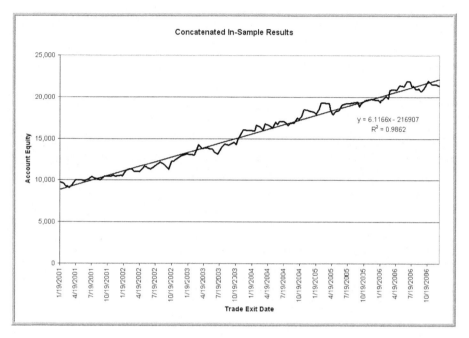

FIGURE 20.20 COMBINED IN-SAMPLE EQUITY CURVE

The annual growth rate over the out-of-sample period is equal to that of the in-sample period. This is unusual. It is an indication that the model has discovered a stable relationship and that it is likely to remain profitable. Since the out-of-sample performance is so good, a drop in out-of-sample profitability will signal that no trades should be taken until the model returns to its 13% annual profitability trend line.

AUTOMATING THE WALK FORWARD PROCESS

The walk forward analysis just described and illustrated was done by hand. Automating the walk forward process both makes it possible to check many alternatives in much less time and with much less effort, and removes some of the bias caused by peeking at the out-of-sample results while adjusting the model.

SECOND EDITION

At the time the first edition of *Quantitative Trading Systems* was written, AmiBroker's automated walk forward feature was still under development. Two programs that did support automated walk forward were mentioned—Intelligent Optimizer and Dakota.

INTELLIGENT OPTIMIZER

Intelligent Optimizer is an add-on to AmiBroker that provides automatic walk forward testing. The current release of it can be downloaded from the Yahoo AmiBroker Group's file directory.

DAKOTA

Dakota, a product of BioComp Systems, Inc., is a stand-alone platform for trading system development, validation, and trading. It uses adaptive techniques to produce 100% out-of-sample results.

AMIBROKER

Automatic walk forward testing was introduced in May 2008 with AmiBroker 5.10. It is included in both standard and professional versions of AmiBroker at no additional cost.

In the example given on pages 273 to 283, the person developing the system manually changed the dates to select different periods for in-sample optimization and out-of-sample testing. In the example that follows, that same analysis is repeated using automated walk forward testing. The AFL code shown in Figure 20.2 is used again, without any changes. The objective function, in-sample periods, and out-of-sample periods are the same as those previously used. These settings are set up using the Analysis menu, Automatic Analysis, Settings. Figures 20.21, 20.22, and 20.23 show the details.

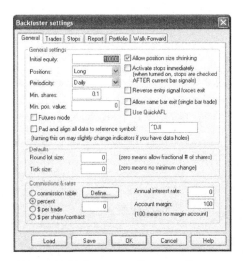

FIGURE 20.21 SETTINGS - GENERAL TAB

FIGURE 20.22 SETTINGS - TRADES TAB

The settings are selected on the Walk-Forward tab, as shown in Figure 20.23. The numbered steps refer to the numbers on that figure.

2. Select the Easy Mode that corresponds to your bar length. If you are using intra-day bars, select Easy mode (intra-day); if you are using end-of-day data, select Easy mode (EOD).
3. Select the date to use as the start of the first in-sample period.
4. Select the date to be used as the end of the first in-sample period.
5. Select the date to be used as the end of the last in-sample period.
6 and 7.   Select the length of the out-of-sample period.

8. Select the objective function.
   Verify that the in-sample and out-of-sample periods are what you want them to be.
9. Click OK to save the settings and exit Settings.

I recommend that you leave Anchored Unchecked.

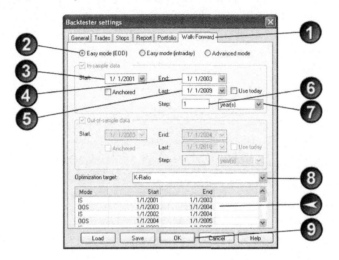

FIGURE 20.23 SETTINGS - WALK-FORWARD TAB

Each in-sample (IS) and out-of-sample (OOS) pair constitutes one step in the walk forward process. When the automatic walk forward is run, AmiBroker accumulates the in-sample equity and out-of-sample equity from each step, concatenates them together, and stores them as "~~~IS-EQUITY" and "~~~OOSEQUITY" in Group253. These two data series are available for later analysis, and they can be plotted automatically during the walk forward run.

As shown in Figure 20.24, and before initiating the walk forward, Insert the Equity function IS_OOS_Equity function so it will plot in a pane on your chart. If you do not already have that function, you can find it in the AmiBroker help files; or simply create it yourself using the Function Editor. That function has only three lines. They are:

```
PlotForeign("~~~ISEQUITY","In-Sample Equity", colorRed, styleLine);
PlotForeign("~~~OSEQUITY","Out-Of-Sample Equity",colorGreen, styleLine);
Title = "{{NAME}} - {{INTERVAL}} {{DATE}} {{VALUES}}";
```

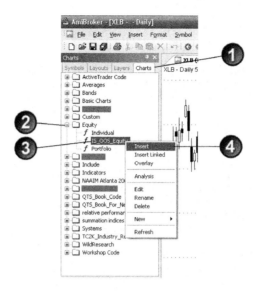

FIGURE 20.24 INSERT THE IS_OOS_EQUITY PLOT

Initiate the walk forward run by using the Optimize pull-down menu, then click Walk-Forward Optimization, as shown in Figure 20.25.

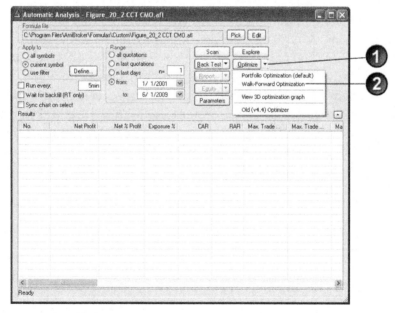

FIGURE 20.25 INITIATE THE WALK FORWARD OPTIMIZATION

The results of the walk forward steps are shown in Figures 20.26. These can be found on the Walk Forward tab of the main chart.

Mode	Begin	End	No.	Net Profit	Net % Profit	Exposure %	CAR	RAR		pds	AMAAvg
IS	1/1/2001	1/1/2003	212	3166.67	31.67	35.20	14.79	42.02		21	96
OOS	1/1/2003	1/1/2004	1	2317.25	23.17	33.33	23.31	69.94		21	96
IS	1/1/2002	1/1/2004	21	3967.67	39.68	49.40	18.24	36.92		91	6
OOS	1/1/2004	1/1/2005	1	-213.49	-2.13	48.81	-2.14	-4.39		91	6
IS	1/1/2003	1/1/2005	205	4115.66	41.16	33.33	18.84	56.51		61	91
OOS	1/1/2005	1/1/2006	1	1006.68	10.07	37.30	10.18	27.30		61	91
IS	1/1/2004	1/1/2006	183	3258.87	32.59	33.33	15.19	45.58		61	81
OOS	1/1/2006	1/1/2007	1	970.51	9.71	40.64	9.85	24.23		61	81
IS	1/1/2005	1/1/2007	33	3923.60	39.24	43.13	18.13	40.18		101	11
OOS	1/1/2007	1/1/2008	1	1172.29	11.72	49.00	11.83	24.13		101	11
IS	1/1/2006	1/1/2008	7	5745.50	57.45	49.00	25.60	52.24		61	1
OOS	1/1/2008	1/1/2009	1	-2179.99	-21.80	49.01	-21.85	-44.59		61	1
IS	1/1/2007	1/1/2009	7	50.90	0.51	50.20	0.25	0.51		61	1
OOS	1/1/2009	1/1/2010	1	-202.26	-2.02	48.04	-4.95	-10.30		61	1

FIGURE 20.26 WALK FORWARD RESULTS

Figure 20.27 shows the in-sample and out-of-sample equity curves from the automatic walk forward run in mid-2009 and presented with the addendum to the first edition.

The system that was described in the original printing of *Quantitative Trading Systems* showed good profit growth and a smooth equity curve. The manual walk forward run used data that ended January 22, 2007 – Point "A". The system continued to be profitable throughout the remainder of 2007 and well into 2008 – area "B". Performance fell off around July 2008 – Point "C". As noted in the original text, page 273, this system had exceptionally smooth results. When the equity curve deteriorated at Point "C", the system should have been taken offline. It should be periodically reviewed and not traded again until the results show that market conditions have returned to the state that this system can again be safely traded.

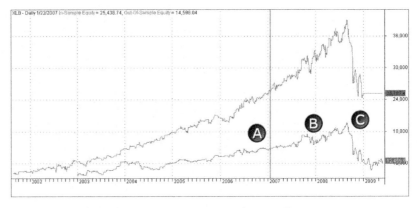

FIGURE 20.27 IN-SAMPLE AND OUT-OF-SAMPLE EQUITY

Note that the 2007 out-of-sample performance was achieved using the best parameters found by testing and optimizing the 2005 and 2006 in-sample period. The 2008 out-of-sample performance was achieved using the best parameters found by testing and optimizing the 2006 and 2007 in-sample period. When the 2007 and 2008 data was used as in-sample data, searching for the best parameters to use to trade in 2009, the in-sample performance deteriorated badly. This is an indication that even using the best set of arguments, the model cannot be brought into sync with the data, and the system should not be traded.

Observant readers will note that the parameter values chosen as best differ slightly between the manual test and the automatic test. This is probably due to slight differences in the historical price data between the two runs. Which reinforces the recommendation that the historical data used to develop a system and the current data used to generate trading signals come from the same data vendor.

This system was brought up to date again in May 2011. Figure 20.28 shows the in-sample and out-of-sample equity curves.

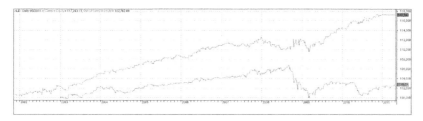

FIGURE 20.28 IN-SAMPLE AND OUT-OF-SAMPLE AS OF MAY 2011

Performance out-of-sample, as it might have been traded, is excellent for the period through mid-2008, then falls off. It recovers in 2009, falls off again, and recovers in 2010.

We would all like to see out-of-sample equity curves that are smooth and upward sloping without interruption. But that seldom happens. One of the keys to successfully trading a system like this one is being able to determine when the system is performing well and when it is broken. Applying statistical tests to the out-of-sample results will show when that the model and the data have fallen out of sync, and when they are back together.

Allowing the walk forward parameters finer resolution, and adding a profit target and a maximum holding period, the results improve. Figure 20.29 shows the results for long positions.

FIGURE 20.29 IS AND OOS RESULTS - LONG - FINER RESOLUTION

Figure 20.30 shows the results for short positions. While you might not be trading the short positions, the equity curve is so stable that signals to go short can be used as signals to exit long positions, which may help overall performance.

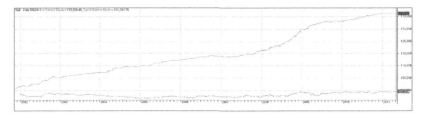

FIGURE 20.30 IS AND OOS RESULTS - SHORT

REMEMBER – if you do not have acceptable test results on a truly out-of-sample data period, then out-of-sample testing begins tomorrow with real money.

21

Survivor Bias

IN MANY PROFESSIONS, such as music, law, and physics, success is based on skill. A person who is untrained and unskilled is unlikely to succeed. Even less likely is that a high percentage of practitioners in any of those fields could be unskilled and still succeed in them.

In financial management skill is not required to be successful. Certainly some managers, advisors, and traders are both skilled and successful. Others are skilled but not successful. Still others are unskilled but lucky.

Fund managers, investment advisors, newsletter writers, and individual traders who were in the right place during the right time were very likely to have made a lot of money. 1988 through 1999 was a great time to hold long equity positions. Those who made the wrong choices were very likely to have lost money, perhaps a lot of money. If we look up the performance statistics for currently active managers and advisors for that period of time, we will see the results for those who were successful. Those who were not successful have gone on to other careers and their records are not available.

Similarly for hedge funds. Those that do well attract more money to manage. Those that do poorly, even after doing well for a long period, often go out of business, perhaps to be reincarnated by the same people, but with a new name and a new performance report. The history of poor performance disappears.

Both broad and focused indices also suffer from survivor bias. A common method of selecting companies to test trading systems is to choose those which are members of the S&P 500 index, S&P 100 index, or the NASDAQ 100 index. When we test long-only positions from 1990 to date for companies that are members of the index, we will see better results than we would if we formed a group of all members of the index as of 1990 and traded them forward. The companies that drop to the bottom of the ranking are dropped from the index and replaced by companies that the index manager thinks will do better in the future. This manipulation of the membership of the index is carried to an extreme with the Dow Jones Industrial Average, which is so managed that it is almost meaningless.

And it is not just indices — mutual fund managers rebalance their portfolios to maintain higher weights in top performing stocks. The top ten holdings for any sector fund today are certain to be far different than the top ten holdings a decade ago.

The table 21.1 that follows lists all of the companies that were members of the NASDAQ 100 index in 1999 but are no longer, those that are members as of January 2007 but were not in 1999, and those that have been members throughout. It is interesting to buy each stock as of 1/1/1995 and hold them through 1/1/2007. Compare the RAR columns in Figures 21.1, 21.2, and 21.3.

Stocks in NASDAQ 100						
1999	2007	Both		1999	2007	Both
ADCT	AEOS	AAPL		MCLD	JNPR	PAYX
ADPT	AKAM	ADBE		MKC	JOYG	PCAR
AFM	AMLN	ADSK		MLHR	LAMR	QCOM
ANDW	ATVI	ALTR		MOLX	LBTYA	ROST
ASND	BEAS	AMAT		MU	LINTA	SBUX
ATML	BIIB	AMGN		NET	LRCX	SIAL
BGEN	BRCM	AMZN		NOVL	MEDI	SPLS
BMC	CDNS	APCC		NSCP	MICC	SUNW
CATP	CDWC	APOL		NWAC	MNST	TLAB
CBRL	CELG	BBBY		NXTL	MRVL	XLNX
CE	CHKP	BMET		PHS	NIHD	YHOO
CEXP	CHRW	CSCO		PMTC	NTAP	
CHIR	CKFR	CTAS		PSFT	NVDA	
CMCSK	CMCSA	CTXS		Q	PDCO	
CNTO	CMVT	DELL		QNTM	PETM	
COMR	COST	ERTS		QTRN	PTEN	
COMS	CTSH	FAST		RTRSY	RIMM	

Stocks in NASDAQ 100						
1999	2007	Both		1999	2007	Both
COST	DISCA	FISV		RXSD	SEPR	
CPWR	DISH	GENZ		SANM	SHLD	
DLTR	EBAY	IACI		SNPS	SIRI	
DZA	ERIC	INTC		SPOT	SNDK	
EFII	ESRX	INTU		SSCC	SYMC	
ERICY	EXPD	KLAC		STEI	TEVA	
FHCC	EXPE	LLTC		TCOMA	VRSN	
FORE	FLEX	LVLT		TECD	VRTX	
HBOC	GILD	MCHP		VRTS	WFMI	
IMNX	GOOG	MSFT		VTSS	WYNN	
JCOR	GRMN	MXIM		WCOEQ	XMSR	
JWN	INFY	NTLI		WOR	XRAY	
LNCR	ISRG	ORCL				

TABLE 21.1 NASDAQ TICKERS 1999 AND 2007

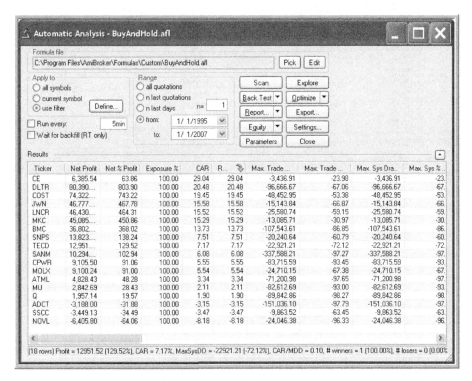

FIGURE 21.1 RESULTS FROM BUY AND HOLD 1999 STOCKS

Ticker	Net Profit	Net % Profit	Exposure %	CAR	RAR
NIHD	447,021.29	4,470.21	100.00	153.78	153.78
SHLD	101,953.34	1,019.53	100.00	93.37	93.37
GOOG	35,891.97	358.92	100.00	90.63	90.63
CTSH	919,638.60	9,196.39	100.00	70.07	70.07
WYNN	67,052.55	670.53	100.00	62.97	62.97
CELG	1,297,500.04	12,975.00	100.00	50.12	50.12
BIIB	1,219,750.00	12,197.50	100.00	49.36	49.36
JOYG	59,155.94	591.56	100.00	41.75	41.75
NVDA	140,447.15	1,404.47	100.00	40.70	40.70
GILD	544,957.28	5,449.57	100.00	39.77	39.77
MEDI	529,499.98	5,295.00	100.00	39.44	39.44
EBAY	142,639.59	1,426.40	100.00	39.04	39.04
AEOS	470,153.87	4,701.54	100.00	38.10	38.10
NTAP	296,875.00	2,968.75	100.00	36.09	36.09
EXPD	314,000.00	3,140.00	100.00	33.64	33.64
SEPR	297,900.00	2,979.00	100.00	33.07	33.07
PTEN	269,879.53	2,698.80	100.00	32.03	32.03
DISH	174,611.66	1,746.12	100.00	28.77	28.77
ATVI	137,480.88	1,374.81	88.57	25.15	28.40
WFMI	174,055.12	1,740.55	100.00	27.49	27.49
ISRG	36,216.87	362.17	100.00	26.46	26.46
ESRX	148,057.39	1,480.57	100.00	25.88	25.88
CHRW	68,786.13	687.86	100.00	25.13	25.13
BEAS	70,641.03	706.41	100.00	23.95	23.95
CDWC	116,702.70	1,167.03	100.00	23.58	23.58
SNDK	92,696.89	926.97	100.00	23.24	23.24
PDCO	95,059.17	950.59	100.00	21.66	21.66
SYMC	88,349.06	883.49	100.00	21.00	21.00
MNST	56,628.57	566.29	100.00	20.77	20.77
COST	74,322.17	743.22	100.00	19.45	19.45
LBTYA	5,237.85	52.38	100.00	17.79	17.79
LINTA	1,089.97	10.90	100.00	17.59	17.59
LAMR	38,437.04	384.37	100.00	16.36	16.36
XRAY	51,042.95	510.43	100.00	16.28	16.28
AMLN	50,116.67	501.17	100.00	16.13	16.13
VRSN	27,695.92	276.96	100.00	16.04	16.04
BRCM	26,140.94	261.41	100.00	15.90	15.90
CMCSA	46,971.74	469.72	100.00	15.61	15.61
CMVT	40,381.86	403.82	100.00	14.43	14.43
VRTX	39,893.33	398.93	100.00	14.34	14.34
LRCX	31,594.08	315.94	100.00	12.62	12.62
CDNS	31,077.98	310.78	100.00	12.50	12.50
PETM	16,404.39	164.04	100.00	8.43	8.43
CKFR	8,679.07	86.79	100.00	5.71	5.71
SIRI	6,619.72	66.20	100.00	4.33	4.33
DISCA	516.34	5.16	100.00	3.47	3.47
XMSR	2,041.67	20.42	100.00	2.60	2.60
JNPR	1,492.72	14.93	100.00	1.87	1.87
EXPE	-1,265.61	-12.66	100.00	-8.96	-8.96
AKAM	6,341.35	63.41	100.00	13.09	13.09

FIGURE 21.2 RESULTS FROM BUY AND HOLD 2007 STOCKS

Formula file

C:\Program Files\AmiBroker\Formulas\Custom\BuyAndHold.afl   [Pick] [Edit]

Apply to
○ all symbols
○ current symbol   [Define...]
⦿ use filter

☐ Run every: 5min
☐ Wait for backfill (RT only)

Range
○ all quotations
○ n last quotations
○ n last days   n=   1
⦿ from: 1/ 1/1995 ▾
   to: 1/ 1/2007 ▾

[Scan]   [Explore]
[Back Test ▾] [Optimize ▾]
[Report... ▾] [Export...]
[Equity ▾]   [Settings...]
[Parameters] [Close]

Results

Ticker	Net Profit	Net % Profit	Exposure %	CAR	RAR	Max. Trade ...	Max
AMZN	218,092.48	2,180.92	100.00	38.38	38.38	-582,196.52	
APOL	443,139.54	4,431.40	100.00	37.44	37.44	-746,860.48	
DELL	394,677.42	3,946.77	100.00	36.14	36.14	-669,516.13	
QCOM	259,928.58	2,599.29	100.00	31.62	31.62	-538,000.02	
YHOO	175,072.47	1,750.72	100.00	31.29	31.29	-831,159.44	
ROST	247,017.54	2,470.18	100.00	31.08	31.08	-99,736.84	
NTLI	9,164.77	91.65	100.00	30.46	30.46	-6,560.36	
SBUX	202,095.81	2,020.96	100.00	29.00	29.00	-60,359.28	
PCAR	144,156.77	1,441.57	100.00	25.62	25.62	-23,040.38	
CSCO	133,842.11	1,338.42	100.00	24.89	24.89	-376,105.29	
CTXS	98,200.00	982.00	100.00	24.01	24.01	-454,240.00	
PAYX	120,495.05	1,204.95	100.00	23.88	23.88	-116,930.69	
ADBE	107,151.00	1,071.51	100.00	22.77	22.77	-94,131.06	
BBBY	97,627.12	976.27	100.00	21.91	21.91	-43,559.32	
ERTS	95,576.52	955.77	100.00	21.71	21.71	-59,916.14	
AMGN	83,832.42	838.32	100.00	20.52	20.52	-64,464.28	
MSFT	81,876.92	818.77	100.00	20.31	20.31	-103,107.69	
SPLS	80,202.70	802.03	100.00	20.13	20.13	-54,966.22	
AAPL	79,399.37	793.99	100.00	20.04	20.04	-36,796.63	
GENZ	72,768.82	727.69	100.00	19.27	19.27	-59,301.08	
ORCL	70,849.06	708.49	100.00	19.03	19.03	-183,915.11	
FISV	70,398.77	703.99	100.00	18.98	18.98	-36,809.82	
ALTR	67,176.47	671.76	100.00	18.57	18.57	-220,156.86	
MXIM	65,049.02	650.49	100.00	18.30	18.30	-156,078.44	
AMAT	64,395.16	643.95	100.00	18.21	18.21	-186,935.48	
FAST	63,827.16	638.27	100.00	18.14	18.14	-31,954.73	
BMET	62,786.60	627.87	100.00	18.00	18.00	-32,204.59	
MCHP	56,194.33	561.94	100.00	17.07	17.07	-36,538.46	
LLTC	46,252.32	462.52	100.00	15.49	15.49	-93,543.60	
INTU	44,677.42	446.77	100.00	15.22	15.22	-55,268.82	
INTC	44,000.00	440.00	100.00	15.10	15.10	-156,186.67	
SIAL	43,600.00	436.00	100.00	15.02	15.02	-13,586.21	
XLNX	42,214.91	422.15	100.00	14.77	14.77	-179,495.61	
IACI	18,744.37	187.44	63.50	9.20	14.49	-24,220.18	
SUNW	38,828.83	388.29	100.00	14.13	14.13	-557,657.64	
ADSK	38,281.62	382.82	100.00	14.03	14.03	-20,930.79	
KLAC	32,196.78	321.97	100.00	12.75	12.75	-59,397.80	
APCC	29,521.97	295.22	100.00	12.14	12.14	-46,434.11	
CTAS	25,455.36	254.55	100.00	11.13	11.13	-22,991.07	
TLAB	5,498.49	54.98	100.00	3.72	3.72	-110,453.18	
LVLT	-8,491.38	-84.91	100.00	-19.44	-19.44	-34,636.31	

FIGURE 21.3 RESULTS BUY AND HOLD STOCKS IN BOTH

The median RAR of those stocks that were members of the 1999 NAS-DAQ100, are not now members, but are still actively traded, is about 7% per year from 1995 to 2007. Those that are now members, but were not in 1999, had an RAR of about 23%. And those that have been members throughout had an RAR of about 19%. Table 21.2 summarizes the results. And clearly, the full extent of the survivor bias is understated, since many of the stocks on the list in 1999 would show negative returns if their data was available.

Median RAR for Survivor Study	
1999	7%
2007	23%
Both	19%

TABLE 21.2

EXPECTATIONS

What rate of return is reasonable to expect? A famous trader turned $10,000 into $1,000,000 in one year, the final equity a factor of 100 times initial equity. Under the assumption that entries and exits are made only when the markets are open, and the fact that there are 252 trading days in a year, then the daily rate of change must be the x in the following equation:

$$x^{252} = 100$$

Logarithms make the solution easy.

$$252 * \ln(x) = \ln(100)$$

$$\ln(x) = \frac{1}{252} * \ln(100)$$

$$\ln(x) = 0.00397 * 4.605 = 0.01828$$

$$x = e^{\ln(x)} = e^{0.01828} = 1.0184$$

$$x = 1.0184$$

The daily rate of change must be 1.84%.

By a similar calculation, the weekly rate of change to turn $10,000 into $1,000,000 in one year is 9.26%.

What does a trading system that produces those results look like? This is one set of performance characteristics that work:

- Has 70% winners.
- Has a payoff of 2 to 1 on winning trades.
- Loses 100% of its equity in all losing trades.
- Trades once a week.
- Bets 20% of the value of the portfolio on every position.

Those are pretty stiff requirements, and the 30% losing trades can come at the wrong time. One in every seven traders who has this system and trades it this way turns $10,000 into $1,000,000 in one year and becomes famous. We do not remember the others.

ONE PERCENT A DAY?

Can a rate of return of "only" 1% per day be sustained? If it could, $10,000 would become $50 trillion dollars – about the total value of all property in the United States in 2006 (also about the total value of the debt of the United States federal government in 2006) – in about nine years.

$$1 * 10^4 * (1.01)^x = 50 * 10^{12}$$
$$(1.01)^x = 5 * 10^9$$
$$x = 2244 \text{ trading days} = 8.9 \text{ years}$$

DRAWDOWN OVER TIME

An earlier chapter discussed the relationship between holding period and drawdown. Following are two graphs – one for a portfolio made up of about 2700 stocks currently listed on the NASDAQ, the other made up of about 2100 NYSE stocks. Beginning 1/1/1990 and continuing every six months through 1/1/2006, the maximum drawdown for each stock for periods of 1, 4, 9, 16, 25, 36, 49, 64, 81, 100, 121, 144, 169, 196, 225, and 256 days ahead is computed. Closing prices are used for the entry and the maximum drawdown. The calculations were done twice a year, on about January 1 and again on about July 1. Whatever stocks have sufficient data were included. The results of all individual drawdowns were averaged together to form a composite for the exchange.

The graphs show several things:

- As expected, the drawdown increases in proportion to the square root of the time the stock is held. That is, the average drawdown should increase by a factor of four when the holding period increases by a factor of 16. That relationship holds reasonably well – at 256 days the drawdown is about four times that of the average drawdown at 16 days.
- The NYSE stocks are less volatile than the NASDAQ stocks.
- Both exchanges show wide variation in drawdown volatility.
- On average, an NYSE stock will experience a 10% drawdown within a holding period of about three months.
- On average, a NASDAQ stock will experience a 10% drawdown within a holding period of about five weeks.

But these figures are all extremely conservative. There is a massive survivor bias. Hundreds of stocks had near 100% drawdowns in the three years from early 2000 through early 2003, and disappeared. Some went bankrupt, some were acquired, some were delisted. If those stocks had been included before they disappeared, there would be many more steep drawdowns, the average drawdown for any given period would be higher, and the length of time before a 10% drawdown would be shorter.

The stock markets have had a very strong upward trend from 1982 through early 2007 when this chapter is being written. So strong that it is difficult to find profitable trading strategies for short positions. High quality, inexpensive data is not available for periods before 1982, so it is difficult to prepare for periods when stocks have a persistent downward trend. Nevertheless, traders should be prepared for periods when short positions are preferred. Perhaps you never would, or never could because of a limitation in the account being traded, take a short position. Even so, it is worthwhile to try to develop trading systems that are profitable, or that at least break even, in falling markets. When those systems generate a signal to enter a short position, it might be a good time to exit or lighten up on long positions.

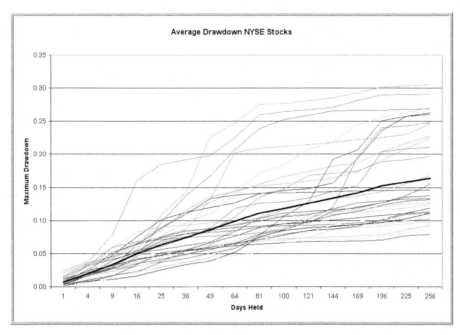

FIGURE 21.4 DRAWDOWN OF NYSE STOCKS

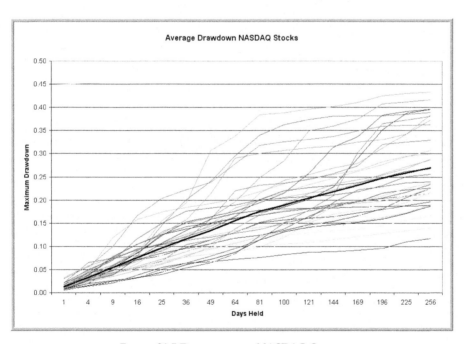

FIGURE 21.5 DRAWDOWN OF NASDAQ STOCKS

To completely overcome the survivor bias of, say, index membership, it would be necessary to have:

- accurate lists of the members as of the start of each test period.
- accurate price history as of the start of each test period – unadjusted for subsequent splits, mergers, and restatements.
- test runs that reflect the then-current conditions as of the start of each test period.

The point is this – even taking a random selection of equities for use in testing is not adequate to overcome the survivorship bias. Any stock or fund that has enough historical data to validate a trading system and is available to trade tomorrow is a survivor and is affected by survivorship bias. The past twenty years have been exceptionally strong for equities. Almost any equity will trade long-only positions well and short-only positions poorly.

Survivor bias produces an overly-optimistic result.

Second edition

The study of drawdown over time presented in the first edition compares the price at the end of the period to the price at the beginning of the period. Intra-period drawdown was not considered.

MTSP presents a similar study of drawdown related to holding period for 1999 through 2010. It confirms that drawdown is proportional to the square root of the holding period, with average drawdown for a one year holding period about 31%. It also found that the average additional drawdown during the year-long holding period is about 8%.

The subtitle to this chapter should be: "History is written by the winners."

22

Monte Carlo Analysis

MONTE CARLO ANALYSIS is based on creating a computer program that models a system we are studying, repeatedly samples possible results from a chance process, and analyzes the results. The process being modeled is the trading system written in AFL. The repeated sampling relies on use of random numbers.

GENERATING RANDOM NUMBERS

When we speak of random numbers generated by a computer, we are speaking of pseudo-random numbers. Truly random numbers can be produced from physical devices, such as flipping coins, throwing dice, or measuring the time interval between counters on a detector of radioactivity. But truly random numbers are both inconvenient to generate and convert to use by a computer program, and non-reproducible.

Various methods have been devised for creating a series of pseudo-random numbers that pass tests of randomness. A common one is called a linear multiplicative congruent generator. A very simple example has been coded into the program shown in Figure 22.4. The constants in the program are chosen to be prime relative to each other. The maximum period – the number of random numbers that can be generated before the cycle repeats – is always less than the constant associated with the modulo operator, 4865933 in this instance.

If longer sequences of pseudo-random numbers are required, there are several methods of increasing the randomness of the numbers generated, and of extending the period beyond the limit of the constant associated with the modulo operator. One is to create a relatively small array of perhaps 1000 elements and prefill the array with random numbers generated by one function. Whenever a random number is required, choose which one to return by selecting it from the array with a random number generated by a different function, then generate a new number to replace the one just used. There are also many other algorithms for generating series of random numbers with very long periods and very random behavior.

If the random number generating program is poorly designed, or if the constants are poorly selected, then the maximum period may be considerably less. The first number to be a duplicate of any number previously generated causes the list of numbers to repeat, and from that point on the random series is only as long as the number of numbers between the two duplicates.

Even if there is a long cycle period, the numbers may have a non-random pattern. One method of visually testing for patterns is to select pairs of numbers, treat them as an x-value and a y-value, and plot the points on a surface. Of course, the non-random pattern could appear first in a three dimensional, or higher, space and be difficult to detect visually.

If you plan to do a lot of testing where random numbers are used, learn enough about the random number generator your software uses to assure yourself that the numbers are sufficiently random and the cycle is sufficiently long for your purposes.

Most pseudo-random number generators produce uniform numbers. Uniform numbers all have the same probability. Throwing a single six-sided die and recording the number on the top face will produce uniform random numbers that range between 1 and 6. The probability density function for that process is shown in Figure 22.1. This is a discrete function, because outcomes can only be integers in the range of 1 to 6.

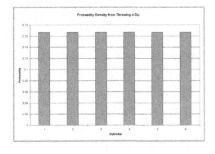

FIGURE 22.1 PROBABILITY DENSITY FROM A SINGLE DIE

Having only six random numbers available is too restrictive for most simulations. So a continuous density function where any outcome can result is used instead. (Since the computations are being carried out on a digital computer which has a finite number of binary digits in the result, strictly speaking the density is still discrete, but the possibilities are so close together that the density is considered to be continuous.) Figure 22.2 shows the density function, usually called the Probability Density Function, pdf, for a continuous density following the uniform distribution. The range is normalized so that every number chosen will be greater than or equal to zero, and less than, but not equal to, one.

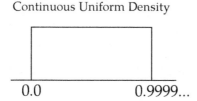

FIGURE 22.2 CONTINUOUS UNIFORM DENSITY FUNCTION

Every density function has a distribution function associated with it. Figure 22.3 shows the distribution function, usually called the Cumulative Distribution Function, CDF, for the uniform distribution.

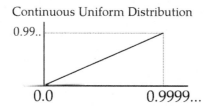

FIGURE 22.3 CONTINUOUS UNIFORM DISTRIBUTION FUNCTION

The process of generating specific random numbers for use in computer simulations is:
   A. Create the CDF for the desired distribution.
   B. Every time a new random number from that distribution is needed:
      1. Pick, or generate, a uniform number between 0 and 0.9999.
      2. Go up the y-axis to that number.

3. Go across, parallel to the x-axis, to meet the line describing the CDF.
4. Drop down to the x-axis.
5. Read off the number from the distribution.

If the desired distribution follows one of the theoretical distributions, such as normal, Poisson, or exponential, it may be possible to compute the CDF. But even some distributions that have mathematical definitions are difficult to compute directly. In all cases where the desired distribution comes from observations, as it could when simulating trading systems, the CDF is developed by sorting observed data into bins and counting the number of observations in each bin. An example using trading data is given in a few pages.

So the keys to running simulations are:
*   Have a CDF for the distribution you want to draw from
*   Have a good uniform random number generator

AmiBroker has a built-in random number function, random(), which can be used to create an array of uniform random numbers, one per bar. To get one random number in AmiBroker, use LastValue(random()). Since we plan to add noise to the data bar-by-bar, we could use the built-in function. But there are times when random numbers are needed at a rate other than one per bar. This can be accomplished using a uniform random number generator that returns a single number with each call.

```
//    UniformRandomNumber.afl
//

global RandomSeed;

function Rand()
//    Uniform random number generator
//    using linear multiplicative congruence method.
//
//    There are no parameters.
//    Each call to Rand generates and returns
//    a new random number from the uniform distribution.
//
//    The congruence method is sensitive to choices for
//    the program constants and degenerates into a very
//    short repetitive cycle when poor constants are
//    chosen.
//    This routine is probably adequate for most informal
//    Monte Carlo analysis to test model sensitivity
//    to small changes in the data.
//    If you plan to do more simulations, you will
//    need a better random number routine.
```

```
{
//   b = 4126537;
//   a = 2323297;
//   m = 4865933;
     Randomseed = (4126537 * Randomseed + 2323297);
     Randomseed = Randomseed % 4865933;
     return (Randomseed / 4865933);
}
```

FIGURE 22.4 UNIFORM RANDOM NUMBER

The RandomSeed is set by a program variable and retains its value between calls to the function. Each different value of RandomSeed creates a series of random numbers that start at a different number. Of course, since the numbers generated always occur in the same sequence for a given RandomSeed, they are not truly random, but pseudo-random. But they are repeatable, which allows comparison of alternatives.

In the case of the program in Figure 22.4, and in most cases, the random number generated is a uniform random number and behaves as a number drawn from the statistical uniform probability distribution. It is always between 0.0000 and 0.9999.

If numbers that appear to have been drawn from other distributions are required, there are several ways to obtain them. Some distributions can be described by a formula that relates the desired distribution to the uniform distribution. For those cases, one or more random numbers are drawn from a uniform distribution and used to compute the associated number from the desired distribution. For both the theoretical distributions that have no formula solutions, and for all empirical distributions – those resulting from collected data – the technique is to first build an array whose components define the Cumulative Distribution Function (CDF) of the desired distribution, then use a uniform number to select a value from the distribution.

Although the normal distribution has well defined mathematical definition, it is difficult to compute the CDF needed. The code illustrated in Figures 22.5 and 22.6 solves the problem by storing the coefficients for the CDF of the normal distribution in the 101 element array. (The values for the CDF of the normal distribution were calculated using a spreadsheet.) After that, it is easy to look up the value required from the array. For more precision, or to extend the function beyond +/- three standard deviations, use an array with more than 101 elements.

Figure 22.5 shows the initialization code. This only needs to be performed one time.

```
//   InitializeNormalCDF.afl
//
function InitializeNormalCDF()
//   Initialize the array that holds the coefficients
//   for the Normal Cumulative Distribution function.
{
    NormCDF[0] = -3.090;
    NormCDF[1] = -2.326;
    NormCDF[2] = -2.053;
    NormCDF[3] = -1.881;
    NormCDF[4] = -1.751;
    NormCDF[5] = -1.645;
    NormCDF[6] = -1.555;
    NormCDF[7] = -1.476;
    NormCDF[8] = -1.405;
    NormCDF[9] = -1.341;
    NormCDF[10] = -1.282;
    NormCDF[11] = -1.227;
    NormCDF[12] = -1.175;
    NormCDF[13] = -1.126;
    NormCDF[14] = -1.080;
    NormCDF[15] = -1.036;
    NormCDF[16] = -0.994;
    NormCDF[17] = -0.954;
    NormCDF[18] = -0.915;
    NormCDF[19] = -0.878;
    NormCDF[20] = -0.842;
    NormCDF[21] = -0.806;
    NormCDF[22] = -0.772;
    NormCDF[23] = -0.739;
    NormCDF[24] = -0.706;
    NormCDF[25] = -0.674;
    NormCDF[26] = -0.643;
    NormCDF[27] = -0.613;
    NormCDF[28] = -0.583;
    NormCDF[29] = -0.553;
    NormCDF[30] = -0.524;
    NormCDF[31] = -0.496;
    NormCDF[32] = -0.468;
    NormCDF[33] = -0.440;
    NormCDF[34] = -0.412;
    NormCDF[35] = -0.385;
    NormCDF[36] = -0.358;
    NormCDF[37] = -0.332;
    NormCDF[38] = -0.305;
    NormCDF[39] = -0.279;
    NormCDF[40] = -0.253;
    NormCDF[41] = -0.228;
    NormCDF[42] = -0.202;
    NormCDF[43] = -0.176;
    NormCDF[44] = -0.151;
    NormCDF[45] = -0.126;
    NormCDF[46] = -0.100;
    NormCDF[47] = -0.075;
```

```
    NormCDF[48]  =  -0.050;
    NormCDF[49]  =  -0.025;
    NormCDF[50]  =  0.000;
    NormCDF[51]  =  0.025;
    NormCDF[52]  =  0.050;
    NormCDF[53]  =  0.075;
    NormCDF[54]  =  0.100;
    NormCDF[55]  =  0.126;
    NormCDF[56]  =  0.151;
    NormCDF[57]  =  0.176;
    NormCDF[58]  =  0.202;
    NormCDF[59]  =  0.228;
    NormCDF[60]  =  0.253;
    NormCDF[61]  =  0.279;
    NormCDF[62]  =  0.305;
    NormCDF[63]  =  0.332;
    NormCDF[64]  =  0.358;
    NormCDF[65]  =  0.385;
    NormCDF[66]  =  0.412;
    NormCDF[67]  =  0.440;
    NormCDF[68]  =  0.468;
    NormCDF[69]  =  0.496;
    NormCDF[70]  =  0.524;
    NormCDF[71]  =  0.553;
    NormCDF[72]  =  0.583;
    NormCDF[73]  =  0.613;
    NormCDF[74]  =  0.643;
    NormCDF[75]  =  0.674;
    NormCDF[76]  =  0.706;
    NormCDF[77]  =  0.739;
    NormCDF[78]  =  0.772;
    NormCDF[79]  =  0.806;
    NormCDF[80]  =  0.842;
    NormCDF[81]  =  0.878;
    NormCDF[82]  =  0.915;
    NormCDF[83]  =  0.954;
    NormCDF[84]  =  0.994;
    NormCDF[85]  =  1.036;
    NormCDF[86]  =  1.080;
    NormCDF[87]  =  1.126;
    NormCDF[88]  =  1.175;
    NormCDF[89]  =  1.227;
    NormCDF[90]  =  1.281;
    NormCDF[91]  =  1.341;
    NormCDF[92]  =  1.405;
    NormCDF[93]  =  1.476;
    NormCDF[94]  =  1.555;
    NormCDF[95]  =  1.645;
    NormCDF[96]  =  1.751;
    NormCDF[97]  =  1.881;
    NormCDF[98]  =  2.054;
    NormCDF[99]  =  2.326;
    NormCDF[100] =  3.090;
    return(Null);
}
```

FIGURE 22.5 INITIALIZATION OF CDF

Figure 22.6 shows the function that generates a single random number from the normal distribution. This is called once for each random number needed.

```
//   NormalRandomNumber.afl
//
function NormalRandomNumber()
//   Normally distributed random number generator
//
//   Returns a random number with mean 0.0 and
//   standard deviation 1.0.
//
//   Before using this routine, a single call to
//   InitializeNormalCDF must be made.
//
{
     Index = int(100* rand()) + 1;
     return(NormCDF[index]);
}
```

FIGURE 22.6 NORMAL RANDOM NUMBER

ADDING NOISE TO DATA

Every data series has two major components – signal and noise. The signal component is that part that we hope contains patterns that can be recognized and traded profitably. The noise component is that part that is random and cannot be traded profitably. To some extent, the separation is arbitrary. Any data from which the trading system cannot extract information and patterns is placed in the noise category.

As the complexity of a trading system increases through the addition of rules, indicators, and filters, and as the number of alternative sets of values for the arguments that are tested increases through extended optimization searches, the likelihood increases that the resulting model has fit itself to patterns that are not persistent beyond the in-sample period.

Filters (the digital signal processing kind) are often applied to the data to remove either the low frequency signal – a detrending operation – or the high frequency signal – a smoothing operation. Both operations are done in hope of leaving a data series that has a higher signal content and lower noise. In order to test the sensitivity of a model to the specific prices in the data, random noise can be added to the data, and the model rerun. If the model performance drops sharply when the noise is added, that is an indication that the model has fit itself to non-persistent patterns and will probably not perform well on out-of-sample data.

Using the two functions just described, the AFL program illustrated in Figure 22.7 adds noise to the data series being used, and reports the performance of the trading system as the level of noise is increased.

```
//   AddNoiseWithIncludes.afl
//
//   Add random noise to price data to test
//   sensitivity.
//
// ------------------------------

global NormCDF;
global RandomSeed;

// ------------------------------

//   Copy the Uniform Random Number code here.
//   (Or use #include)

#include <UniformRandomNumber.afl>

//   ------------------------------

//   Copy, or #include, the code to initialize the
//   NormCDF array and to generate
//   Normal Random Numbers here.

#include <InitializeNormalCDF.afl>
xxnull = InitializeNormalCDF();
#include <NormalRandomNumber.afl>

//   ------------------------------

SetTradeDelays(0,0,0,0);

//   Select a random seed.
//   A different seed will produce a
//   different series of noise.
RandomSeed = 17131;

//   Weight of 0.0 adds no noise.
//   Weight of 1.0 adds one standard deviation of noise.
Weight = Optimize("Weight",0.0, 0.0, 2.0, 0.05);

//   Compute the standard deviation of the Close.
//   Arbitarily use 20 days.
SD = StDev(C,20);

//   Bar by bar, add noise to the Close.
for (i=1; i<BarCount; i++)
{
    NoisyClose[i] = C[i] + SD[i]*Weight*NormalRandomNumber();
}
```

```
//   Tell AmiBroker to use NoisyClose for trades.
BuyPrice = NoisyClose;

//   The trading system rules.
MALength1 = 1; //Optimize("MALength1",1,1,10,1);
MALength2 = 4; //Optimize("MALength2",4,1,10,1);

MA1 = DEMA(NoisyClose,MALength1);
MA2 = EMA(NoisyClose,MALength2);

Buy = Cross(MA1,MA2);

HoldDays = 1; //Optimize("HoldDays",2,1,5,1);
Sell = BarsSince(Buy)>=HoldDays;

Sell = ExRem(Sell,Buy);

//   Examine the noisy data bar by bar.
Filter = 1;
AddColumn(C,"C",1.4);
AddColumn(SD,"StDev",1.4);
AddColumn(NoisyClose,"Noisy",1.4);
Diff = (NoisyClose-C)/SD;
AddColumn(Diff,"Diff",1.4);
```

FIGURE 22.7 ADD NOISE

The procedure to determine the sensitivity of the model to noise is as follows:

1. Set Weight = 0.0 so that no extra noise is added. The Close prices as they exist in the data files will be used to compute the Buy signal.

2. Set the in-sample dates as desired.

3. Set the trading system variables, such as moving average lengths, to Optimize. Optimize to find the best model.

4. Assign the best values to the variables that were optimized so that they will not change during the next step.

5. Set Weight to Optimize. With each pass, a different amount of noise will be added to the closing price. The noisy close will be used to compute the Buy signals and calculate the trading performance.

6. Examine the output from the optimizing runs. If the run with Weight = 0 is at the top of the list and the results drop off rapidly as noise is added, that indicates that the model has fit itself to the noise component in the original data. If the run with Weight = 0 is among runs that form a plateau in the fitness variable, or if the run with Weight = 0 is several places down the list and runs

with small amounts of noise are ranked nearby or higher, then the model is not overly sensitive to noise and is more robust.

As an example, the Russell 2000 index is optimized over the in-sample period of 1/1/1995 through 1/1/2005, then sorted by K-ratio. The best arguments were hard coded in and a new optimization was run varying the weight of the noise. The results show a plateau for noise up to 0.10 standard deviations of the close, then drop off. This model handles small amounts of added noise well.

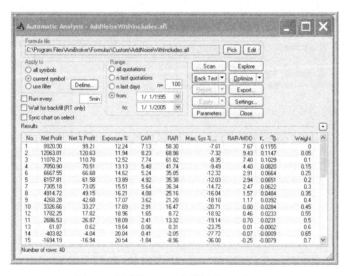

FIGURE 22.8 RUSSELL 2000 WITH NOISE

SIMULATION RUNS USING A SUBSET OF ACTUAL DATA

The S&P 500 index closed on December 29, 1994 at 461.17 and closed on December 29, 2006 at 1418.30. The time period is 12 years, or 3022 trading days. $10,000 invested on 12/29/1994 would be worth $30,754 on 12/29/2006. The annual compound rate of growth is 9.81%. The daily compound rate of growth is 0.000372 or 0.0372%.

Given the annual growth rate of 9.81%, and 9 up years out of 12 years, we might expect that a trading system that is in a long position a randomly selected 20 percent of the time would be profitable. We can test that.

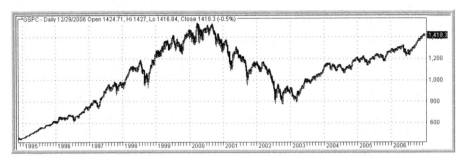

FIGURE 22.9 SP500 PRICE

AmiBroker is used to compute the day to day percentage changes.

```
//   ComputeDailyPercentChange.afl
//
//   Compute the Close to Close percentage change
//   for the series and period provided.
//
SetTradeDelays(0,0,0,0);
BuyPrice = C;
SellPrice = C;
PctChg = (C - Ref(C,-1)) / C; // or ROC(C,1);
Filter = 1;
AddColumn(C,"C",1.4);
AddColumn(PctChg,"PctChg",1.8);
```

FIGURE 22.10 COMPUTE DAILY PERCENT CHANGES

The change data are exported to a CSV file, and imported into a spreadsheet for analysis. The mean and standard deviation of the 3022 daily changes are 0.000315 and 0.010795, respectively. The skewness is -0.202, meaning the distribution has a longer tail to the negative side – the normal distribution has skewness of 0.0. The kurtosis is 3.705, meaning the distribution is more peaked than a normal distribution, which has a kurtosis of 3.0.

The data is sorted into 200 bins, each bin 0.00065 wide, with the minimum bin -0.073 and the maximum bin +0.057. The curve representing the density function of the normal distribution with a mean of 0.000315 and a standard deviation of 0.010795 is superimposed over the histogram of actual observations.

A chi-square test shows that the observed data definitely did not come from a normal distribution. Chi-square is computed to be 322, with 79 degrees of freedom. The 0.005 significance level for 80 degrees of freedom is 116. Since 322 is much greater than 116, we can reject the hypothesis that the observed data came from a normal distribution.

But, not being a normal distribution may not matter at all. So far, nothing we have discussed relies on the distribution being normal. And if something did, we might be able to use repeated sampling to produce a nearly-normal distribution, in accordance with the Central Limit Theorem of statistics.

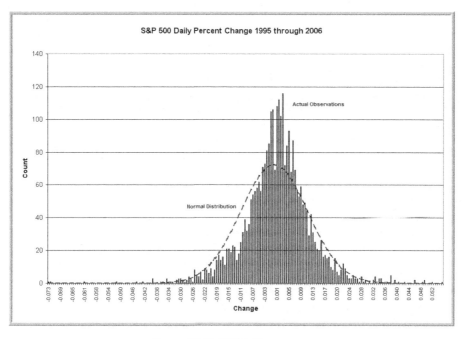

FIGURE 22.11 SP500 HISTOGRAM

The cumulative distribution function (CDF) is formed by adding the count in each "bin" from left to right, then normalizing so that it starts at 0.00 and ends at 1.00.

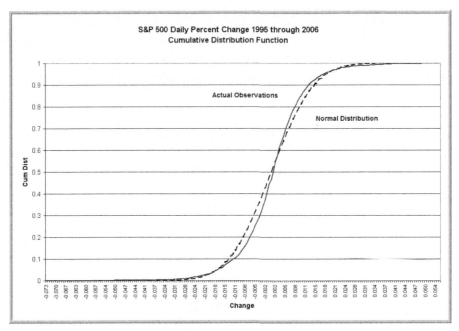

FIGURE 22.12 SP500 CUMULATIVE DISTRIBUTION

The cumulative distribution function can be used to select a sequence of daily changes to simulate trades. The technique is to generate a single random number between 0.0000 and 0.9999 from a uniform distribution, use that number as an index as though it is a cumulative distribution value, go up the y-axis to that value, go horizontally across until the curve is reached, then go down to the x-axis. The value at the x-axis is the corresponding change.

TRADING SYSTEM SIMULATION

As an example, we will examine the possible equity curves from a trading system that takes long positions, holds them just a few days, and is in a long position about 20 percent of the time. Since there are 3022 days in the seven year period, 604 daily values represents 20 percent. Using the average daily rate of change of 0.000315 and 604 days, the final equity should average approximately the initial equity times (1.000315) ^ 604, or about \$12,095 for an account that started at \$10,000.

To create a single simulated run:
  • Start with an initial account of, say, \$10,000.

- For each of 604 days:
  - Randomly draw a daily change from the observed data.
  - Add 1.00 to the change and multiply by the running account value.

The last value, after day 604, gives the final equity for one simulated run. The intermediate equity values can be used to calculate drawdown and other statistics, if desired.

Make several runs and examine the distribution of the equity curves. The following chart shows the equity curves from a run of 50 simulations.

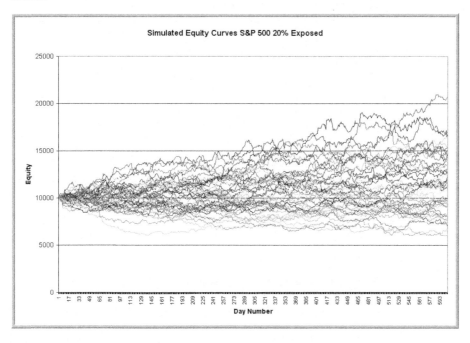

FIGURE 22.13 SIMULATED EQUITY

After making many runs of 200 simulations each, the average final equity is about $12,100, as expected. Maximum final equity is usually about $22,000 and the minimum final equity is usually about $5,500. About 30 percent of all simulation runs have a final equity less than $10,000.

USING AMIBROKER DIRECTLY

Although AmiBroker does not have extensive native Monte Carlo capability, it is possible to do an analysis directly in AmiBroker that provides some of the same information.

The following AmiBroker program uses a random entry, along with a three day holding period, to create a trading system that holds a long position about 20 percent of the time.

```
//    SimulateRandomLongReport.afl
//
//    Use random entry to long positions.
//
SetTradeDelays(0,0,0,0);
BuyPrice = C;
//    Use the Optimize statement to get a report
//    listing of the results.
Seed = Optimize("Seed",13331,13331,13530,1);
//    Exit after a fixed holding period.
HoldDays = Param("HoldDays",3,1,100,1);
//    Buy 10% of the days.
RandomBuy = Random(Seed)<= 0.10;
//    Do not allow overlapping trades.
Buy = (RandomBuy AND Ref(BarsSince(Randombuy),-1)>HoldDays);
Sell = BarsSince(Buy) >=HoldDays;
Sell = ExRem(Sell,Buy);
```

FIGURE 22.14 SIMULATE RANDOM LONG REPORT

Run this as an optimization. For each pass, the variable Seed will be assigned a different value, and a different series of entry dates will be generated. The Exposure% column shows that a long position is held about 20 percent of the time. The best results for this series show a profit of $12,434, or a final equity of $22,434. AmiBroker computes drawdown and other metrics.

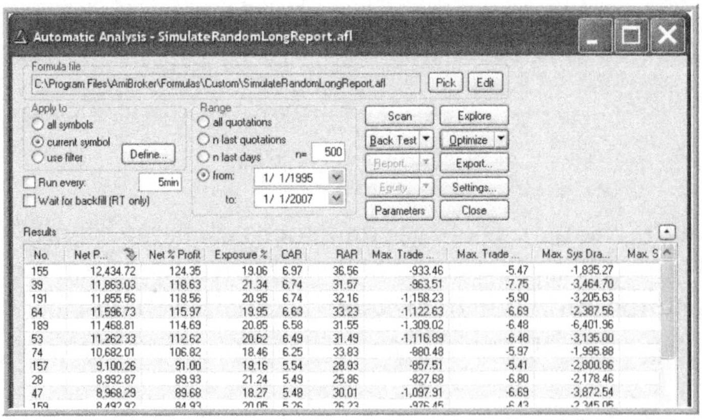

FIGURE 22.15 AMIBROKER SIMULATION REPORT

A variation on the AFL code produces a graphical output.

```
//   SimulateRandomLongGraphic.afl
//
//   Use random entry to long positions.
//
SetTradeDelays(0,0,0,0);
BuyPrice = C;
//   Use the Param statement to view the result
//   in a window pane.
Seed = Param("Seed",13331,13331,13530,1);
//   Exit after a fixed holding period.
HoldDays = Param("HoldDays",3,1,100,1);
//   Buy 10% of the days.
RandomBuy = Random(Seed)<= 0.10;
//   Do not allow overlapping trades.
Buy = (RandomBuy AND Ref(BarsSince(Randombuy),-1)>HoldDays);
Sell = BarsSince(Buy) >=HoldDays;
Sell = ExRem(Sell,Buy);
Plot(C,"C",colorBlack,styleCandle);
shape = Buy * shapeUpArrow + Sell * shapeDownArrow;
PlotShapes( shape, IIf( Buy, colorGreen, colorRed ),
                   0, IIf( Buy, Low, High ) );
GraphXSpace = 5;
e = Equity();
Plot(e,"Equity",colorRed,styleLine|styleOwnScale);
```

FIGURE 22.16 SIMULATE RANDOM LONG GRAPHIC

From the Charts menu, select SimulateRandomLongGraphic, right click, then Insert. As each new symbol is selected from the Symbols menu, the random entry system will be applied and the equity curve displayed. Right Click the pane, select Parameters, then use the Slider to change the value of Seed. A new equity curve will be computed and immediately displayed, as shown in Figure 22.17.

FIGURE 22.17 AMIBROKER SIMULATION GRAPH

CONCLUSION: One test run may not be enough. See MTSP for detailed techniques you can use to analyze distributions.

MARGIN AND POSITION SIZING

MARGIN FOR EQUITIES

When trading equities, there is limited opportunity to increase leverage. In real life, an account can use margin – that is, borrow from the brokerage firm to increase the trading account. In the US at the present time, margin is limited by law to 50; where 100 means the retail account funds the account completely and 50 means the retail account funds fifty percent of the account, with the remainder borrowed. To use margin in AmiBroker, on the Backtest menu, select Settings. On the General tab, enter the figure in Account Margin. See figure 22.18. To trade a $10,000 account as though it has $20,000, set Account margin to 50.

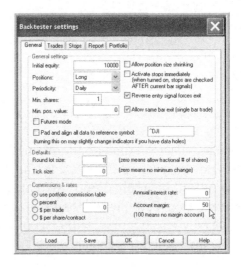

FIGURE 22.18 ACCOUNT MARGIN

POSITION SIZING FOR EQUITIES

Investment advisors and trading coaches recommend that the risk of every trade be limited to some small percentage of the trading account – typically from 1% to 5%. Risk is measured by the amount that will be lost when the stop-loss logic causes an exit. A trade that buys 100 shares at $50.00 is making a purchase of $5,000.00. If the trading system has a Maximum Loss stop set to 5% (see Figure 22.19), that trade has a risk of $250.00. Note that placing a stop-loss order with your broker does not guarantee that the exit price will be limited to 5% — in the event of a fast market or overnight gap, the price at which the order is filled could result in a loss exceeding 5%.

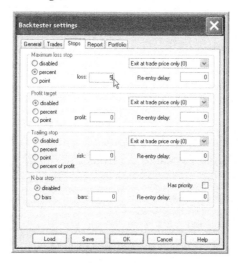

FIGURE 22.19 MAXIMUM LOSS STOP

Alternatively, the maximum loss stop can be set within the AFL code, as is demonstrated in the next section. Setting the stops within the AFL makes them more readily available for testing and optimization.

Computing the risk for the entire trading account with several trades open simultaneously is much more complicated than for a single issue. If the techniques of Modern Portfolio Theory are used, it is necessary to know the correlation between open trade equity for the positions. But correlations are not stationary. The conditions under which they change most dramatically are precisely when the changes cause the portfolio risk to increase the most—during times of extreme market volatility. Consequently, I do not recommend creating portfolios expecting safety in diversity. Having said that, if you want to analyze behavior of a portfolio, I recommend Monte Carlo simulation.

RISK AND STOPS

One of the major points of this section is that **Stops Hurt Systems**. Along the route to giving some evidence for that statement, some alternative schemes for allocating funds are presented.

If a trading account has an initial equity of $50,000 and the trader plans to hold five positions, a common allocation scheme is to divide the funds equally. The AmiBroker code to do this is:

```
PositionSize = -20;   //   20% of equity in each
```

Or the following, which allows testing and optimization of the profitability of the portfolio as a function of the number of positions:

```
NumberPositions = 5; //   Can be optimized
SetOption("MaxOpenPositions",NumberPositions);
PositionSize = -100/NumberPositions;
```

Another allocation scheme determines the number of shares to trade by the risk. The AmiBroker code to do this, where risk is measured by the average true range, is:

```
//   TestingRiskPerTrade.afl
SetOption("InitialEquity",50000);
RiskPerTrade = 0.02;  //2%
RiskInPoints = 2.0 * ATR(20);
e = Equity();
Shares = RiskPerTrade * e / RiskInPoints;
SetPositionSize(shares,spsShares);
Buy = Cross(MA(C,8),MA(C,7));
Sell = Cross(MA(C,7),MA(C,8));
```

FIGURE 22.20 TESTING RISK PER TRADE

The code in Figure 22.20 sets the position size according to the potential risk, but does nothing to exit losing trades based on adverse price movement. Figure 22.21 is the same, but adds a maximum loss stop.

```
//   TestingRiskPerTradeWithStop.afl
SetOption("InitialEquity",50000);
RiskPerTrade = 0.02;  //2%
RiskInPoints = 2.0 * ATR(20);
e = Equity();
Shares = RiskPerTrade * e / RiskInPoints;
SetPositionSize(shares,spsShares);
ApplyStop(stopTypeLoss,stopModePoint,RiskInPoints);
Buy = Cross(MA(C,8),MA(C,7));
Sell = Cross(MA(C,7),MA(C,8));
```

FIGURE 22.21 TESTING RISK PER TRADE WITH STOP

Try various combinations of risk level, stop setting, and holding period. You will find that stops hurt systems. The trading system used is trivially simple. Replace it with your own and try again.

There is one way to enter a trade – by the Buy signal that the model generates. There are several ways to exit the trade:

• By the Sell signal that the model generates.

- By a profit target.
- By a maximum holding period.
- By a trailing stop.
- By a maximum loss stop.

The worst way to exit is the maximum loss stop. For one reason or another, you may be required to have a maximum loss stop in your code, but try to design your trading systems so that one of the other methods causes almost every exit.

My research indicates that stops hurt all systems.

Continuing on with position sizing, a more sophisticated position sizing can combine equal allocation with risk allocation.

```
//   EquityAllocation.afl
//
//   Allocating capital in an account
//   based on a combination of equal division
//   and risk.
//
//-------------------------------------------
//   Compute the allocation of funds
//
SetOption("InitialEquity",50000);

//   Allocate a maximum of 20% of the equity
//   in a single position
AllocationPercentage = 0.20;
        //Optimize("AllocPct",0.20,0.05,0.50,0.05);

//   Risk at most 2% on any trade
RiskPerTrade = 0.02;
        //Optimize("RiskPerTrade",0.02,0.005,0.1,0.005);

//   Compute the stop in several ways
//   Number of points as measured by ATR
ATRMultiplier = 2.0; //Optimize("ATRMult",2.0,0.5,5.0,0.5);
RiskByVolatility = ATRMultiplier * ATR(20);

//   Number of points as measured by Maximum Risk
RiskByMaximumRisk = C * RiskPerTrade;

//   Use the smaller number of points
RiskInPoints = Min(RiskByVolatility, RiskByMaximumRisk);

//   Set the built-in stops
//   The default exit is ExitAtStop=1 -- stop out intraday
ApplyStop(stopTypeLoss,stopModePoint,RiskInPoints);
ApplyStop(stopTypeTrailing,stopModePoint,2*ATR(20));//   Chandelier

//   Keep track of the account equity
e = Equity();
```

```
//   Compute how many shares to buy
SharesByCapital = AllocationPercentage * e / C;
SharesByRisk = RiskPerTrade * e / RiskInPoints;

//   Use the smaller number of shares
Shares = Min(SharesByCapital, SharesByRisk);
SetPositionSize(Shares,spsShares);

// ------------------------------------------
//   The trading system follows
//   Replace this one with a better one of your own
MALength1 = 8; //Optimize("MALength1",16,1,20,1);
MALength2 = 7; //Optimize("MALength2",15,1,20,1);
MA1 = MA(C,MALength1);
MA2 = MA(C,MALength2);

Buy = Cross(MA1,MA2);

HoldDays = 100; //Optimize("HoldDays",1,1,20,1);
Sell = Cross(MA2,MA1) OR (BarsSince(Buy)>=HoldDays);

Buy = ExRem(Buy,Sell);
Sell = ExRem(Sell,Buy);
```

FIGURE 22.22 EQUITY ALLOCATION

Disable the stops, either by setting them very wide or commenting out the ApplyStop statements. Select values for the parameters that optimize the fitness of the system. Code those values so they will not change, then explore the alternative exit methods.

Why is this material in the chapter on Monte Carlo Analysis? Because setting position size, determining exit methods, and setting stop levels requires a lot of thought, testing, optimization, and what-if analysis. Future developments that expand the capability to do that analysis within AmiBroker will be welcome.

SECOND EDITION

Originally, AmiBroker had a random number generator that, each time it was called, returned an array of uniform random numbers, one per bar. Figure 22.4 gives AFL code for a simple random number generator that returns a single random number for each call. The purpose of this is to provide for generating only a few random numbers, but be faster than the built-in function since it was not generating a number for each bar; or for generating a lot of random numbers, where more were needed than the number of bars.

With AmiBroker version 5.00, released in September 2007, AmiBroker has "Mersenne Twister" random numbers. The Mersenne Twister is very good – that means that the sequence passes tests of randomness and has a long period (approximately $2.9 * 10^{6012}$) before repeats. If you need random numbers in AmiBroker, use Mersenne Twister in preference to both the previous version of Random built in to AmiBroker and the routine shown in Figure 22.4.

Here is an excerpt from the release notes that describes the Mersenne Twister.

MTRANDOM – Mersenne Twister random number generator
Syntax:

mtRandom (seed = Null)

mtRandomA(seed=Null)
Returns:

NUMBER or ARRAY
Function:

mtRandom(seed=Null) – returns a single uniform random number (scalar) in the range [0,1).

mtRandomA(seed=Null) – returns an array, whose length is equal to the number of bars in the price data series, each element being a uniform random number in the range [0,1).

Seed is the random generator seed. If you don't specify one, the random number generator is automatically initialized using the current time as a seed. That guarantees both that the sequence is unique, and also that the sequence cannot be replicated.

Modeling Trading System Performance discusses use of Monte Carlo simulation in depth, including techniques to estimate both profit potential and risk.

Appendix A

Extending AmiBroker

Custom metrics

While AmiBroker computes a large number of metrics without any extension, the metric that best fits your trading may not be among them. Particularly if an automated walk-forward test and validation process will be carried out, the preferred metric must be computed for each optimization run.

This example follows the example given in the AmiBroker User Guide very closely. It adds *expectancy* as a custom metric. Expectancy is the amount that, on average, each trade returns. A system with a negative expectancy is a losing system, and no position sizing technique can overcome that. The long-term profitability of a system with a positive expectancy can be enhanced by intelligent position sizing.

Expectancy = %winners * average profit + %losers * average loss

Where average loss is a negative number.

Write the AFL code shown in Figure A.1, and save it as you would any other trading system.

```
//    CustomMetric.afl
//
//    Add a custom metric to the backtest report
//
//    The first part defines the custom metric
//
SetCustomBacktestProc("");

if (Status("action") == actionPortfolio)
{
    bo = GetBacktesterObject();

    bo.backtest();

    st = bo.getperformancestats(0);

    expectancy = st.getvalue("WinnersAvgProfit")
                    *    st.getvalue("WinnersPercent") /100
                    +    st.getvalue("LosersAvgLoss")
                    *    st.getvalue("LosersPercent") / 100;

    bo.addcustommetric("Expectancy", expectancy);
}
//
//    The second part is the trading system
//
fast = Optimize("fast",11,1,20,1);
slow = Optimize("slow",50,5,50,5);
MAF = MA(C,fast);
MAS = MA(C,slow);
Buy = Cross(MAF,MAS);
Sell = Cross(MAS,MAF);
```

FIGURE A.1 CUSTOM METRIC

When this system is run as a backtest, expectancy is added to the Report. When this system is optimized, expectancy is added as a column in the Optimization Report.

Bars...	# of losers	% of Losers	L. Tot. Loss	L. Avg. Loss	L. Avg % Loss	L. Avg. Bars...	Expectancy	fast	slow
107.45	19	63.33	-9,329.62	-491.03	-2.60	25.68	321.06	11	50
95.43	13	48.15	-10,937.95	-841.38	-4.43	24.62	312.65	17	50
94.23	16	55.17	-9,904.99	-619.06	-3.41	27.94	294.68	12	50
98.92	15	55.56	-10,086.41	-672.43	-3.73	30.47	287.14	20	50
90.36	13	48.15	-10,433.41	-802.57	-4.36	29.23	285.59	19	50
81.00	12	41.38	-9,548.85	-795.74	-4.32	23.83	283.97	15	50
07.64	17	54.84	10,227.45	601.61	3.21	25.76	275.03	13	45

FIGURE A.2 CUSTOM METRIC OPTIMIZATION

Expectancy can also be coded as a percentage, as illustrated in Figure A.3.

```
//   ExpectancyPercent.afl
//
//   Add a custom metric to the backtest report
//
SetCustomBacktestProc("");

if (Status("action") == actionPortfolio)
{
    bo = GetBacktesterObject();

    bo.backtest();

    st = bo.getperformancestats(0);

    ExpectancyPercent = st.getvalue("WinnersAvgProfitPercent")
                *    st.getvalue("WinnersPercent") /100
                +    st.getvalue("LosersAvgLossPercent")
                *    st.getvalue("LosersPercent") / 100;

    bo.addcustommetric("ExpectancyPercent", ExpectancyPercent);

}
```

FIGURE A.3 EXPECTANCY PERCENTAGE

There are other definitions of expectancy. But if you agree that these are correct, there is no need to code either A1. or A.3. AmiBroker already reports Average Profit / Loss and Average Profit / Loss %, which are expectancy and expectancy percent.

CUSTOM METRIC WITH PENALTY FUNCTIONS

The next example is more complex, and is based on the desire to incorporate several goals in the objective function.

I have chosen the K-ratio as the primary metric from among those built-in to AmiBroker. The K-ratio is the ratio of the slope of the equity curve to the standard error of the equity curve. A steep slope is good, and a small standard error is good. The additional terms of this custom metric reward results with values in a range that I prefer and penalize values that fall outside that range. In some cases, the penalty is complete rejection, in others it is a reduction of the objective function. (It is difficult to meet all of these conditions without penalty, but worth trying.)

Features I want are:

- Average Percentage Gain per Trade at least 1.0%.
- The Exposure - the time the system is in a position - between 10% and 20%.
- The average holding period between 3 and 7 days.
- The percentage of trades that are winners at least 65%.
- A Risk Adjusted Return value of at least 20%.

The objective function is calculated as:

Obfn = KRatioVal * AvgPctGainMult * ExposureMult *
    HoldingPeriodMult * PctWinnersMult * RarMult;

If there are no penalties, the objective function is the K-ratio of the system. For each feature, I have created a weighting function which defines the desired range and assigns penalty weights for being outside that range. Each multiplier is a number between 0.0 and 1.0. A multiplier of 1.0 assigns no penalty; a multiplier of 0.0 completely rejects the set of arguments associated with it.

Take, for example, the Exposure. If the exposure is between 10% and 20%, multiply the objective function by 1.00 – no penalty. Exposure cannot be less than 0%. If the exposure is less than 10%, multiply the objective function by a linear factor between 0.50 and 1.00, depending on how much less than 10% the exposure is. If the exposure is between 20% and 40%, decrease the multiplier linearly to 0.50. If the exposure is greater than 40%, multiply by 0.50.

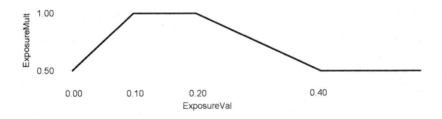

FIGURE A.4 PENALTY FUNCTION FOR EXPOSURE

The calculation of the ExposureMult term computes the weighting depending on which of the four parts of the line ExposureVal falls into.

```
// ExposureMultPseudoCode

ExposureVal = 0.01 * st.getValue("ExposurePercent");

ExposureMult = IIf(exposureVal<0.10,
                    part1,
               IIf((exposureVal>=0.10 AND exposureVal<=0.20),
                    part2,
               IIf((exposureVal>0.20 AND exposureVal<0.40),
                    part3,
                    part4 )));
```

FIGURE A.5 EXPOSURE MULT PSEUDO CODE

It takes a little geometry and a little algebra to write the formula for each part. Assume ExposureVal is about 0.32, or 32% exposure. That falls in the third line segment.

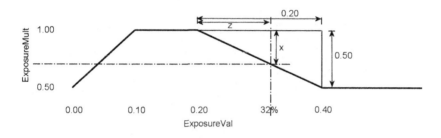

FIGURE A.6 PENALTY FUNCTION FOR EXPOSURE PART 3

We need to know the value of x, so that it can be subtracted from 1.00.

   ExposureMult = 1.00 - x

By similar triangles, we know

$$\frac{x}{z} = \frac{0.50}{0.20}$$
$$x = \frac{0.50}{0.20} * z$$

We know that ExposureVal extends past 0.20 by z.

   ExposureVal = 0.20 + z

   z = ExposureVal − 0.20

So, we can put everything together and compute ExposureMult

$$ExposureMult = 1.00 - \left(\frac{0.50}{0.20}\right) * (ExposureVal - 0.20)$$

The complete program, shown in Figure A.7, combines all of the desired features and produces a single-valued objective function. All of the constants have been left in place to make modifications easier. If desired, the code could be simplified to

$$ExposureMult = 1.50 - 2.5 * ExposureVal$$

But that would make understanding and modification much more difficult. Actually, the AFL compiler simplifies expressions before execution, so they can be left as they are with little adverse effect on running time.

Insert the objective function calculation portion ahead of the trading system being tested or optimized.

```
//    CustomMetricWithPenalty.afl
//
//    Add a custom metric to the backtest report.
//    The metric is the K-ratio, multiplied by a
//    penalty function based on:
//        the average percentage profit or loss per trade.
//        the percentage the system is exposed to the market.
//        the holding period per trade.
//        the percent of trades that are winners.
//        the RAR value.

KRatioVal = 0;

SetCustomBacktestProc("");

if (Status("action") == actionPortfolio)
{
    bo = GetBacktesterObject();

    bo.backtest();

    st = bo.getperformancestats(0);

    KRatioVal = 100.0 * st.getvalue("KRatio");

    AvgPctGainVal = 0.01
            * st.getvalue("AllAvgProfitLossPercent");
    ExposureVal = 0.01 * st.getvalue("ExposurePercent");
    HoldingPeriodVal = st.getvalue("AllAvgBarsHeld");
    PctWinnersVal = 0.01 * st.getvalue("WinnersPercent");
    RarVal = 0.01 * st.getvalue("RAR");
```

```
AvgPctGainMult = IIf(AvgPctGainVal<0.01,
            0.0,
        1.00);

ExposureMult = IIf(ExposureVal<0.10,
            1.00-(0.50/0.10)*(0.10-ExposureVal),
        IIf((ExposureVal>=0.10 AND ExposureVal<=0.20),
            1.00,
        IIf((ExposureVal>0.20 AND ExposureVal<0.40),
            1.00-(0.50/0.20)*(ExposureVal-0.20),
        0.50 )));

HoldingPeriodMult = IIf(HoldingPeriodVal<3,
            1.00-(0.50/3)*(3-HoldingPeriodVal),
        IIf((HoldingPeriodVal>=3 AND HoldingPeriodVal<=7),
            1.00,
        IIf((HoldingPeriodVal>7 AND HoldingPeriodVal<14),
            1.00-(0.50/7)*(HoldingPeriodVal-7),
        0.50 )));

PctWinnersMult = IIf(PctWinnersVal<0.50,
            0.50,
        IIf((PctWinnersVal>=0.50 AND PctWinnersVal<=0.65),
            1.00-(0.50/0.15)*(0.65-PctWinnersVal),
        1.00 ));

RarMult = IIf(RarVal<0.10,
            0.50,
        IIf((RarVal>=0.10 AND RarVal<=0.20),
            1.00-(0.50/0.10)*(0.20-RarVal),
        1.00 ));

ObFn = KRatioVal * AvgPctGainMult * ExposureMult
        * HoldingPeriodMult * PctWinnersMult * RarMult;

bo.addcustommetric("ObjectiveFunction", ObFn);
}

//   The trading system starts here

fast = Optimize("fast",16,1,20,1);
slow = Optimize("slow",8,1,20,1);
MAF = DEMA(C,fast);
MAS = DEMA(C,slow);

HoldDays = Optimize("HoldDays",1,1,20,1);
Buy = Cross(MAF,MAS);
Sell = Cross(MAS,MAF) OR BarsSince(Buy)>=HoldDays;
Sell = ExRem(Sell,Buy);
e = Equity();

//Plot(C,"C",colorBlack,styleCandle);
//shape = Buy * shapeUpArrow + Sell * shapeDownArrow;
//PlotShapes( shape, IIf( Buy, colorGreen, colorRed ),
//      0, IIf( Buy, Low, High ) );
Plot(e,"Equity",colorGreen,styleLine|styleOwnScale);
//GraphXSpace = 5;
```

FIGURE A.7 CUSTOM METRIC WITH PENALTY

A trading system using this objective function was optimized using the S&P 500 from 1/1/1995 to 1/1/2005. The trading system itself is not important. The results were ranked in order using the objective function described. The equity curve for each of the top seven parameter sets was plotted. They are displayed in order of preference as measured by the objective function.

FIGURE A.8 TOP RANKED

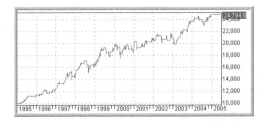

FIGURE A.9 SECOND RANKED

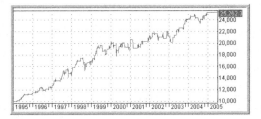

FIGURE A.10 THIRD

FIGURE A.11 FOURTH

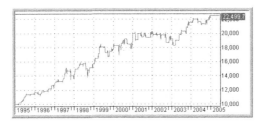

FIGURE A.12 FIFTH

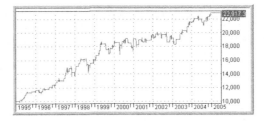

FIGURE A.13 SIXTH

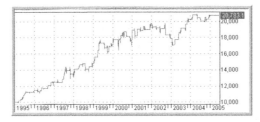

FIGURE A.14 SEVENTH

If I have confidence that the objective function accurately reflects my preferences, I should prefer each equity curve to the one below it. More importantly, I should be willing to accept the parameter set that is highest ranked as the best and the one to walk-forward, validate, and potentially trade.

ENABLE CUSTOM BACKTEST PROCEDURE

Once you are satisfied with your custom metric, your can set an option that instructs AmiBroker to always add your custom metric to all backtests and optimizations without need to paste the code into your system, or even to #include it. On the Automatic Analysis menu, Settings menu, Portfolio tab, check Enable custom backtest procedure. Then using the Pick button, browse to your custom metric AFL, Open it, and Click OK.

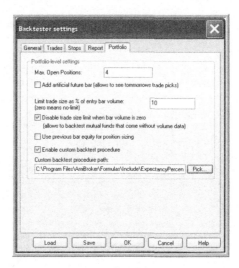

FIGURE A.15 ENABLE CUSTOM BACKTEST PROCEDURE

CREATE DLL PLUGIN MODULES

AmiBroker is easily extended by the end user through plugin modules compiled into DLLs. The plugin DLL can be created using any C or C++ compiler, or other language capable of creating regular DLLs. DLLs have several advantages over AFL program modules:
- They run faster.
- They can be called recursively.
- The code they contain is hidden from view.
- They can perform tasks that are difficult using only AFL.

Download the AmiBroker Application Development Kit (ADK) from the AmiBroker website, *www.amibroker.net.* Adk.exe is about 200 KB and is installed by double clicking it. The installation procedure creates a subdirectory to the AmiBroker directory. Read the Plugin Interface document that opens when you install the ADK.

FIGURE A.16 INSTALL ADK

Download the free BloodShed C++ compiler from *www.bloodshed.net*. The compiler comes as either a zip file or a self installing exe. Version 4.9 is stable and the exe file is about 9 MB. Double clicking the exe installs the compiler into a directory of its own – not into Program Files as is usual.

While you are at the BloodShed site, check some of their excellent documentation and tutorials for C++ in general and for BloodShed C++ in particular.

FIGURE A.17 INSTALL DEVCPP

Use Windows Explorer to make a copy of the Sample subdirectory that was installed with the ADK. It is easy to inadvertently change one of the files, and having a backup of the files at they were distributed is good insurance.

Double click sample.dev to cause DevCpp to open the sample project. The .dev extension is specific to the BloodShed compiler.

Click functions.cpp to open the functions module. With the exception of a two line modification to plugin.cpp to identify your project to AmiBroker, all of the code you write will go into this module.

From the DevCpp menus, select Project, then Project Options.

FIGURE A.18 PROJECT OPTIONS

Select the Parameters tab. Select the entire string of command line options in the Compiler window, copy them, and paste them into the C++ window. Click OK. Select the File menu and click Save All.

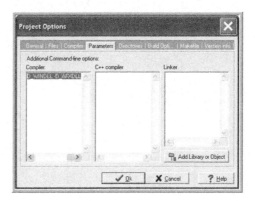

FIGURE A.19 PROJECT OPTIONS

Click Plugin.cpp to open it up. The two lines that you will change describe the plugin to AmiBroker. Change them to reflect your project.

FIGURE A.20 PLUGIN CPP

Click functions.cpp to open it. Functions.cpp contains code for ExampleMACD, ExampleMA, and ExampleEMA. It might be helpful to print out a copy of Functions.cpp.

Without changing anything, select Execute, then Compile.

FIGURE A.21 EXECUTE COMPILE

Select Compile Log and look at the notations made by the compiler. If Total Errors is 0, the compile was successful.

FIGURE A.22 COMPILE LOG

Look in the ADK directory you are working with. The DLL that was just created, sample.dll, is in that directory.

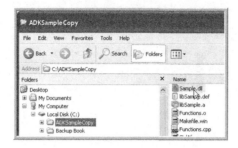

FIGURE A.23 FIND SAMPLE DLL

Copy sample.dll to the AmiBroker\Plugins directory.

FIGURE A.24 COPY DLL TO PLUGINS

Open AmiBroker, select tools, then plugins.

FIGURE A.25 TOOLS PLUGINS

The first time a previously unrecognized plugin is loaded, AmiBroker asks for your permission. Click OK, then look at the list of plugins. The one that you just compiled is listed.

The AmiBroker User Manual has the following to say about third-party plugins:

> Using third-party plugins:
>
> To use third-party plugin DLL just copy the DLL file to the Plugins folder in the AmiBroker directory. Then run AmiBroker. Then choose Tools->Plugins menu. In the Plugins window you should see the list of all loaded plugin DLLs. If AmiBroker was running when you copied the DLL you should click on "Unload" and then on "Load" button. This will force rescanning the Plugins folder and loading the DLLs.
>
> When the plugin DLL is loaded the new functions exposed by this DLL become available to all your AFL formulas. For the list of functions exposed by plugin you should consult the documentation of the plugin itself.
>
> IMPORTANT NOTE: AmiBroker makes no representations on features and performance of non-certified third-party plugins. Specifically certain plugins can cause instabilities or even crashes. Entire use of non-certified third-party plugins is at your own risk.

Be aware of potential for conflicts among the names of global variables in the plugins. Some third-party plugins have exposed global variables that they use to communicate between two or more of their modules. If you name a variable in your DLL with the same name, there could be a conflict. If that happens, change the name of the variable of yours that is in conflict.

FIGURE A.26 PLUGIN LIST

The functions that are contained in that plugin are available to AFL routines, but the names of the functions do not appear in the list of AFL functions – you have to know they are there. One of them is exampleMACD – a function that accepts no arguments, but has the two values it uses assigned within the DLL. Here is a simple AFL program that refers to exampleMACD.

FIGURE A.27 TESTING DLL

And here is how it looks in the AmiBroker window panes.

FIGURE A.28 USING DLL

Z-Score example

The previous steps demonstrate that the ADK kit and BloodShed C++ work together to create DLLs that AmiBroker can use. The steps that follow add a fourth function to Sample.cpp – one that computes the z-score of whatever series it is given.

To begin with, we'll write the zscore function in AFL, and apply it. The code is written in AFL in the same steps that we will write it in C++.

```
//   zscore.afl
//
//   demonstration of z-score
//
//   z-score is a measure of the distance a single element
//   of a data series is from the mean, measured in
//   standard deviations.

function zscore(price,Length)
{
    av = MA(price,Length);
    st = StDev(price,Length);
    zs = (price - av) / st;
    return zs;
}

zz= zscore(C,20);

Plot(C,"C",colorBlack,styleCandle);
Plot(zz,"z-score",colorRed,styleLine|styleOwnScale,-2,2);
Plot(0,"0",colorRed,styleDots|styleOwnScale,-2,2);
Plot(1,"1",colorPink,styleDots|styleOwnScale,-2,2);
Plot(-1,"-1",colorPink,styleDots|styleOwnScale,-2,2);
```

FIGURE A.29 ZSCORE

When writing in C++, we will be looping through the data under control of our own code. As an intermediate step, here is the same zscore written in AFL, but using looping instead of the higher level functions. The two versions of z-score are plotted together – one using just dots, the other a dashed line – to demonstrate that they overlay exactly.

```
//
//   demonstration of z-score
//
//   z-score is a measure of the distance a single element
//   of a data series is from the mean, measured in
//   standard deviations.

/////////////////////////////////

function zscore(price,Length)
{
    av = MA(price,Length);
    st = StDev(price,Length);
    zs = (price - av) / st;
    return zs;
}
```

```
///////////////////////////

function zsloop(price,Length)
{
    //   step through the data computing some
    //   intermediate values
    i = 0;
    sm[i] = price[i];
    sq[i] = price[i] * price[i];
    Sumsq[i] = sq[i];

    for (i=1; i<Length; i++)
    {
        sm[i] = sm[i-1] + price[i];
        sq[i] = price[i] * price[i];
        Sumsq[i] = Sumsq[i-1] + sq[i];
    }

    for (i=Length; i<BarCount; i++)
    {
        sm[i] = sm[i-1] + price[i] - price[i-Length];
        sq[i] = price[i] * price[i];
        Sumsq[i] = Sumsq[i-1] + sq[i] - sq[i-Length];
    }

    //   step through the data again, this time
    //   computing the mean and standard deviation
    av[0] = price[0];
    sd[0] = 1.0;

    for (i=1; i<Length; i++)
    {
        av[i] = sm[i] / i;
        sd[i] = sqrt((Sumsq[i]/i)-(av[i]*av[i]));
    }

    for (i=Length; i<BarCount; i++)
    {
        av[i] = sm[i] / Length;
        sd[i] = sqrt((Sumsq[i] / Length) - (av[i]*av[i]));
    }

    //   step through the data a third time,
    //   computing the z-score.
    zs[0] = 0.0;
    for (i=1; i<BarCount; i++)
    {
        zs[i] = (price[i] - av[i]) / sd[i];
    }

    return zs;
}
```

```
//////////////////////

zz= zscore(C,20);
z1 = zsloop(C,20);
zscpp = ExampleZScore(C,20);

Plot(C,"C",colorBlack,styleCandle);
Plot(zz,"z-score",colorRed,styleDots|styleNoLine
            |styleOwnScale,-2,2);
//Plot(z1,"z-score loop",colorBlue,styleDashed
            |styleOwnScale,-2,2);
Plot(zscpp,"z-score cpp",colorGreen,styleDashed
            |styleOwnScale,-2,2);
Plot(0,"0",colorRed,styleDots|styleOwnScale,-2,2);
Plot(1,"1",colorPink,styleDots|styleOwnScale,-2,2);
Plot(-1,"-1",colorPink,styleDots|styleOwnScale,-2,2);
```

FIGURE A.30 ZSCORE LOOP

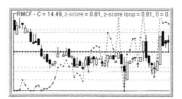

FIGURE A.31 ZSCORE CHART

Here is the same algorithm, this time written in C++.

```
//   ExampleZScore
//
//   usage:   zz = exampleZScore(price,length);
//
AmiVar VExampleZScore( int NumArgs, AmiVar *ArgsTable)
{
    AmiVar zs;

    zs = gSite.AllocArrayResult();
    int nSize = gSite.GetArraySize();
    float *price = ArgsTable[0].array;
    int length = (int) ArgsTable[1].val;

    int i;
    int j;

    //   allocate temporary storage
    double* sm = new double[nSize];
    double* sq = new double[nSize];
    double* sumsq = new double[nSize];
    double* av = new double[nSize];
    double* sd = new double[nSize];

    j = SkipEmptyValues( nSize, price, zs.array);
```

```
//   step through the data computing some
//   intermediate values
i = j;
sm[i] = price[i];
sq[i] = price[i] * price[i];
sumsq[i] = sq[i];

for (i=j+1; i<j+length; i++)
{
    sm[i] = sm[i-1] + price[i];
    sq[i] = price[i] * price[i];
    sumsq[i] = sumsq[i-1] + sq[i];
}

for (i=j+length; i<nSize; i++)
{
    sm[i] = sm[i-1] + price[i] - price[i-length];
    sq[i] = price[i] * price[i];
    sumsq[i] = sumsq[i-1] + sq[i] - sq[i-length];
}

//   step through the data again, this time
//   computing the mean and standard deviation
i = j;
av[i] = price[i];
sd[i] = 1.0;

for (i=j+1; i<j+length; i++)
{
    av[i] = sm[i] / (float)i;
    sd[i] = sqrt((sumsq[i] / (float)i) - (av[i] * av[i]));
}

for (i=j+length; i<nSize; i++)
{
    av[i] = sm[i] / (float)length;
    sd[i] = sqrt((sumsq[i] / (float)length) - (av[i] * av[i]));
}

//   step through the data a third time,
//   computing the z-score.
zs.array[j] = 0.0;
for (i=j+1; i<nSize; i++)
{
    zs.array[i] = (price[i] - av[i]) / sd[i];
}

delete[] sm;
delete[] sq;
delete[] sumsq;
delete[] av;
delete[] sd;

return zs;
}
```

FIGURE A.32 ZSCORE CPP

The code uses the sqrt function. To instruct the compiler to have that function available, add the line #include "math.h" near the beginning of functions.cpp.

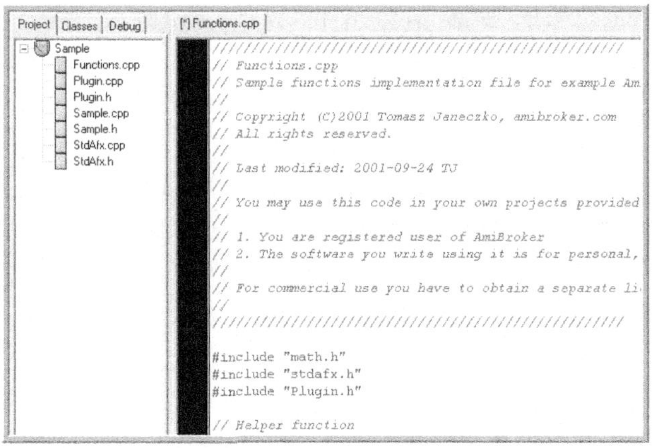

FIGURE A.33 MATH.H

To make the new function visible to AmiBroker, include an entry for it in the gFunctionTable near the end of functions.cpp.

```
/////////////////////////////////////////////
// Function table now follows
//
// You have to specify each function that should be
// visible for AmiBroker.
// Each entry of the table must contain:
// "Function name", { FunctionPtr, <no. of array args>, <no. of string args>, <no. of float ar

FunctionTag gFunctionTable[] = {
                    "ExampleZScore",        { VExampleZScore, 1, 0, 1, 0, NULL },
                    "ExampleMACD",      { VExampleMACD, 0, 0, 0, 0, NULL },
                    "ExampleMA",        { VExampleMA, 1, 0, 1, 0, NULL },
                    "ExampleEMA",        { VExampleMA, 1, 0, 1, 0, NULL }
};

int gFunctionTableSize = sizeof( gFunctionTable )/sizeof( FunctionTag );
```

FIGURE A.34 FUNCTION TABLE

And here is the AFL code that calls the ZScore function written in C++.

```
//  ZScoreCpp.afl
//
//  demonstration of z-score
//
//  z-score is a measure of the distance a single element
//  of a data series is from the mean, measured in
//  standard deviations.
```

```
zscpp = ExampleZScore(C,20);

Plot(C,"C",colorBlack,styleCandle);
Plot(zscpp,"z-score cpp",colorGreen,styleLine|styleOwnScale,-2,2);
Plot(0,"0",colorRed,styleDots|styleOwnScale,-2,2);
Plot(1,"1",colorPink,styleDots|styleOwnScale,-2,2);
Plot(-1,"-1",colorPink,styleDots|styleOwnScale,-2,2);
```

FIGURE A.35 ZSCORECPP

And the results in the AmiBroker Window.

FIGURE A.36 ZSCORE IN CPP RESULTS

ExampleZScore is now available as a function whenever it is needed.

Appendix B

Glossary

alpha   The rate of return of an asset, relative to the market. The intercept of the regression line describing the relative rates of return of the asset and the market.

argument   In more formal terms, a procedure has formal parameters that describe the process being programmed, and actual arguments that are used to evaluate the procedure for a specific case. Most of us are rather informal about the distinction between parameters and arguments. When the distinction is unimportant, either term may be used.

asset   A resource having economic value. A resource that is bought or sold.

bad tick   An erroneous tick that does not represent a trade.

back test   Testing the profitability of a trading strategy on prior periods of time.

bar   A consolidation of all ticks received over a given period of time into a single graphic element with values for the open, high, low, and closing values during that period.

beta   The volatility of an asset, relative to the market. The slope of the regression line describing the relative rates of return of the asset and the market.

breakout   A trade at a price higher than the highest high over a given period, or lower than the lowest low over a given period.

close   The price of the final tick or transaction in a bar.

commodity   A basic economic good that is traded as a futures contract.

constant expiration   A method of computing the prices of a synthetic futures contract based on an average of all active contracts.

continuous contract   A synthetic futures contract constructed by splicing together individual contracts as they roll over.

contract   A single unit of a commodity or future, such as 42000 gallons of crude oil, traded on one of the futures exchanges.

correlation   A statistical measurement of the similarity of two data series, measured over a selected period of time.

curve-fit   The term applied to a model that fits the data points too well, probably modeling the noise rather than the signal, and unlikely to represent the general patterns in the data.

data mining   Searching data series for patterns. Sometimes a derisive term implying a search for correlated data without regard for probable underlying association.

day trading   Buying and selling within a single trading day based on signals taken from analysis of intra-day data.

degrees of freedom   A statistical measurement based on the relationship between the number of independent observations in a data series and the number of parameters that are estimated using that data. The number of data points minus the number of estimates is called the residual degrees of freedom. The lower the residual degrees of freedom, the less likely that the model has learned a general pattern.

delayed real-time   Real-time data that has been delayed, usually by about 20 minutes, before being broadcast.

diffusion index   An index formed by comparing the number or total amount of increases with the number or total amount of decreases over a group of tradable issues.

DLL   Dynamic-Link Library. An executable file that allows programs to share code.

Donchian   A trading system method that buys on a breakout to new highs and sells on a breakout to new lows. Based on work done by Richard Donchian in the 1970s and 80s.

drawdown   The peak to trough decline in the value of a position or an account, usually measured as a percentage.

efficient   The central point of several theories of market prices and movements. Proponents of the strong form of efficiency believe that all information, whether public or private, is represented in the price of the asset at all times, and that there is no profit to be made by analyzing prices, earnings, estimates, or anything else. Quantitative analysis and technical analysis are based on the belief that the markets are sufficiently inefficient that analysis of price patterns will lead to profitable trades.

end-of-day   Data reported after the market has closed, and representing one day's activity. End-of-day data for stocks and futures is usually reported as a set of four data points, the opening trade, the high, the low, and the closing trade. Mutual fund data is usually only the closing price.

equity curve   The value of the trading account over time, often presented as a graph.

evolutionary operation   A search technique that fixes the values of all variables except one, and searches for the best model by varying that one. Then repeats for all other variables, and continues to cycle through until an optimum solution has been found. This method works well in industrial processes, but not for financial data.

exchange   The organization responsible for regulating the trading of stocks, futures, or options.

exhaustive search   A search technique that examines every possible data point.

expectancy   The average amount or percentage won or lost on an average trade by a trading system. The expectancy must be positive for a system to be profitable.

expiration   The time at which an individual futures contract or option ceases to exist.

exploration   The AmiBroker term for the analysis of a group of issues, resulting in a report listing information about each item. The report can contain anything that AmiBroker has access to or can compute, including indicators and buy and sell signals.

exposure   The percentage of time a given trading system is in a position. Whenever it is not exposed, the system has no position and is flat.

first notice   The date when holders of futures contracts are notified that the specific contract they hold will be expiring shortly, and they need to either exit their position or prepare for delivery of the commodity which that contract represents.

fold   A method used to develop out-of-sample periods from a set of data. The data is divided into several periods, each in turn reserved as out-of-sample data while the remaining data is in-sample. This method is not appropriate for modeling financial trading systems.

forex   Short for Foreign Exchange. Trading of currencies, usually as pairs with a transaction being the purchase of one currency and the simultaneous sale of the other.

friction   The costs of trading – primarily slippage and commission.

front month   The futures contract that is most active and closest to expiration.

function   In AmiBroker, a method of encapsulating a calculation into a single segment of code that can be called using its name. An example is the square root function.

future   A tradable asset that represents the future delivery of some physical commodity or financial asset.

future leak   A future leak occurs when a trading system looks ahead to data that will not be available in real-time to make its buy and sell decisions.

high   The highest price traded for the period defined.

historical data   The data series comprised of the historical records of all the individual reports for trades for an asset.

holding period   The amount of time a position is held from buy to sell.

indicator   In AmiBroker, a representation of some characteristic of a tradable issue. Indicators are often mathematical in nature, such as a moving average, and are displayed graphically. The states or values of indicators are key components of trading systems.

in-sample   During the model development process, data is divided into two sections. The in-sample data is used to develop the model, the out-of-sample data is used to verify that the model has detected patterns in the data that are predictable and profitable.

intra-day   When referring to data bars, data that is shorter than a full day. When referring to trading, trades that are made during the trading day rather than at the open or close of trading.

jackknife   Same as fold.

K-ratio   A metric used to measure the goodness or fitness of a trading system developed by Lars Kestner. K-ratio is essentially the slope of the equity line divided by the standard error of the equity line.

leverage   The relationship between the value of the asset being traded and the amount of money the trader has put up for that trade. Unless margin is used, stock trades are unleveraged. Futures trades are leveraged.

limit-if-touched order   An order placed with a broker that becomes a limit order when a trade occurs at the price specified.

limit-on-close order   An order placed with a broker that becomes a market-on-close order if the closing price is within the limit specified.

limit-on-open order   An order placed with a broker that becomes a market-on-open order if the opening price is within the limit specified.

limit order   An order that is placed with a broker to buy at a price below the lowest offer, or to sell at a price above the highest bid.

long   A long position has purchased the asset, but not yet sold it.

low   The lowest price traded for the period defined.

market   When referring to orders to buy or sell, a market order is executed at the current bid or offer. When referring to tradable assets in general, the market is the broad category to which the tradable belongs.

market order   An order placed with a broker to buy or sell at the current offer or bid price.

market-if-touched order   An order placed with a broker that becomes a market order when a trade occurs at the price specified.

market-on-close order   An order placed with a broker to buy or sell at the closing price.

market-on-open order   An order placed with a broker to buy or sell at the opening price.

mean   The arithmetic average.

mean reversion   A trading system method based on an expectation that prices return to a mean level. Mean reversion systems buy weakness and sell strength.

metric   A measure. The term is often used when discussing the fitness of a trading system.

model   The idea or method that becomes the computer code portion of a trading system.

Monte Carlo   A technique used in system validation that makes repeated selections from random data to test the stability and sensitivity of trading systems.

non-exhaustive search   A search technique that does not examine every possible data point. An initial, often randomly selected, set of points is evaluated. This is followed by several iterations where a new set of points is selected through use of some heuristic. When the search concludes the result is a local maximum that is often the global maximum.

objective function   A single-valued measurement of the fitness of a trading system. Optimization techniques are guided by maximizing the value of the objective function.

one-cancels-all order   A set of orders placed with a broker. When any one of the orders is executed, all of the others are canceled.

ohlc   The four data points associated with a bar of data – open, high, low, and close.

open   The first price traded for the period specified.

open interest   For futures contracts, the number of contracts that exist.

optimal f   A position sizing technique based on methods developed by Ralph Vince that computed the optimal number of contracts to hold for any given trade in order to maximize future account equity.

optimization   The organized search of alternative values of variables in a trading system.

outlier   A legitimate data point that is outside the normal range of data points.

out-of-sample   During the model development process, data is divided into two sections. The in-sample data is used to develop the model, the out-of-sample data is used to verify that the model has detected patterns in the data that are predictable and profitable.

parameter   In more formal terms, a procedure has formal parameters that describe the process being programmed, and actual arguments that are used to evaluate the procedure for a specific case. Most of us are rather informal about the distinction between parameters and arguments. When the distinction is unimportant, either term may be used.

pattern system   A trading system based on the assumption that recognizable price patterns precede opportunities to make profitable trades.

perpetual contract   The same as continuous contract.

pessimistic return ratio   A metric designed by Ralph Vince that attempts to estimate the out-of-sample performance of a trading systems by adjusting statistics measured from in-sample performance.

phantom signal   A phenomenon of walk-forward testing (or trading systems that have future leaks) where a signal or position changes without warning.

real-time   When referring to price quotations, data that is reported and broadcast as soon after the transactions take place as is possible.

regression   A modeling technique that computes the best fit of a line or curve to the data.

rollover   Rollover takes place when one futures contract expires, or drops off significantly in volume, and the next in time sequence becomes the front month.

scan   In AmiBroker, running a program that checks the group of tickers for signals.

seasonality system   A trading system based on the premise that prices move up or down at predictable times of the day, month, year, or other time period.

sensitivity   A technique used in modeling to test the ability of the model to detect general patterns. Values of parameters are changed by small amounts to see if the fitness values remain at or near optimum.

Sharpe ratio   A measure of performance based on the ratio of the return of the portfolio to the standard deviation of the return. The return is adjusted to be the excess return minus a risk-free rate, such as short term treasury bills.

short   A short position has sold the asset, and will need to purchase it back later to close out the trade.

signals   A trading system analyzes the data according to its rules and issues buy and sell signals.

snapshot data   Snapshot data is real-time, or delayed real-time, data that is checked periodically intra-day, but does not contribute toward building a real-time intra-day database.

Sortino ratio A measure of market risk similar to the Sharpe ratio, but using only the downside volatility in the denominator rather than the standard deviation.

standard deviation A statistical measure of the variability or volatility of a set of data. The square root of the variance.

standard error A statistical measure of variability somewhat similar to the standard deviation, but based on repeated measurements. The standard error can be thought of as the standard deviation of the means of repeated samples.

stationary The statistical concept that the characteristics of the data being modeling change very little over time. Financial time series are notoriously non-stationary.

stop and reverse A trading method where the exit from a long trade signals the entry to a short trade, and the exit from a short trade signals the entry to a long trade. The system is always in a position.

stop order An order placed with a broker to buy or sell at the market when a trade occurs at the price specified.

stop limit order An order placed with a broker to trade, but only at a limit price, when the market trades at the price specified.

symbol space Just as the range of values for any variable being optimized can be thought of as a numeric space, the range of tickers available for testing can be thought of as the ticker space or symbol space.

system A trading system, in the context of this book, is a combination of a model and a data stream.

tick The report of a single transaction. The minimum upward or downward movement in the price of a security.

tradable Any asset that can be bought and sold, and modeled as a component of a trading system.

trading frequency The number of times per day, month, or year that a trading system issues buy or sell signals.

trading range   Every market can be characterized as being in either trending mode, where prices predominantly move in one direction, or a trading range mode, where prices return to the recent average.

trailing stop   For a long position, the trailing stop rises as the price and the trade's profit rises, but never drops back when the price falls. If the price drops to the level of the trailing stop, a market order to exit the position is issued.

trend   Every market can be characterized as being in either a trending mode, where prices predominantly move in one direction, or a trading range mode, where prices return to the recent average.

trend following   A trading system method that recognizes that the market is in a trending mode and takes a position in the direction of that trend. Trend following systems buy strength and sell weakness.

Treynor ratio   A risk adjusted measure of return for a trading system similar to the Sharpe ratio, but using beta as the measure of volatility instead of standard deviation.

ulcer index   A metric that uses the depth and length of drawdowns as a measure of the performance of a trading system.

validation   Validation is the process of applying statistical tests to data from the out-of-sample trading to estimate the likelihood that a trading system will be profitable in the future.

VAMI   Value Added Monthly Index – a measure of portfolio performance based on monthly changes in the portfolio equity.

variance   A statistical measure of variability or volatility of a set of data. The sum of the squared deviations of the individual data points from their mean.

volume   The number of shares or contracts traded over a given period.

walk forward   The technique of repeatedly optimizing over an in-sample period, testing over an out-of-sample period, and moving both periods forward in time. The concatenated results from the out-of-sample periods are used to estimate the likelihood of future profitability.

Appendix C

Resources

BOOKS, JOURNALS, AND MAGAZINES

Active Trader Magazine, (800) 341-9384, *www.activetradermag.com.*

Aronson, David, *Evidence-Based Technical Analysis,* Wiley, 2007.

Bandy, Howard, *Introduction to AmiBroker,* Blue Owl Press, 2008.

—, *Modeling Trading System Performance,* Blue Owl Press, 2011.

Bernstein, Peter, *Against the Gods,* Wiley, 1996.

Drobny, Steven, *Inside the House of Money,* Wiley, 2006.

Ehlers, John, *Rocket Science for Traders,* Wiley, 2001.

—, *Cybernetic Analysis for Stocks and Futures,* Wiley, 2004.

Formula Research, Nelson Freeburg, 800-720-1080, *www.formularesearch. com.*

Fox, Justin, *Myth of the Rational Market,* Harper, 2009.

Futures Magazine, (800) 458-1734, *www.futuresmag.com.*

Hulbert Financial Digest, (866) 428-6568, *www.marketwatch.com.*

Jones, Ryan, *The Trading Game,* Wiley, 1999.

Mallaby, Sebastian, *More Money than God*, Penguin Press, 2010.

Patterson, Scott, *The Quants*, Crown, 2010.

Taleb, Nassim, *Fooled by Randomness,* Norton, 2001.

Technical Analysis of Stocks and Commodities, (800) 832-4642, *www.traders.com*

Tharp, Van, *Trade Your Way to Financial Freedom, Second edition*, McGraw-Hill, 2007.

Vince, Ralph, *Portfolio Management Formulas*, Wiley, 1990.

—, *The Mathematics of Money Management*, Wiley, 1992.

—, *The New Money Management*, Wiley, 1995.

—, *The Handbook of Portfolio Mathematics*, Wiley, 2007.

—, *The Leverage Space Trading Model*, Wiley, 2009.

PROGRAMS, DATA

AmiBroker, *www.amibroker.com.* Publisher of AmiBroker.

BioComp Systems, Inc. *www.biocompsystems.com.* Publisher of Dakota.

Bloodshed, *www.bloodshed.net.* Publisher of BloodShed C++ compiler.

CNN Money. *money.cnn.com.* Free delayed real-time quotations and fundamental data.

Commodity Systems, Inc (CSI). *www.csidata.com.* Subscription end-of-day data for stocks, indices, futures, and mutual funds. Covers all world markets.

eSignal. *www.esignal.com.* Subscription real-time streaming quotes for stocks and futures. Covers US and major European markets.

FastTrack. *www.fasttrack.net.* Subscription end-of-day data for stocks, indices, and mutual funds.

Google. *finance.google.com.* Free delayed real-time quotations and fundamental data.

Interactive Brokers. *www.interactivebrokers.com.* 100 symbol streaming real-time quotes for IB customers.

Interest rate historical data. *www.federalreserve.gov/releases/* Government data

Investopedia. *www.investopedia.com.* Terms and definitions.

Market Watch. *www.marketwatch.com.* Free real-time quotations and fundamental data.

msn Money. *moneycentral.msn.com.* Free real-time quotations and fundamental information. Free end-of-day data for indices, stocks, and mutual funds. Automatic downloading through AmiQuote.

Premium Data. *www.premiumdata.net.* Subscription end-of-day data for stocks, funds, and futures. Covers major world markets.

Quotes Plus. *www.qp2.com.* Subscription end-of-day data for stocks, indices, futures, and mutual funds.

Reuters. *today.reuters.com.* Free delayed real-time quotations and fundamental data.

Reuters Datalink. *www.equis.com.* Subscription real-time and end-of-day data for equities, indices, mutual finds, and futures. Covers all world markets.

TC2007. *www.tc2000.com.* Subscription end-of-day data for stocks, indices, and mutual funds.

Yahoo. *finance.yahoo.com.* Free delayed real-time quotations and fundamental data. Free end-of-day data for indices, stocks, and mutual funds. Automatic downloading through AmiQuote.

Yahoo Groups. *Groups.yahoo.com.* Discussion groups covering many topics, including AmiBroker.

Index

Psychology, 33

Quality of entry signals, 104-107
Quantitative analysis, 9-11, 13-24, 195-199
Quote.com, 61
Quotes Plus, 28, 61

Random entry, 91-93, 104, 107, 320-321
Random numbers, 305-312, 326-327
Real-time, 26-28, 57-61, 183, 190
Real estate, 21
Real money, 23, 39, 151, 294
Recognizing goodness, 49
Regression analysis, 18-19, 346
Repeated sampling, 305, 317
Research reports, 13
Restatements, 15, 304
Retracements, 11, 18, 203
Reuters, 28, 59
Risk, 19, 35, 37, 324-327
Risk adjusted return (RAR), 50-52, 170, 176, 209, 242
Robustness, 19
Rollover 30-31
Rotational systems, 55, 207-212
Roulette, 54
Runs test, 248-250
Russell 2000, 50, 315

S&P 500, 15, 31, 46, 137-138, 155, 200-203
Sales, 13
Scaling in, 93-94
Scaling out, 97-98
Seasonality procedure, 154
Seasonality systems, 153-172
Second Edition, 55-56, 137-142, 151-152, 170-172, 211-212, 260-264, 274, 288, 304, 326-327
Stop and Reverese (SAR), 98-99
Scanning, 57-58
Seasonality system, 147-164
Sector analysis, 195-206